PUSHKIN PRESS

MAZEL TOV

'So much more than a good read... What makes *Mazel Tov* especially attractive is that the author effortlessly succeeds in depicting real-life characters'   *Cutting Edge*

'In our hyper-partisan times there is hope to be found in the friendship between Margot and the Schneiders, however complicated and difficult it is to maintain'   *Culturefly*

'A must-read for everyone'   *De Standaard*

'A compelling and confronting story... beautifully written'
De Sleutel

'Captivating and inspiring'   *De Morgen*

'A beautiful story about friendship and overcoming cultural differences'   *Tertio appa Libri*

D0068448

J. S. MARGOT (b. 1967) is a freelance journalist and a writer based in Antwerp. An award-winning contributor to leading national newspapers, she has also written five novels and lectures regularly in both the Netherlands and Belgium. In 2017 she was awarded the E. du Perronprijs and the prize for the best religious book from the VUKPP for *Mazel Tov*, which was also highly acclaimed in the Dutch and Belgian press. *Mazel Tov* has been translated into German, French and Polish and won the Best Book Award in Poland; it is her first book to be translated into English.

JANE HEDLEY-PRÔLE studied German and Dutch in the UK, after which she settled in the Netherlands. Alongside her job at the Dutch Ministry of Foreign Affairs she works as a literary translator. Her translations include *We Are Our Brains* by D.F. Swaab, *What About Me?* by Paul Verhaeghe, *The Republic: A Novel* by Joost de Vries, *The Fetish Room* by Rudi Rotthier and Redmond O'Hanlon and *Hitler's Horses* by Arthur Brand.

MAZEL TOV

The Story of my Extraordinary
Friendship with an
Orthodox Jewish Family

J.S. MARGOT

Translated from the Dutch by Jane Hedley-Prôle

PUSHKIN PRESS

Pushkin Press
71–75 Shelton Street
London WC2H 9JQ

Original text © 2017 by Margot Vanderstraeten
English translation © 2020 Jane Hedley-Prôle

Mazel Tov was first published as *Mazzel tov* by Uitgeverij Atlas Contact in Amsterdam, 2017

First published by Pushkin Press in 2020
This edition first published in 2021

This book was published with the support of Flanders Literature
(www.flandersliterature.be)

1 3 5 7 9 8 6 4 2

ISBN 13: 978-1-78227-528-2

All rights reserved. No part of this publication may be reproduced, stored in a retrieval system or transmitted in any form or by any means, electronic, mechanical, photocopying, recording or otherwise, without prior permission in writing from Pushkin Press

Designed and typeset by Tetragon, London
Printed and bound by CPI Group (UK) Ltd, Croydon, CR0 4YY

www.pushkinpress.com

MAZEL TOV

PART I

1987–1993

One

It must have been the beginning of the month. The new academic year hadn't yet begun and I was heading for the canteen, feeling relieved, having just resat the Spanish grammar exam. To get there, I had to walk through the hall of the university building, past benches where dozens of students sat chatting and smoking. The route to the canteen was more exciting than most lectures.

Noticeboards lined the walls, full of intriguing announcements: "Who wants to swap my landlord for theirs?", "Feel like coming to Barcelona with us? Room for <u>one</u> more person. Conditions apply. Call me" and "Free sleeping bag for anyone who'll join me in it."

A single corner was reserved for the university's job agency.

If one of the jobs displayed in a lockable, plastic showcase looked interesting, you'd note down the number of the vacancy and go to the little social services office a bit farther along. There a lady with a long-suffering expression would tell you the details, which usually boiled down to her giving you the name, address and telephone number of the employer. Then, sighing under the weight of her boring job, she'd wish you good luck with your application.

The agency had provided me with a lot of temporary jobs in the previous two years, from chambermaiding to dishing out detergent samples, from headhunter's assistant to museum attendant.

When I came across a handwritten job vacancy. "Student (M/F) required to tutor four children (aged between eight and sixteen) every day after school and coach them with their homework", I immediately wrote the number on my palm. An hour later the lady from the job agency gave me the contact details of the family in question. I will call them the Schneiders, which is not their real name, though their name also sounded German, or German-ish.

The Schneiders, the lady said, were Jewish, but that shouldn't be a problem, and if it *was* a problem, I could always come back and she'd try to see if we could work something out, but she couldn't guarantee anything, because you never knew with people like that—which she apparently *did* know, just as she knew that the Schneiders would pay me 60 Belgian francs an hour, which wasn't a lot, but could have been worse. When it came to money, she informed me, Jews were a bit like the Dutch.

When I stared at her in surprise, she seemed taken aback by my ignorance. "Why do you think so many Dutch people come here to study interpreting? Because it's a good course and it's cheap. As soon as they've got their diploma, they whizz off back to their country. So we're basically training our biggest competitors. Luckily the university gets a subsidy for foreign students, so it's not all bad. What I want to say is: don't let yourself get pushed around. Don't accept an unpaid trial period. Even if you decide to stop after the first week, they have to pay you for the hours you've worked." I did quick sums in my head as she babbled on, calculating that I could earn 600 Belgian francs a week: 2,500 a month. Back then, when the rent of a small flat was about 6,000 francs a month, it all added up.

Two

"Hello *Mevrouw*. Could I please speak to Mr or Mrs Schneider?"

"Mrs Schneider speaking."

"Good afternoon. I believe you're looking for a student who can help your children with their homework?"

"We have been looking for such a person for *un certain* time."

"I only saw the vacancy this week."

"Last year we had six students. They gave up after a few evenings."

"Why did they give up?"

"Tcha, why. Why not, *n'est-ce pas*? They did not do a good job, I can tell you."

"You have four children."

"Two sons and two daughters."

"How old are they?"

"Between eight and sixteen. It says so in the vacancy. You call me for what reason, if you have not read it? You are how old?"

"Twenty…"

"That is only four years older than our oldest child. You are studying at which university?"

"Antwerp University. The Higher Institute of Interpreting and Translation Studies."

"That is not a university, it is a higher institute."

"In Belgium it's technically part of the university."

"Belgium is bizarre."

"I'm studying French and Spanish."

"French is good. Your Spanish is of no use to us. At home we speak French with the children. But their *yeshiva*, school, is Flemish, or I should say 'Dutch-language', *n'est-ce pas*? My husband is not at home now. You need to speak to my husband."

"I'd like to come over and introduce myself. When would suit you?"

"You have experience with children?"

"I really like children. And I like teaching. Shall I come on Friday?"

"You never come to us on a Friday. You have experience with teaching?"

"I sometimes helped my cousins with their homework. And my sister, and my friends."

"Then you cannot know whether you like teaching, *n'est-ce pas*."

"I *think* I like it."

"Friday our holiday begins already, the preparations for it. That day, the children never have school in the afternoon. But on Wednesday afternoon they do. Shabbat lasts, simply explained, from Friday when the sun goes down to Saturday when the sun goes down. Saturdays you therefore cannot come, as we devote the day to rest. But it is the intention that you also come to us each Sunday forenoon. To help the girls. You think that this you can do?"

"That shouldn't be a problem."

"You think you can respect us?"

"What do you mean?"

"We are not like everyone, *n'est-ce pas*. We will explain that to you later. I would first like to know: students have the habit to go out on Saturday evenings. And they would rather not get up on Sundays."

"I'm an early bird," I lied.

"When you can come to introduce yourself?"

"Would Wednesday afternoon suit you, *Mevrouw* Schneider?"

"I just said: the children have lessons on Wednesday afternoons. And it is better you see the children."

"In the late afternoon I mean," I corrected myself. "At five o'clock? I have your address."

"What is your name, please?"

Three

You'd think no one could possibly remember what the weather was like, say, thirty years ago, but that Wednesday in September the sun shone and the sky was bright blue—the kind of warm blue that heralds cold autumn weather—as I walked down Belgiëlei, the wide, busy avenue that cuts the Jewish neighbourhood in two, terminating in the handsome masonry of the railway embankment that runs between Zurenborg and the imposing edifice of Antwerp Central Station.

I never came to this side of the city. The only street I knew here was Pelikaanstraat, crammed with little jewellers' shops, where, on Sundays especially, people flocked to shop or just browse.

I was amused to see hordes of immaculately dressed infants on scooters. Girls and boys—with or without side curls—raced recklessly but alertly along the pavement, nearly taking off my toes as they shot past. Outside some buildings—schools and crèches?—there were clusters of over a dozen scooters and as many children's bikes. Very few were locked or chained.

Men with big white, grey or black beards strode along, seemingly in a tearing hurry. They had the air of people who knew where they were going; they didn't look at me, but turned their gaze the other way. Their beards and sidelocks, reaching from the tops of their ears to their shoulders, were blown around not by the wind, but by the speed with which they walked. Like funeral directors late for an appointment. Some wore white stockings under black breeches. Their jet-black coats (silk, satin or polyester?) all looked identical. Though they hung below the knee, not a single one was unbuttoned. Mustn't these men be stiflingly hot and sweating under their black top hats?

Practically all the women I saw had the same hairstyle: a sort of pageboy cut that just cleared their shoulders. The same colour too, pretty much: chestnut brown or black. It was obvious that some were wearing cheap wigs. Others had tucked their hair under a kerchief—the kind my mother and grandmother wore during spring cleaning, when they repainted their ceilings. Blondes appeared to be a rarity in this neighbourhood. Skirts and dresses were nearly all ankle length. Despite the warm weather, many of the women wore tights: black, dusky pink or brown, occasionally white. Garments were buttoned up to the neck. The only woman I saw in a colourful outfit was a passing cyclist with earphones on her head, listening to a Walkman.

I spoke into the intercom of a town house with a broad facade, gleaming as if newly renovated. A many-branched candelabrum stood on the window ledge next to the door, in front of the net curtain. Above the doorbell hung a transparent tube in which there seemed to be a piece of rolled-up paper. I took it to be a kind of fortune cookie, a note with a thought-provoking saying to cheer up your day. It struck me as a nice idea.

A female voice repeated my name—it resonated through the intercom—and asked me to "look at the eye". It was the same voice as on the phone a few days earlier.

It took a while before I realized that the doorbell was linked to a security camera, and that I was being filmed. In the late 1980s, a camera system like that was a high-tech gadget, something you'd only expect to see at the entrance to a jeweller's or a big corporation; certainly not at the door of a town house surrounded on all sides by other houses. My parents, who lived in a detached house in the countryside, only locked the back door in the evening, after the dog had been fed. During the day it was left open. When visitors rang the door of my flat in Antwerp, I would throw my keys out of the window, knotted up in a tea towel.

"Could you please go a bit lower? You are too high for the eye," the voice said. The "too high for the eye" made me smile.

I bent my knees slightly and looked into the protruding eye. For at least five minutes, things went silent on the other side.

I didn't really know what I was supposed to do as I waited. Every now and then I would look at the camera, smiling awkwardly. It was irritating, but when you're applying for a job you don't want to mess up. They might get annoyed, I thought, if I rang again too soon. Then I thought perhaps they'd already opened the door for me via the intercom and I just hadn't realized it; perhaps I should have pushed harder against the door, have pressed my whole weight against it…

I gazed at the houses and apartments on the other side of the street. There, too, I saw many-branched candelabras, each one bigger than the last. I counted the arms: seven, occasionally nine.

The neighbours opposite seemed to have the same little tubes on their doorposts. A man in a long black coat and a wide-brimmed hat entered a house. Rummaging in his satchel for his keys, he turned towards the street, where the light was better. I gave him a friendly nod, but he feigned not to see me. Before he and his hat disappeared behind the door, he briefly touched the tube.

Two women appeared at one of the windows of the building that he'd entered, pretending not to look at me, but inspecting me carefully. They didn't press curious noses against the windowpane; they belonged to the other kind of spies: the ones who stand a few paces back from the window, because they think that from there they can watch without being seen. Which isn't true.

Just as I was about to ring the bell a second time, chains began to rattle behind the heavy wooden door. I heard the shove and clink of bolts, both at the top and bottom of the door, the click of keys, a bleeping—the intercom, presumably.

Two pale, giggling girls with blue skirts and white, long-sleeved blouses buttoned up to the neck looked at me, amused and curious, and I looked back at them with the same eager curiosity. One was a larger version of the other.

"*Entrez*, please, *entrez*," said Little, who had a little voice.

"Our parents are expecting you," Large added. Her voice was little too.

Four

For the first half-hour I sat opposite Mr Schneider in a room that was called "the office", on the far side of the ground floor, just past the lift.

The lift! That such decadence existed was new to me: that there were people living in the city, people without physical disabilities, who had a lift in their house.

Another thing that greatly impressed me was the thick white carpet: your feet sank right into it. My mother believed in tiles: you could throw a bucket of soapsuds over them and scrub them clean in a trice. In this house, people had lined the access routes with deep-pile white carpet.

The CCTV images flickered on the wall of the corridor, showing the street from various angles. A hazy passer-by walked past. Someone stuffed leaflets into letterboxes.

In the office stood a desk and a bookcase, only a single shelf of which was filled. I recognized a French grammar book and a French dictionary. The other books were Hebrew works, I assumed: fat tomes whose leather spines were embossed with gold lettering and curlicues.

The windows stretched from floor to ceiling and overlooked the courtyard garden whose main feature—in the middle of the city!—was a pond with a footbridge. On the edge of the big marble terrace was a basketball stand and hoop, and farther down the garden, a swing hung from a shiny red metal frame. The lawn was immaculate: bright-green grass, freshly mown.

Mr Schneider turned out to be a tall, thin man in a white shirt, dark suit and dark-blue *yarmulke*. He didn't have sidelocks and his black beard, speckled with grey, was fluffy and didn't hang down like a bib between his chin and his chest.

Mr Schneider had a powerful voice, and his French accent was less marked than his wife's. He looked a bit like my father, but a Jewish version, and with somewhat deeper grooves in his forehead and around his eyes. Some people's cheeks are never red, and Mr Schneider appeared to me to be such a person. His skin looked to be permanently pale grey. His moustache and beard framed his mouth, lending colour to his face.

"We'll do this just once, shall we?" Mr Schneider asked after we'd shaken hands. I didn't know what he meant. He took off his jacket and draped it slowly over his chair, taking care to align the shoulders exactly with the corners of the chair back, then asked me to take a seat.

"If you hold out your hand to me, I will shake it, *juffrouw*," he said, having apparently read the confusion on my face. "Because I respect you and your customs, *n'est-ce pas*? But as a precaution we, Orthodox Jews, do not shake women's hands. It has to do with ritual cleanliness and suchlike. But we will not speak of that now. It would be nice if you could respect our tradition."

I smiled at him. Sheepishly, I imagine. I looked at my right hand and wondered how it could be unclean. Though admittedly, my fingers did bear traces of Tipp-Ex.

On a wide shelf of the bookcase, surrounded by three round hatboxes, lay a black hat with a broad, stiff brim. I'd once snapped up a similar hatbox at a flea market; in it I stored all the personal letters I'd received in my life.

Mr Schneider started on a long monologue. He did not leave any space for interruption, and when I attempted to ask him a question he responded like politicians in chat shows, suffering the intervention and then continuing unperturbed.

"I have four wonderful children," he said, "two exemplary sons and two equally exemplary daughters. All four of them are different, which is logical, and I shall try to shed some light on that."

My heart sank. I couldn't stand exemplary children. Never got along with them, could spot them a mile off: by their shoes, by the way they walked, the way they looked at you. I could measure their obedience just by the angle of their chins.

"Simon is our eldest," Mr Schneider began. "He is now sixteen. He is most like—in terms of character I mean—his mother, my spouse. He is gentle and tough at the same time, *vous comprenez?* You will understand when you meet my spouse. A hard worker who prefers to be silent than to talk, that's his way. But you should not underestimate him; both his heart and his tongue are well cut." As if he were talking about a diamond. It made me smile.

"If Simon opens his mouth, *juffrouw*, it is not to talk, but because he has something to say, if you know what I mean. *N'importe*: you will not have much to do with him, he is studying maths and science. His subjects are too difficult and too specialized for you; you have a flair for languages, I understand, you have a different type of brain, *n'est-ce pas*, you can only help our Simon with French and Dutch, perhaps also with history and geography. Our elder son will himself indicate when he has need of you. But if he does, we want him to be able to count on you, *n'est-ce pas*."

"Of course," I said.

"Jakov is our second oldest," he went on. "We had two boys, one after the other, and two girls. It could not have been better. First the sons. Then the daughters. We are blessed, my spouse and I. Jakov is thirteen, he will turn fourteen next month. He is the spitting image of me at that age: a scamp who is very popular with his schoolmates. Jakov has many friends, just like I did. He connects very easily with others. A sociable boy. We have to take care that he does not connect *too* quickly, also with girls, if you get my meaning. When I was young, I was content to wait. But my spouse and I married in the 1970s. Since then everything has changed, the world is moving too fast, and Jakov likes speed. He is very bright. He always wants to try out new things and he likes excitement. So he will push boundaries, challenge rules. I don't know if Jakov will have need of you. He is wilful. Nevertheless, we would like you to test him regularly on his study materials. He needs to be taught discipline. You will have to be strict with him, but not too strict—you need to find the golden mean."

I nodded, somewhat bored. I would rather see his sons, those exemplary boys, than listen to him singing their praises, but I didn't dare say so.

"You have already met Elzira and Sara," Mr Schneider continued.

I realized that I was nodding again.

"Elzira is our elder daughter; Sara—the little rascal—our younger. Elzira turned twelve in August. She's just two years younger than Jakov. And I would never say this in their hearing, but Elzira is cleverer than her two brothers put together. It's just that she can't concentrate—she has fits of nerves, and that worries us."

He paused briefly. A tall boy walked across the garden.

"At school they recommended that we have some psychological tests carried out, which we did. There's nothing wrong with her. She's just a bit different."

Once again he paused.

"Most of your time will be spent with Elzira; our daughter lacks self-confidence, you know, like all teenage girls, of course. She's very uncertain, and Simon and Jakov undermine what self-confidence she has, even though we tell our *garçons* they shouldn't, *n'est-ce pas*. I can give you an example: Jakov refuses to play chess with Elzira, even though they are well matched. He doesn't want to play with her because he knows she will knock over half the chess pieces..."

He stared silently into space for at least half a minute. Those thirty seconds seemed very long.

"I will, in the strictest confidence, tell you that Elzira has dyspraxia. The diagnosis is official. I do not know if you are aware of that condition. Her handicap—although we never refer to her condition in that way when she is present—has nothing to do with her intelligence, *n'est-ce pas*. Her motor skills regularly go haywire, *c'est tout*. She loses dexterity and has difficulty with balance and coordination. She has a tremor, like people who suffer from Parkinson's. Sometimes her hands shake, she can't control her muscles, she often drops things and therefore can appear clumsy. One part of her brain doesn't always communicate smoothly with the other, that's how you have to imagine it, like a short circuit, but that clumsiness has nothing to do with her intelligence, *n'est-ce pas*, I say it again, I would like to say it all the time, there is nothing wrong with her intelligence."

I'd sat up straighter, because Mr Schneider had started to talk faster and faster, and because he was saying *"n'est-ce pas"* more and more often.

"You know, of course, *juffrouw*, that to develop, a person must have self-confidence, motivation and ambition. Well, we are worried that our daughter, because of this so-called defect, will become withdrawn and fearful. She must not lag behind the other pupils in her class. That would not do her justice. We do not want her to suffer. We do not want her to become the subject of discussion. That is your main task: be patient with Elzira, enable her to excel."

His eyes had become damp, and he coughed between sentences, but he did not slow down.

"And then last but not least: Sara, without an 'h'. Sara is only eight. She is a champion gymnast, as agile as a snake. We do not know from whom she has inherited this bizarre and useless talent, not from me at any rate, and my spouse has many talents, but agility of body is not one of them. If it were left to Sara, sport would be her only occupation. That is of course out of the question for people like us. We do not wish to encourage her at all in that direction. Not even if she had the potential to be a world-class gymnast. We want her to train her brain. Now she is only eight. But soon she will be eighteen, you understand—I take it you understand me."

"Yes," I heard myself say.

"Just to make sure, I shall summarize what we expect from each other, *juffrouw*: we from you, our children from you, all of us from each other," he continued. "We give our sons and daughters to you. And you give them attention. You help them with their schoolwork. You are their tutor. You follow their lesson timetable and stick to it. You ensure that they pass with flying colours, *n'est-ce pas*. And we recompense you for all your efforts. You keep a list on which you write the hours that you have worked, and you also describe, using *mots clés*, keywords, how you spent those hours with them, is that agreed? Can my spouse and I count on you?"

I was beginning to feel a bit dizzy. As I sat listening to Mr Schneider's litany, I longed for some fresh air. The little room had grown stuffy. Through the window I could see an upper balcony, where a woman was shaking out a tea towel. It occurred to me that Mr Schneider had always said "my spouse" and never "my wife".

I fidgeted in my chair. I was eager to meet the four children. To talk to Little and Large. And see those fantastic sons in person. I also wished that Mr Schneider would ask me some questions. It wasn't for nothing that I'd rehearsed a series of answers to imaginary queries: do you think the pay is reasonable, what are your strengths and weaknesses, how good are your language skills, explain why you think you're the right person for our children…

Mr Schneider began talking again. It was apparent from what he said that I'd already got the job, and could start immediately. His assumption that I was okay with this—without asking whether I *wanted* it—made me rebellious. I decided it was time to go home.

Before I could get up, there was a knock at the door. A woman entered the room. Her hair was concealed under a chequered kerchief and she wore an apron round her plump middle. After putting two steaming cups of coffee and two wedges of cheesecake down in front of us she disappeared again without a word.

"Do you know the joke about Moshe, who's dying, and who calls his business partner Abe to his side?" Mr Schneider asked. And he began to tell the story. About Moshe, who doesn't want to die before asking Abe forgiveness for certain wrongdoings.

"Do you remember when our first business went bust? That was my fault, Abe, and I'm sorry. I embezzled money and falsified the accounts."

"I forgive you, Moshe," Abe reassures him.

Moshe: "And that night when that car got totalled. That was me, Abe, I wasn't wearing my glasses and I'd had too much to drink…"

"Let's forget that," says Abe.

"That time that 100,000 francs went missing from the safe: it was me who took the money, I had to pay off my son's gambling debts."

"Ach," says Abe, "don't worry about it, Moshe, I forgive you everything. Because, you know, I'm the one who put that arsenic in your coffee."

After telling the joke, Mr Schneider cracked up laughing. Because he kept on looking at me expectantly, I pretended to laugh too.

"I will leave you now," he said as abruptly as he had launched into the joke. He hadn't touched his cheesecake.

He stood up, adjusted his *yarmulke*—attached to his curly crown with a hairpin—and put his jacket back on. Fresh underarm sweat stains marked his shirt.

"My spouse will come and speak with you in a moment. I wish you every success."

I automatically stuck out a hand, which he shook heartily.

I could have kicked myself.

Five

Mrs Schneider, whose first name turned out to be Moriel, was younger than I am now. When she introduced herself to me she had just turned forty. Which made her exactly twice as old as me.

My grandmother had once explained to me—and working out she was right kept me quiet for a week—that you can only be twice someone else's age for a single year of your life. Once past that date (in the best-case scenario) the years gradually creep towards each other. People move closer together as if, like trees, they're collecting annual rings that make them stronger, plant them more firmly in the ground, make their crowns broader so that others can shelter under them better. The twenty years that separate a fifty-year-old from a seventy-year-old are nothing compared to the twenty-year gulf between a ten-year-old and a thirty-year-old.

Mrs Schneider was of average height and somewhere between fat and thin. Her appearance was chic, almost intimidatingly so. You could see she set high standards for herself and others. Her movements, her voice, her jewellery, her clothes—her entire presence—radiated distinction.

She wore a classic, dark-blue suit with a skirt that reached below the knee: discreet with a modern twist. Her hairstyle—shoulder-length and bouffant—reminded me of Pam Ewing's in *Dallas*. When she moved, her skirt rustled.

She didn't look motherly, more ladylike. Her skin, too, was pale, with a faint tinge of blue, the colour of her blouse.

Once again I held out a hand. Once again the gesture was returned. Once again I could have kicked myself: this reflex was more ingrained than I'd realized. Though maybe it was okay; perhaps women were allowed to touch each other and this rule only applied to the opposite sex.

"You are studying," she said, sitting down on the chair that her husband had just been using, though not before first carefully smoothing down the back of her skirt.

"To become a translator."

"Your exam results, you have them with, *n'est-ce pas?*"

"No… you didn't ask me to bring them…"

"That you are a good student we cannot know, if you have not your results with you. Aaron says you speak French."

I answered that my knowledge of French was passive, rather than active. "Dutch will always be my mother tongue. I only translate from French into Dutch, never the other way—I'd make a real mess of that!"

"Then the language you do not know."

"Oh but I do. I understand the language, how it's constructed. I read French literature. And I really like grammar," I said. That wasn't a fib. The more irregular the better.

"Our children you can help with their French home tasks."

Mrs Schneider appraised me like an insurance agent assessing damage to a building. A gap here, a split there, two or three cracks that cannot be overlooked. She spoke all her sentences as if they were conclusions, without any upward intonation. Never a trace of a question. I wasn't sure whether her manner of speaking was deliberate or due to her shaky command of Dutch. She clearly wasn't a native speaker, though this hadn't seemed so obvious during our phone conversation. Perhaps she didn't know the rules about word order. Or perhaps, like many of the French-speaking bourgeoisie in Flanders, she just didn't care. I was happy to teach her too.

"Of course I can help them with their homework."

"You speak beautiful Dutch."

"Thank you."

"You have a beautiful name."

"So do you."

"Thank you. For my name, Moriel, I cannot take credit. I have my parents to thank for it." She smiled tentatively. "Many people think I am called Murielle. But it is Moriel, with *o* and without double *l* and an *e* at the end."

Now it was my turn to smile tentatively.

"On weekdays at five or five thirty you come, and stay until eight, at least. On Sunday mornings you come at ten and leave when our daughters you have helped. Our sons need you not help, on Sundays they go to Bible class. My husband, Aaron, or I, we pay you each week."

She *did* call her husband by his first name. And just like her husband, she had decided, without bothering to check with me, that I would enter into their service.

"You have hobbies, *n'est-ce pas.*"

"Reading. Going to the cinema or the theatre. Travelling as often as possible to countries whose language I'm learning. Having friends round."

"You have many hobbies, but none is to children connected."

"I think children are great."

"You have no experience with children."

"I did a lot of babysitting when I was younger. I'd read the children stories. And then we'd act them out. Or we'd make up a sequel, or add another character to the story."

"That you here need not do."

"Babysit?"

"Make up stories. That we do not want you to do. School is not a game. And tutoring is not the same thing as babysitting. You are good at keeping silent?"

"Uh…"

"We do not want that you speak with the children about your personal life—about your world, I mean to say. The idea is you work with their learning materials."

"That shouldn't be a problem."

"Your life is your life and stays your life. You are *seule*, single?"

"I'm a student."

"You are not married."

"I live with my boyfriend."

"Your parents approve."

I nodded and had to bite my tongue so as not to blurt out that my parents had given up trying to interfere with my life and as a result approved of everything I did.

"Your parents, they are still together?"

"You mean, are they divorced? No."

"With how many children are you at home?"

"Three."

"All three healthy?"

"Yes, as far as I know."

"Your husband works."

"He's looking for a job."

"He has graduated, *n'est-ce pas*."

"No, he did one year of law."

"So he is younger than you…" Now her voice did go up at the end of the sentence, by a good few centimetres.

"No, he's seven years older. My boyfriend's a political refugee. He faced persecution in his country, so he fled. He might go back to university, study industrial engineering, he's not sure yet. It depends on other factors and on his linguistic ability. Dutch isn't an easy language to…"

I was at it again. The least suspicion that someone looked down on Nima and I'd get defensive, would stress that he was a political, not an economic refugee. As if I myself needed confirmation that someone who fled for political reasons was superior to someone who fled to escape poverty and a lack of prospects.

"*Donc*, he no longer studies law."

"He could only study law in a language he spoke really well. That's difficult here."

"Your husband, he is from another country."

"From Iran," I said, all too familiar with the reactions this could trigger.

"Iraaaannn," she repeated, ruminatively.

"Tehran," I added.

"Your husband is Muslim, *n'est-ce pas*," she said.

"He's not my husband, he's my boyfriend. And he's not a practising Muslim," I said. That, too, I had learnt since I'd been with Nima. That it could be helpful to say as soon as possible that although my boyfriend was a Muslim, he did not practise his religion actively: he did not pray three to five times a day, he did not observe Ramadan, and sharing his life with a non-Muslim didn't bother him at all.

He was, in short, too left-wing to be religious. Just like the label of political refugee, that of "non-practising Muslim" was considered meritorious, a medal on his lapel, a passport in my circle of friends and acquaintances.

Sometimes, but not now, I lied that his parents were Zoroastrians. Some of Nima's friends were Zoroastrians, and I knew a little bit about their faith, which was based not on the Bible or the Koran but the Avesta. Zoroastrianism usually met with a sympathetic response, especially if you explained that the term came from Zarathustra, meaning you could link the religion to Nietzsche, who in certain circles was revered more than any deity.

"You are a young and sensible woman. And your husband lives in the country of the ayatollahs…"

Another reaction I'd got tired of hearing. I gave it short shrift: *"Mevrouw,* my boyfriend lives in Belgium precisely because he has fled from the likes of Khomeini."

I didn't tell her that Nima, who had come to Belgium with his older sister, was from an affluent family, nor that his resistance to the Islamic regime had been limited; unlike many of his friends, his ideological battle had cost him no more than a blacklisting and few nights in jail, after which he very soon left the country.

His parents were worried he'd be called up to fight in the war against Iraq. It was one of the factors that prompted them, like many other middle-class Iranian families, to send their son to the West, along with their daughter. Under the Shah's regime they had enjoyed considerable freedom, including freedom of thought. Tehran, to them, was the Paris of the Middle East. They had abhorred the authoritarian, dictatorial Shah, but they abhorred the reactionary Islamic state even more. They wanted their children to savour the taste of Paris, rather than the bitterness of a Shiite dictatorship, if needs be in another country.

Mrs Schneider did not ask my friend's name.

"You live with someone of a different faith."

"Yes."

"You are not a Muslim."

"I was brought up as a Catholic."

"You do not intend to covert."

"I'm not religious. Any more. If I ever was…"

"And your parents…"

"My parents were churchgoers. They observed all the main Catholic traditions. Easter. All Saints. Christmas. Now that we children are more or less grown up, they no longer attach such importance to church services or belief…"

She toyed with her bracelet, as delicate as the two rings she was wearing: fine silver with a minuscule gemstone. You have jewellery that whispers and jewellery that shouts; Mrs Schneider's jewellery whispered so clearly as to drown out any shout.

"Your husband fled his religion."

"He fled a religious state."

"And his parents?"

"Are still there."

"Your husband, he is an Arab."

Oh no, I thought, not this again too. "The people of Iran are not Arabs but Persians. He doesn't speak Arabic, he speaks Persian." The word "Persian" worked its usual magic, thanks to the association with handwoven carpets. They were seen as a good investment, especially in Belgium, where house ownership is a national obsession. So much so that Belgians are said to be "born with a brick in their stomachs".

"Our children, Aaron has told you about them."

"About all four."

"My husband didn't ask you anything."

"He talked the whole time," I said. And it was a relief to be able to say it.

"I thank you," she said, all of a sudden. "I will ring for the maid. Krystina will show you out. I wish you a pleasant day. *Merci et bonne journée.*"

She pressed a button under the desktop and with a brief nod left me sitting there, somewhat bemused, in a fine cloud of her perfume, which I couldn't identify. Anaïs Anaïs was the only scent I knew, as I occasionally sprinkled it on my neck and wrists. Not so much because I liked its heavy, floral fragrance, but because I wanted to spread the aura of the writer Anaïs Nin.

Krystina was not the woman who had served me the delicious cheesecake.

Six

A good three weeks later I was rung by Mrs Schneider. After a few evenings of tutoring, the three students who *had* passed the Schneiders' application procedure had stopped coming. Mrs Schneider didn't give me any details, and I didn't trouble to find out whether they'd been fired or had left of their own accord. Clearly, the departure of the third student had made emergency measures necessary. That was where I came in.

During the call, Mrs Schneider made no mention of my failed job interview. Speaking to me as if for the first time, she stressed the need for her children to receive the best possible education. There was no time to waste, she said, every day and evening needed to be spent profitably, *n'est-ce pas*?

Would I consider coming, she wanted to know.

"My boyfriend's still from Iran, you know," I couldn't help saying.

"Aaron will continue the conversation," she responded. Her husband would prefer to receive me in his office near Pelikaanstraat, she added. As soon as possible: would tomorrow at four be convenient? Did I need picking up, or a taxi to be sent, *peut-être*?

After the chicness of the Schneider home, the un-chicness of Mr Schneider's workplace was startling. Housed in a building along with—to judge by the number of doorbells and letterboxes— dozens of other businesses, his office contained little more than a cluttered black metal desk and four chairs. It was stuffy, as if the only window, streaked with dirty rainwater, hadn't been opened in years, and as if the concrete decay visible from the outside was seeping through the walls. The building's secretaries, as unstylish as the interior, were common property, just like certain office equipment: the typewriters, photocopiers and IBM computers. Through the dirty window I could see the dome of Antwerp Central Station.

All kinds of magnifying glasses, pincers and tweezers lay on a table against the wall, along with prehistoric-looking microscopes. The harsh fluorescent lighting over the centre of the table, banishing all shadow, made everything even uglier than it already was.

"I am a diamond merchant," Mr Schneider said.

I could not suppress a smile.

"This amuses you?"

"I was just reminded of that scene in *Cheese* where the main character says 'I am a cheese merchant'."

Mr Schneider looked a little blank.

"Do you know the book I mean? We studied it at school. It's by Elsschot."

"Elsschot?"

"A Flemish author, it doesn't matter," I mumbled.

"Oh, I've read Elsschot's books, you know! And Simon, our elder boy, chose Elsschot in his Dutch literature classes. I suspect that Jakov will too. It's not that the pupils choose this writer because they love his work so much, of course, but because Elsschot wrote thin books in language that is easy to understand!"

Mr Schneider laughed, his whole body shaking.

"Elsschot came from Antwerp, *n'est-ce pas*," he continued. "He was a gifted chess player. Sapira, a Polish Jew, was for a while a family friend of the De Rudders—Elsschot's real name, if I'm not mistaken."

"De Ridder," I corrected. But I was amazed. I'd never expected to be taught something about Elsschot by a Jewish man with a *yarmulke* and a beard. I'd written a thesis on the author, so I knew a fair bit about his life. When I cycled through the city, if the weather was nice I'd sometimes make a detour through the neighbourhood where he'd lived and where his favourite cafe was. I'd never read that he had a Jewish friend, or friends.

As soon as I was installed on a squeaky leatherette chair, Mr Schneider embarked on yet another monologue, this time on the might of the Persian empire. He talked about someone called Haman, the vizier of the King of Persia, who, in the biblical book of Esther, tries to persuade the King to kill all the Jews, because the Jew Mordechai had refused to bow to him.

I'd never heard any of these names or stories. Nor had I heard of Purim, the Jewish carnival, a religious holiday that, according to Mr Schneider, had something to do with Haman and Mordechai. At the time, it didn't interest me. I was there about a job.

But Mr Schneider was off again. He just couldn't stop talking, and I got the impression that he wanted to placate me, to make up for some perceived faux pas of his wife's. He talked about the richness of Persian civilization and about the importance of the Mizrahi Jews in Iran and the wider region. From the terror under which the Iranian population was suffering he switched to Jewish cuisine and the influences of Lebanon and the Middle East. He even spoke of the Persian intellect, of Persian culture and tradition. Lavished more praise than Nima, even in his most chauvinistic moods, had been able to muster for his fatherland. I found it slightly ludicrous.

Mr Schneider went on to hint that he'd perhaps done business with the Shah—not directly, no of course not, what an idea. It was even possible, he said, that some of the gems he sold now were being bought by relatives of the late Shah, though he could not be sure: in his business, secrecy was as precious as the raw diamonds in which he traded. But one of his regular customers, a diamond cutter, paid visits to the home of Farah Diba, the Shah's widow, which in the old days had meant travelling to Tehran, but after the Islamic Revolution and the flight of Reza and Farah Pahlavi to the West, this jeweller only had to go to Paris—much more convenient.

Paintings of gold letters on a dark-blue background hung on every wall. I didn't know the Hebrew alphabet—or even the Persian alphabet, for that matter, though Nima had made a couple of attempts to teach me. A framed photo of the Belgian King and Queen adorned the wall behind Mr Schneider.

The picture frames wobbled every time a train went past. Seeing that, I shivered. Why, I wondered—as Mr Schneider held forth on the Diamond High Council and the Antwerp Diamond Bourse, and on the Jewish tradition in the diamond sector—had the Jews of Antwerp chosen to resettle *here* after the war, in their old neighbourhood near the railway line? It seemed so masochistic. Who would do that to themselves? Why hadn't they moved to another neighbourhood? Why would you want to be confronted every day with the horror of your own, decimated people? To see the trains, those potent symbols of the sufferings of your people, your family, rolling past. To hear their rumble—feel it, even: the window of his office vibrated in its frame.

Sixty-five per cent of Antwerp's officially registered Jewish population had been—I looked it up after my failed job interview—deported by rail to concentration and extermination camps, mainly from the Dossin barracks in nearby Mechelen. Of those thousands, the vast majority never came back. After 1945, most of those Jewish children who had survived the war in hiding had lost a parent or been orphaned. It was likely that Mr Schneider belonged to this group. Yet Mr Schneider's office was near Simonsstraat, one of the main streets of Antwerp's Jewish diamond district. Named after Pieter Simons, the engineer who built the first railway line between Antwerp and Mechelen. Mechelen, the place from which, a century later, many Jews were transported.

I grew suspicious. I suspected Mr Schneider of something, I didn't know what. At the same time I mistrusted myself.

I thought of my grandfather. From his rocking chair next to the stove he would tell stories about the war and about POW camps. He loathed Nazis so much that as he lay dying, he summoned up his last remaining strength to send the very nice district nurse away: "No collaborator's daughter sets foot in this house!"

I also thought of Yehudi Menuhin. Nima and I had a few CDs of duets by that brilliant violinist and the equally brilliant Indian sitar player Ravi Shankar. To us, the music of these two virtuosos was a symbol of harmony between East and West, a harmony that we strove to achieve in our private life, often—but by no means always—successfully.

The liner notes in one of these Menuhin and Shankar CDs gave a brief summary of their lives. Menuhin was the first Jewish musician to perform in Germany after the Holocaust. As early as 1947, scarcely two years after the end of the Second World War, he allowed the people who had tried to exterminate his people to enjoy his genius and his art.

I couldn't comprehend such forgiveness. There were days when I saw it as a form of treachery. Whenever I shared my doubts about Menuhin's integrity with Nima, he said I was blowing the issue out of all proportion. But he loved it when I got all passionate about something, he said, it really turned him on.

"Our children go to Jewish schools," said Mr Schneider, interrupting my thoughts.

"Jewish schools? Private schools?" I asked, all ears again.

"No, not private education. They go to a Jewish school that is recognized and subsidized by the Flemish government. But it is a

Jewish school that centres on Jewish culture, our way of thinking and behaving. Is there anything else you want to ask?"

"I didn't know such schools existed."

"In addition to being educated in the Jewish religion and culture, all pupils are taught the regular secular curriculum. The same education you had."

"That seems like a lot."

"Jews like to study. We can handle that type of workload."

"And on top of that, there's me? More lessons *after* school?"

"What use has a child for precious objects? Jewels, expensive cars and suchlike? They should develop their minds to the full—*that* is truly precious."

"Do only Jewish children go to these schools? Or are they mixed schools, accessible to all?"

"Indeed."

"What do you mean?"

"Exclusively Jewish pupils."

"Then it *is* a private school?"

"No. As I said, the pupils follow the education ministry's official curriculum. The government scrutinizes our attainment targets. We do what is expected of us."

"But the children don't come into contact with non-Jewish peers?"

"Liberal Jewish children sometimes go to regular secondary schools. But Orthodox Jews prefer schools that honour their tradition and religion. We don't want to equip our children with a watered-down version of our belief and culture. Our sons and daughters go to the Yavne school, which is strict Orthodox, but less strict than the Jesode Hatora–Beth Jacob school."

"And the teachers? Are they all Jewish?"

"The teachers of lay subjects usually aren't."

"Lay subjects?"

"Maths, French, Dutch... Religion is taught by Jewish people. Secular subjects usually aren't."

I must have looked dubious: I'd never heard anything so strange. And yet at the same time it wasn't entirely unfamiliar. I myself was the product of a Catholic school where eighty per cent of the pupils came from migrant worker families, most of them Muslim. It was the 1970s, and the school was in Meulenberg, Limburg, a neighbourhood built to house miners' families. It was a purely practical choice: we lived in a "white" village not far away, but my mother had always taught in Meulenberg. So back then, long before multicultural schools were a concept, my classroom featured all kinds of nationalities, dress, smells, tastes, languages and religions. In the playground we spoke our own language, an argot of the streets. "Your mother's a whore!" we would shriek, and "Pull your lip over your head and shut up!" Anyone who didn't stand up for themselves was a goner. Threats of physical violence—"I'll beat you up at the school gates!"—were standard fare. Just like the delicious, exotic food items shared in the canteen. Until it became too expensive (or the authorities found it too progressive) there was even a Koran teacher. He taught after normal school hours, so his pupils stayed behind, along with the children receiving instruction in their native languages: Spanish, Turkish, Arabic. But at these Jewish schools, if I understood it correctly, secular and religious teaching intermingled throughout the day, throughout the year, throughout an entire school career.

"Why don't your children go to ordinary schools and learn Jewish religion and Hebrew after school?" I asked. The tables had turned since a few weeks ago. The Schneiders now wanted something from me; I had nothing to lose.

"We have our own traditions. And our own history," Mr Schneider said.

"Who doesn't?" I blurted out.

He smiled.

"Are non-Jewish children allowed to register at your schools?"

"Officially, yes. Of course they are, we owe that openness to the state that subsidizes. We're no different from Catholic schools."

"Would I be admitted to your children's school?" I asked.

"In theory, yes. In practice, it's very rare."

"Is only secondary education segregated?"

"Do you mean boys and girls being educated separately? No, we separate them at an early age."

"By segregated I meant separated from other religions and the rest of the world. Does that start in secondary school?"

"Children also go to Jewish primary schools."

"So there aren't any non-Jewish pupils there?"

"There could be, but that doesn't really happen in practice."

Just like when I'd been struck by the proximity of the railway line, a feeling of oppression washed over me. So religious Jews separated themselves from the rest of the population very deliberately and from a very young age. What possessed them? How could a minority seek to distinguish itself so strongly from the majority? Who, apart from the whites in South Africa, sought to protect their identity by isolating themselves? How self-righteous—or fearful—would you have to be for that? How blind to your own history? It wasn't so long ago that Germany and its cohorts had viewed this tight-knit people as public enemy number one. Yet now, not fifty years later, they still wanted to isolate themselves? In the army, everyone knew that camouflage could save lives. But these people, of all people, with a history of persecution, were trying to do everything they could to be noticed? Or was there something I was failing to understand? To see? Did the problem lie with me? Why was I focusing on outward differences, anyway? It was assimilated German Jews, after all, whom the Nazis perceived as the greatest threat: the many who had worked themselves up unobtrusively to the highest echelons of society.

As all these confused thoughts bubbled up, I bit my lip. I knew I'd sound anti-Semitic if I blurted out what I was thinking. There were times when Nima was proud that he could distinguish himself from us Westerners. But at the same time he was maddened by people constantly reminding him that he wasn't "one of us".

My fellow students hadn't been able to hack it, and I wasn't going to be able to hack it either. How could I work with people who made their belief and their origins the focus of their lives?

"Do you know the joke about Moshe?" Mr Schneider asked.

He didn't give me time to answer.

"Moshe is on his deathbed, and he calls his business partner Abe to his side."

He told the whole joke again. When he got to the punchline he again guffawed and again looked at me expectantly. Again I laughed, feeling desperately awkward.

"When can you start?"

"This evening," I answered.

I said goodbye without a handshake. Just before Mr Schneider shut the door of his office, he called me back. Could I write my boyfriend's name down on a piece of paper?

Seven

When I got home, Nima and I had a terrible row, the worst in the two years we'd been together.

"Why did you give him my name? These people—what are they called, Schneider—don't have the right to ask for my personal details. Even if the *police* were to ask you my name, you wouldn't be obliged to answer, *ma chère*, you should know that! We're not married, are we? So it's only our business who you live with, right? Really, how could you be so naive? I should be teaching *you*, instead of you tutoring those Jewish children. You don't know the first thing about human rights! Lesson one: never say more than is strictly necessary, because everything you say can be used against you, especially if you're an immigrant or political refugee!"

I'd never seen Nima—with whom I spoke French, English and Dutch alternately—so angry and unreasonable as on that evening. His usual serenity deserted him. And it wasn't so much Mr Schneider's impertinence that infuriated him. He was mainly mad at me, at the cultural divide that I (like it or not) stood for.

No longer was I the woman he'd spent months wooing, whom he'd showered with poetic declarations of love. I was the spoilt Westerner who utterly lacked political and historical awareness; I embodied the American imperialism that imposed its political, ideological and economic systems on the rest of the world; even culture was dictated by the Americans, because how many people would still go to the movies if they weren't made in Hollywood?

He left no frustration unvoiced.

Did I have *no* idea how much Israel, that tiny little strip of a country, influenced world politics, particularly in the Middle East? Didn't I *know* what Mossad was? Had they written down the names of *their* lovers for me on a piece of paper? Had they said to me: "Here are *our* particulars, check out who *we* are with the intelligence services"? Did I only read Noam Chomsky's linguistic treatises? Shouldn't I familiarize myself with the political works of this remarkable, left-wing, anti-imperialist Jewish intellectual?

Privacy wasn't about what you had to hide. Privacy was about everything you wanted to keep to yourself, because that was your right. Your own space. Your own security. Your own freedom: the most precious thing in the world. Why had he fled his own country, did I think? Was he—he really couldn't believe it himself—*really* having to explain this, the foundation of all civic freedoms?

"You've just got a grudge against *Jews*," I exclaimed. "You just don't want me to teach *Jewish* children. Put on your 'Free Palestine' T-shirt, why don't you? Tell me where it is, I'll get it for you. Or have you mislaid it, and is that *Israel's* fault, like everything else?"

He didn't find that funny.

We didn't find anything funny.

"You're not listening," he said.

"I heard you."

"You heard what you want to hear. I've got nothing against Jews, *nothing*—please get that into your head once and for all! But I *do* have a problem with the state of Israel, with a government that doesn't want to negotiate with Palestinian representatives, and with the whole mess that America and Europe have created in the

Middle East. Marx was a Jew. Trotsky was a Jew. I owe my *ideology* to Jews! Well, its basic premises, at least."

"I've given your name to a Jewish father of four children, that's all. Now Mossad is on your case and I'm partly to blame for all the deaths in the Middle East."

"My best boxing partner was a Jew!"

"Where?"

"In Tehran. Where else? You come across a lot of Jews in the ring. They're excellent boxers."

"You're lying."

"Ask Mr Genius Schneider. Ask him if Jews are good boxers."

"He told me about the Jews in Iran."

"Twenty thousand Jews live in my country! But that's not interesting, I know. Only fanatical Muslims are interesting."

And so it went on.

The upstairs neighbours stamped on their floor, our ceiling.

"Look at me!" I shouted at Nima. He didn't. He never looked at me when his emotions got the better of him. Even when he missed his family so much it choked him; after the telephone sessions with his mother, for instance, who, after she'd talked to him for an hour, would pass him over to his father, who'd talk to him for five minutes at most. Twice I'd seen him bang his head against the wall. Once when he found out that his favourite uncle had died: as long as the radical Islamists called the shots, attending a relative's funeral was out of the question. The other time was when it dawned on him that Khosrov, an Iranian friend with whom he played chess every week in the Full Moon cafe, was gay.

"Lots of Jews stayed in Iran after the Islamic Revolution. They don't have it easy. But they're a lot better off than Palestinians in Jewish occupied areas, that's for sure."

"How can you be so certain? Have you been to Israel?"

"I know the Middle East."

"Jews are entitled to their own country, you know that very well."

"I'm not claiming they aren't. But there's no dialogue with the original inhabitants. America looks down on the Middle East, so Israel does too."

"What was your boxer friend called?"

"Raoul Eskenazy."

"Where is he now?"

"How should I know? The ayatollahs are bad. But you lot are even worse. You've let yourselves sink into a kind of torpor. Despite all the possibilities you have."

"So why did you flee here, if we're all such losers? If only you'd stayed in your own terrific country!"

"I bet those Schneiders or Schleipers are helping finance the state of Israel."

"Oh, is *that* suddenly the issue?"

"Have you ever wondered why Israel takes part in the Eurovision Song Contest?"

"What does the Eurovision Song Contest have to do with it, for heaven's sake?"

"Israel, the conscience of Europe, isn't even *in* Europe! So why does it take part every year? Because Europe wants to forget the extermination of the Jews. And how does Europe settle this debt? By allowing people in neighbouring countries to be exterminated. Has Israel ever entered a Palestinian candidate for the contest? A Muslim? A Palestinian from the West Bank, East Jerusalem or Gaza? Have you ever heard of a Jew who didn't get a Belgian residence permit? A Jew who's been deported? But take a Palestinian or a Lebanese Muslim with exactly the same social, economic and intellectual background as his Jewish neighbour, and he'll be sent back on the first plane."

"Everything is the fault of the Jews."

"You shouldn't have given my name to those Schleipers."

"Schneider, they're called Schneider. And Mr Schneider is very nice."

As we made love afterwards, once again reconciled, it seemed unwise to confess to Nima that I'd gone so far as to write his name twice, the second time in capital letters, to make it easier for Mr Schneider to read.

Eight

I was aware that Nima's fears weren't entirely unfounded.

He'd even had dealings with officers of the BOB, the Surveillance and Investigation Brigade of the Belgian gendarmerie, and the National Security Agency.

Once I'd gone with him to their regular meeting place, deep down in the bowels of the Brussels metro. I'd insisted. Not that I suspected Nima of inventing these spy stories, yet at the same time I didn't quite believe them entirely.

I stood a few metres from Nima and the secret agent on the narrow, smelly, draughty platform of Madou station. He wasn't going to tell the spy about me, or that I was there. Anyway, if the agent knew his job, he wouldn't need to.

The man—a white guy with a moustache, in civilian clothes—didn't wear a hat or a long beige raincoat, nor did he have the obligatory briefcase that spies in films always carry around with them. He just looked like a regular commuter.

I watched them as unobtrusively as possible, squinting over the upturned collar of my jacket. They talked to each other the way spies do. The contact gazed at the ground and the train rails, Nima stared straight ahead at the opposite wall; when a train stopped, blocking his view, he hardly shifted his gaze.

The whole scene was funny and scary at the same time.

Funny because it was so unreal. Scary because the Belgian secret police had power over Nima and not the other way round.

I fantasized about how anyone could be a secret agent. The woman a bit farther down the platform, wearing a bus driver's uniform. The guy with gelled-up hair who was emptying the waste bins. The student sitting on a bench, hunched over a sociology textbook.

It was no coincidence that the BOB had contacted Nima. They'd picked him because they felt his left-wing sympathies might make for a mutually beneficial partnership.

Not that Nima had told them his ideological views, or that they were set out in his asylum dossier. The BOB had managed to winkle this information out of him without him realizing. A remarkable achievement, given how alert he was when it came to privacy issues.

The BOB's technique involved having their agents attend evening classes in French and Dutch for newcomers to the country. They would sign up under an assumed name and profession. During the breaks they'd hand out chewing gum and cigarettes: this and the fact they joined in the smoking sessions loosened tongues.

Nima was learning French. An occasional smoker, he'd once told some undercover BOB officer about the political posters he'd put up in Tehran. About his role in the student movement of the law faculty. Not knowing who he was dealing with, he'd even shown him the scar on his side, running from his right nipple to his back: "Souvenir of a jail sentence."

A little later they exchanged telephone numbers. "I play chess, so if you're looking for a partner, *appelle-moi*."

The man rang him a few days later. How would Nima like to infiltrate the ultra-left wing of the Iranian students' association in Brussels?

Nima, furious, had immediately hung up.

But a few months later the same man rang him again. "As I said, we want you to brief us on ultra-left groups at the university. But they're not the ones we're really interested in. Where progressives and atheists assemble, religious fanatics—fundamentalists—are never far away. It's *them* we want to know all about."

This time Nima didn't hang up immediately.

In exchange for passing information to the secret police, the Belgian state would pay for his studies. If he proved useful, they'd pay him a monthly allowance. Expenses, too, were negotiable. "It can take more than a couple of drinks to get to the truth."

The secret agent knew that Nima's sister, Marjane, who was two years older than him, also lived in Belgium and, like her brother, had been granted political refugee status. "But it's obvious she's an economic refugee." He assured Nima that the Belgian judicial authorities would leave Marjane in peace. The veiled threat was clear. Nima, meanwhile, just stalled and strung the BOB along. To me he said: "You don't betray your own people. And if something needs settling between Iranians, we'll see to that ourselves." For months, he played the security service's game, but with different objectives. He tried to find out exactly what it was they wanted to know about his left-wing compatriots, and what their methods were. Eventually, everyone in left-wing Iranian circles knew what these undercover officers looked like, and where they operated.

So "Fuck you" were the last words that Nima said to the agents of the state security service.

After that meeting in Madou station we went and drank a *geuze* in a cafe on the Grand Place. Or maybe in Bar Ommegang, I can't remember any more.

Nine

The first time Jakov and I really talked was on a cold day in January. I was waiting for Elzira.

One of the housekeepers told me Elzira had gone to an appointment that was running very late: "But *Madame* and *meydl* will be home soon."

I found Jakov in the garden. When not in school uniform—black trousers and jacket, white shirt—he always wore a basketball outfit. So there he was shooting hoops, in T-shirt and shorts, despite the winter cold. He had hairy legs and feet like boats. Sometimes he adjusted the red baseball cap under which his *yarmulke* hid.

In his sports kit, Jakov reminded me of Sig Arno, the German Jewish comic film actor. With his dark hair and beaky nose, Arno looked so Jewish that he made these characteristics his trademark. Like in the film where he competes in a race and, thanks to the length of his nose, is the first to reach the finish.

"Hello," I said.

"Hey," said Jakov, without looking at me. He bounced the ball hard on the tiles. Compared to Arno's great schnozz, Jakov's was a miniature.

I'd never talked to Jakov before without someone else being around. He never asked me to help with any of his school assignments and he'd made clear to his parents, despite their protests, that he would only call on me if he failed a test.

Though he did drop by every now and again, when I was tutoring Elzira. He would say hello and ask, without attaching too much importance to the answer, how I was—how's things, *ça va*, everything okay?

He took a shot, but just missed the net. Time and again. After each shot he sniffed and straightened his spectacles.

"May I?" I asked.

Jakov made a few feints and burst out laughing when I reflexively put my hands out to catch the ball. I was struck by how tall and gangly he was. He must have been at least six feet.

"Do you play basketball at school?" I asked.

"I support Maccabi," he said. He came and stood in front of me. "Look, a Maccabi cap. Maccabi is Hebrew." He threw the ball in the air and caught it again. "In our books, Maccabi stands for a strong Jewish nation."

"Oh," I said. I wanted to try a shot. I'd been good at basketball as a teenager, though volleyball took over when I got on a team.

Jakov's nose was red from the cold.

"The Maccabees were fighters. Before the birth of Christ, even, they revolted against the Greeks and their Syrian allies."

"Throw me the ball instead of giving me a history lesson," I joked. His patriotism, or need for identity or whatever you'd call it, didn't interest me at all.

"And the Maccabees refused to adapt to their Greek overlords. They were very strong, I admire them." Jakov, too, spoke Dutch with a French accent. As a family, the Schneiders spoke French, Hebrew and Yiddish, sometimes English. Almost never Dutch.

He spun on his heel, ran to the net and threw the ball, once again missing. After catching it, he threw me a pass that landed painfully in my solar plexus.

"Ow," I said.

"Assimilation is death to us," he said.

"That hurt, actually," I said, now holding the ball.

"Did you hear what I said?" he asked.

"That assimilation is death to you," I repeated. "That's a pretty big claim. What made you say that all of a sudden? Hitler was *against* assimilation. The Aryan race wasn't *allowed* to mix. Just saying."

"I'm talking about separate sports clubs."

"Oh. Is that why you have your own sports clubs? Because anything's better than mixing with non-Jews? Like your schools, where non-Jews aren't welcome?" Rage was rising in me as fast as the mercury in the thermometer was sinking, that chilly week. "Do you never doubt, then? Do you never ask yourselves whether the way you live now is the right way?"

"What do you mean?"

"How can humanity strive for unity if certain groups try ever harder to distinguish themselves?"

"You don't know our history," he said, his hands in the air, ready to block my throw. "Jewish athletes weren't allowed to join non-Jewish clubs. We have to look after ourselves, because others never will."

I took a shot. The ball rolled round the metal hoop a few times, then dropped neatly into the net.

"A fluke," Jakov sniffed. "A fluke can be pretty." He collected the bouncing ball and turned around: "*À la prochaine.*"

"Shall we have a competition? Ten shots each?"

"I've got other stuff to do," he said. He went inside.

Half an hour later, when I was sitting in the office next to Elzira, hunched over her homework—French, the simple future tense—I heard water from the bath or shower running through the pipes.

I thought it a pity he'd brushed me off so soon. I'd have liked to talk longer with him.

Ten

"So you can read Hebrew too?"

Once again, I was waiting for Elzira. Of late she'd had a few weekly appointments somewhere after school. I wasn't told what they involved. Something to do with young Jewish girls, I guessed.

This time Jakov wasn't playing basketball. Muffled up against the cold, he was fishing all kinds of debris out of the garden pond, in which three big, colourful fish were swimming. He looked at me from the little bridge. He was wearing a multicoloured, crocheted *yarmulke*; there was even a bit of red in it.

"Of course," he answered. "Every Jewish boy can. We start learning Hebrew from the age of three, we're taught the alphabet, then we study the Torah! When we're thirteen, we're called up to read aloud in the synagogue. By then we *have* to be able to read Hebrew perfectly. Our family's reputation depends on it!" He spoke in exclamation marks, as if he were standing in a pulpit.

"What about girls?" I asked. "Can they read Hebrew?"

"Girls don't have to read aloud in the synagogue. But at our school, the Yavne, they learn modern Hebrew too. Just not as thoroughly as us boys, I think. Men have to be smart."

"*We* boys, Jakov. They don't learn Hebrew as thoroughly as *we* learn it, not 'us'. And I think your mother's smart. Elzira and Sara too," I said.

"When I get married, I'd like a smart wife."

"Smarter than you?"

"Being able to read the Hebrew alphabet doesn't mean you know the language, right? I don't always know what I'm reading." He was changing the subject again.

"Oh, I know what you mean," I said. "I can read a difficult Spanish text aloud fluently without always knowing what it's about. But I do love the feel of the language rolling over my lips; sometimes it even gives me butterflies."

He grinned. "In *shul*—that's to say, in synagogue—we talk about what we read, and we debate it. We don't have a fixed truth, like you. We discuss texts, we discuss their exegesis, their interpretation, their commentaries. We have interpretations about interpretations about interpretations. You people aren't like that."

He fished a fat, slimy, dark-green strand out of the pond, pulling a face as he did so.

"'You people', you say. Just who do you mean, exactly?" I asked. I went and stood beside him. The fish gleamed under the surface. Two were white with orange patches. My coat touched Jakov's. He continued to peer intently at the water, stroking the surface with the net, not budging aside at all. I noticed a constellation of spots on his red nose and forehead. He'd have to be careful not to get acne.

"You, the other people."

"The non-Jewish population?"

"Catholics, certainly. And Muslims."

"Do you think I'm Catholic?"

"You're not a Muslim!" His joke seemed, like a deep sigh, to release some inner tension.

"In what language do you converse in the synagogue?"

"In Yiddish, modern Hebrew, French, English. There are many Jews who speak better English than French."

"Don't you ever talk Dutch?"

"Sometimes. Yes, of course. But by no means all Jews were born here or went to school here. We come from all over, as you know."

The fish swam in circles. Occasionally the silver one, the only one that didn't have orange blazes on its scales, gulped for air. Jakov danced round him with the net, working carefully.

"Ancient Hebrew isn't the same as Ivrit, modern Hebrew. It's the language of the Torah, our Holy Writ. It's not a spoken language. Jews stopped speaking Hebrew long before the birth of Christ. Of course you know that very well, you study languages."

As you know. Of course you know. These asides of his pricked me like fishhooks.

"So all those Antwerp Jews who speak Hebrew are in fact using a new form of an ancient language?" was all I could think of to say.

He stopped sweeping the net and turned round, raising his eyebrows exaggeratedly. A mocking, superior smile played on his lips. His glasses were smeared. I found the contrast touching.

"Or am I wrong?" I asked, beginning to get tired of waiting for Elzira. Was I allowed to count time spent waiting as time spent working? I should be. Every evening I arrived at their door at half past five. And according to Jakov's bright-red Swatch it was now nearly six thirty. His watch was modern. Everything else about him was Orthodox.

"Don't tell me you don't know that Yiddish is the most commonly spoken language in Antwerp's Jewish community!"

He'd hooked me again.

"Elzira told me Yiddish wasn't taught at your school."

"At our school, the religious subjects are taught in Hebrew."

"Why?"

"We're not Hasidic Jews," he said, once again with that knowing air of mystery he cultivated. It made him seem opinionated, tough, scared and vulnerable all at once. "Haredi and Hasidic Jews belong to another group."

"Am I supposed to know what you mean?"

"Haredi and Hasidic Jews are ultra-Orthodox Jews. They have their own *rebbes* and their own *shuls*."

"You don't?"

"We're Modern Orthodox. We go to different synagogues and have different rabbis. Hasidic children go to different schools, which are much stricter about religion than ours. Assuming they go to a school that teaches secular subjects in the first place. In Belgium, children must be educated, but they don't have to go to school. So in the very strictest groups, some children are home-schooled. They don't have a curriculum; they only study the Torah and the Talmud—the interpretations of the Torah. Those are their frames of reference, those they will study and discuss throughout their lives, from the moment they get up to the moment they go to sleep. We are not like them. We do not close our eyes to modern society, we form part of it."

"Hasidic Jews are the ones with the sidelocks, right? I've never seen boys wear such a jolly *yarmulke* as you," I teased him.

He started, began to blush, felt to see if it still sat properly on his head and laughed. "A fine *yarmulke*, you must admit. Given to me by my grandmother. She brought it back from Israel, from a famous shop in the Mea Shearim neighbourhood in Jerusalem; there they sell almost nothing but hats and *yarmulkes*, thousands and thousands of them. In theory we can wear all colours. Haredi and Hasidic Jews can't, they only wear black. And their *kippahs* are never crocheted, like mine. They're made of velour."

"When do you say *kippah* and when *yarmulke*?"

"There's no difference, *kippah*, *keppeltje*, *yarmulke*, it's all the same."

"You could have your name crocheted in a *yarmulke*."

"My name's on the inside. Embroidered."

"May I see?"

"No."

"Say something to me in Hebrew."

"Everyone has a different accent in Hebrew." He turned back to the pond. The surface was clean. He checked the air pump and opened the tap to refresh the water.

"What sort of accent do you have, then?" I asked.

"The accent of a French-speaking Flemish Jew born in Antwerp, with roots that started off somewhere in Hungary, but also lie in the Netherlands," he said.

"So you have family in the Netherlands?"

"Had. The Netherlands, Jews, war."

"What do you mean?"

"Anne Frank wasn't the only person to be betrayed by the Dutch, in case you thought that."

"I *don't* think that."

"You should listen carefully when you hear Hebrew or Yiddish being spoken. Georgian Jews roll their 'r's. Jews from Morocco, Tunisia and Algeria have a guttural 'r', they gargle like the Arabs."

"As if I could hear that. As if I knew what country a Jew was from. To me, you all look alike!"

Once again, his eyebrows went up very pointedly.

"Some rabbis *détestent* modern Hebrew," he went on. "They can't abide that their holy language is reduced to a tool with which to *papoter*... That's why the language of communication is Yiddish and not modern Hebrew."

"*Papoter* is French. You mean 'chat'."

"It takes aeons for the finest diamonds to reach their full brilliance. To me, ancient Hebrew is such a diamond. So I get it that people think you shouldn't touch it. But let's talk about something else, it's not good to talk about this all the time."

"Why not?"

"You're not a Jew."

This defensive, slightly superior attitude was familiar to me. Nima and I sometimes played the same game. He said I had no right to talk, because I was an outsider. I retorted in kind.

Like when someone rang the doorbell whom I didn't feel like seeing. Nima just couldn't understand why I wouldn't answer. In his country that was unthinkable. He would quote an old Persian proverb: "A good hostess knows there is always enough water for an unexpected guest." It meant that a meal for two could easily be turned into a meal for four if you added water to the dish.

"You're not in Iran now," I would respond. "Here, things are done differently. You couldn't know, you weren't born here."

For my part, I couldn't understand his boundless generosity. One day, when we were visiting my sister in Ghent and it turned out, while cooking a meal for us, that she'd run out of olive oil, Nima said, "I'll just nip out and get some." He came back with a five-litre can. Me: "Isn't that a bit over the top?" Him: "In my country, you can never give too much, only too little." "But we can't even make ends meet ourselves!" "An Iranian doesn't think like that."

"These are koi," Jakov said. "We'll have to put wire netting over the pond, otherwise they'll get eaten by herons. Herons just love kosher koi." He laughed.

"Kosher koi? Surely you don't eat them!"

"Joke. But we're allowed to eat them. Koi are carp. We buy them in Israel. They're just as good as the ones from Japan, but only half the price."

"Aren't those fish too big for a heron?"

"You never know. Prevention is better than care."

"Prevention is better than *cure*."

"You're a *goyte*," he said. He walked to the garden shed and hung the fishnet on a hook on its wall.

"What's a *goyte*?"

"Feminine of goy."

"And as a *goyte* I'm inferior? And you're superior?"

"I'm not saying that."

"What *are* you saying, then?"

"You don't believe in the Messiah."

"I don't believe in anything."

"Anything at all?"

"Well, if you must know, I believe in my boyfriend, Jakov. In love."

Eleven

Elzira was right-handed.

And it was her right hand that failed her the most.

Yet even at the age of twelve, Elzira showed extraordinary feistiness. I've seen her, surrounded by relatives, open cards and parcels with beads of sweat pearling on her forehead, not from the heat or excitement about the contents, but because she knew everyone was looking at her: the more eyes on her, the more her hands would shake.

Though it cost her a huge effort to prise open the gift wrapping, though it would have been much easier for her to accept all the help that was offered, or to rip open an envelope in one go, she refused to let her deficient motor skills get the better of her and opened presents by herself, as calmly as she could. You could see from her seriousness that this battle between her and the wrappings was nothing less than a point of honour.

It had started suddenly, when she was five. At first, her parents thought their daughter was just highly strung. Or that she suffered from growth spasms. Maybe a nerve had got trapped somewhere. But when the tremor continued, day after day, they were worried enough to go to their doctor. The doctor sent them to a neurologist, the first in a long line of specialists the Schneiders consulted at home and abroad, Jewish and non-Jewish.

All the experts came up with much the same diagnosis: dyspraxia, a genetic disorder that has links with dyslexia.

59

The more tests that Elzira had to undergo, the clearer it became that her motor skills had been impaired right from birth.

She'd never managed to handle a knife and fork with ease. In shoe shops she chose moccasins, or shoes that fastened with Velcro, avoiding shoelaces and zips. She pretended not to like ball games, to mask her lack of skill. When, as a five-year-old, she refused to learn to ride a bike, her father and mother thought this was from religious motives: some of her little playmates came from ultra-strict families and they could neither ride bicycles nor sit on the back. The notion of their legs whirling about on the pedals, or dangling from the carrier, was anathema to Him.

One evening I found her sitting in her room crying, almost inaudibly. Perhaps she'd got a bad mark for her test, I thought. But the marked paper was lying in front of her, and I could see she'd done very well.

"What's the matter?" I asked.

She didn't answer. She wiped away her tears. New ones immediately appeared.

Trembling, she began to hit her right hand with her left. Cautiously, I took hold of both her hands. She didn't resist.

"Are you cross about something?" I asked.

She clenched her fists. "I go to the physiotherapist," she said. "Twice a week after school. He was supposed to *me guérir*, to cure me. But it's not getting better. And sometimes I go to a psychologist."

That explained the mysterious appointments.

"Does the physiotherapist give you exercises to do?"

"All the time. And I have to do them at home. Throw balls and catch them, so that my eyes and hands react together, or something like that. Write down words. Tell the time. I have a book with exercises."

"And the psychologist?"

"Talks to me."

"And you talk back?"

"As much as I can. Sometimes I can't."

"Can't or won't?"

"With me, that's sometimes the same."

"So this psychologist, is he Jewish?"

"Yes. And it's not 'he' but a 'she'. Most of her clients are Jewish. She speaks Yiddish and Hebrew. I speak to her *en français*."

"Do you like talking to her?"

"She's *gentille*."

"Do you feel relieved afterwards?"

"I go on shaking."

"You'll have to be patient. Did she tell you whether you can expect to improve, and when?"

"She says she can't guarantee anything."

"But?"

"But what?"

"Did she say that the exercises will help? That talking will help?"

"I don't know. I'm tired."

"Shall we do some exercises together?" I suggested. "Where's that booklet you got from your physiotherapist? Shall we play catch in the garden for half an hour?"

Elzira stared outside, every muscle tensed. Her skin was so translucent I could see the blue veins in her neck and temples.

"Are you crying because you're scared your hand might never be steady?"

"Daddy will buy me an electric typewriter one day," she said.

"That ought to make you happy," I smiled.

"Daddy doesn't want to buy the typewriter yet. Like you, he believes in exercise. He thinks I'm giving up if I stop writing by hand. If I can, at my young age, already replace my pen with a machine, he regards that as... He thinks then that I succombeer..."

"That I'm giving up: *succomber* means 'to give up, to surrender'."

"Yes, *une défaite*, he will think it a defeat."

"The shaking will get less as you grow older," I said reassuringly. "Your mummy and daddy told me. And they know, because of the doctors and test results."

"But it will never go away altogether."

Now we both stared outside.

"Congratulations on your French test," I said after a while. "You got eight out of ten for verb endings! Not many girls could do that."

"Could you please teach me to ride a bike?" she asked.

Twelve

After badgering them for weeks, Mr and Mrs Schneider finally gave me permission to teach their elder daughter to ride a bike. We were allowed to spend two hours a day on this activity every Sunday, from eleven to one, on condition that I took Elzira to a place where she could fall safely, away from traffic, and where she couldn't suffer loss of face.

The idea of their daughter lying on the ground with her legs in the air in one of the streets of the Jewish neighbourhood horrified the Schneiders. In a neighbourhood where no one knew her, no one could gossip about her.

I walked alongside her, pushing her brand-new bicycle, heading for a park near the banks of the Scheldt.

Christmas trees had been put up in some of the streets.

"Jews don't celebrate Christmas, right?" I said.

"I think those lights are very pretty," Elzira said. Her breath made little clouds in the cold air.

She walked with short strides. She was wearing a long, black velvet pencil skirt that restricted her leg movements. Pretty and modest, but decidedly impractical for cycling. We both wore leather gloves: mine were red, hers black.

Elzira, it soon turned out, had never before crossed the avenues that bisected the city centre by herself. "Not even with friends." She'd never before gone on foot to this side of Antwerp. On the rare occasions that she visited a non-Jewish neighbourhood, she would travel by car, on the back seat of her father's white Volvo. The Schneider girls seldom went by bus or tram, certainly not on their own. If it was raining very heavily, they would take a taxi to and from school. They would find these taxi firms in the Jewish community's own telephone book, or in *Koopjesplus*, the Antwerp Jewish Advertiser, which plugged cheap reflexology sessions, group tours to Switzerland, special offers on detergents or kosher cake for special events in Hebrew, Yiddish, English, French, Dutch and even Georgian.

They were regular customers of Antwerp Taxi. The operator of the city's largest taxi firm knew not to send certain drivers to certain addresses. Just as he knew when it would be better to send a people carrier: large families didn't fit into a standard cab, and if they had to go to Zaventem airport there could be scenes when the head of the family wanted to lash all the suitcases and buggies to the roof of the cab with rope or bungee straps, and you had to tell him that safety regulations didn't allow it.

Elzira didn't look around her, but marched on. She seemed to be in a hurry.

The area around Verschansingstraat and the old Waterpoort city gate was home to a large Moroccan and Turkish community. The men sat in coffee and tea houses whose windows were covered with opaque plastic, and sometimes bore the letters VZW, standing for "not-for-profit organization", not always in the right order. The women were nowhere to be seen. In summer, surrounded by children, they would sit chatting on stools on the pavement, newly washed mats and rugs spread out around them to dry. They drank mint tea, unfailingly accompanied by sweet, orange-coloured pastries. In winter they vanished indoors. The streets were almost deserted. The only shops open were Turkish ones. I could hear Arabic or Berber; I couldn't distinguish the one from the other.

Elzira asked: "Is it dangerous here?"

"Dangerous? Why?"

"Only non-Jews live here."

"That applies to most places in the city."

"*Je sais.*"

"Do you feel uneasy?"

"I don't know."

"Every city has its neighbourhoods."

"Yes."

"My boyfriend Nima is Iranian; you know that."

"But he's with you."

Never a great talker, Elzira suddenly started to rattle away without stopping. She told me that she had been given her pink bicycle for her *bat mitzvah*—a kind of confirmation ceremony for girls. That she'd tried to ride it a couple of times. That it hadn't worked. That she hadn't been able to keep her balance. That she'd never managed to pedal and steer simultaneously, because of her handicap. She repeated the word handicap, pronouncing it in a French way. She said she'd once smashed her bike against the garage wall in front of her parents and run off to her room in a rage. Told me that Daddy had put the bike in his car and that they'd driven to a park outside the city a few times. That the last time she'd burst into tears and Daddy had said, "You don't have to, it's all right."

She explained to me what *bar mitzvah*, "son of the commandment" meant. She did it really well, going into detail, as if giving a mini presentation. In short it amounted to this: *bar mitzvah* was the solemn ritual ceremony at the synagogue for thirteen-year-old boys, marking their transition to religious adulthood. From then on they no longer fell under the religious custodianship of their parents, but took personal responsibility for keeping the 613 Jewish commandments, *mitzvoth*, which I knew existed, but not that there were so many of them.

Elzira: "'*Bat mitzvah*', with a 't', means 'daughter of the commandment'. But in public Jewish life, men are more important than women. So boys get a bigger party. And more and bigger presents. But girls *do* have this celebration earlier, when they're twelve."

"I think your bike's a big present, you know," I responded.

She nodded. Here, plucked from her familiar environment, she looked extra vulnerable. She placed her hand on the bike saddle. It was a Kalkhoff, a brand you hardly ever saw in Belgium. Kalkhoffs were made in Germany.

My grandfather regarded all German companies as tainted. No German products crossed *his* threshold. For the Schneiders, though, the fact that Kalkhoff workers might have contributed to the extermination of the Jewish people was apparently no reason to boycott the brand. I had yet to meet a Jew who drove a Mercedes, but in the case of this bicycle they hadn't even bothered to paint over the name on the frame.

At the baker's in Verschansingstraat, near the Royal Museum of Fine Arts, I bought two croissants and two *pains au chocolat*.

Elzira didn't want to go inside with me. "You go, I'll stay with my bike." Her head was hidden by her down hood.

"Have one," I urged her before we set off. I held the bag, with its fragrance of fresh pastry, under her nose.

She shook her head.

"Go on, I didn't buy them for nothing."

"No thank you." She pushed the bike's kickstand up again and asked what direction we should go in.

"The croissants here are really tasty," I tried once more.

She had already walked on. She said nothing more, but I could see from her pace that she wanted to get going.

As we waited at a zebra crossing she looked at me. "Could I perhaps just taste a *pain au chocolat*? But don't tell Mummy or Daddy."

"Sure. Here. Enjoy. They're really good. But why aren't your parents allowed to know? Are you on a diet?"

"It's not allowed."

"What's not allowed?"

"The baker isn't kosher..."

"But there can't be anything wrong with a croissant. There's no fish, meat or milk in them."

"There are eggs and butter in them. Eggs have to be checked by the rabbi. Only he can say whether they're kosher."

"Checked for what?"

"Traces of blood. We don't eat eggs *qui sont des poussins.*"

"Eggs that are chickens? There aren't any chickens in these eggs!"

"You shouldn't mock us."

"I'm not mocking you, sorry, I didn't mean it like that. I just find it, er, a bit absurd. But if I'd known you weren't allowed to eat anything from our bakers, of course I wouldn't have bought something here or offered it to you..."

"With us, all *produits laitiers* have to be separated from everything else. That includes the kitchen, our own kitchen. Have you seen that there are two dishwashers in our kitchen? One for *produits laitiers* and one for everything else. We've got two sets of pots and pans."

"I've never been in your kitchen. And it's 'dairy products', Elzira. *Produits laitiers* is dairy products. Eggs aren't dairy."

"Butter's a dairy product. I'll show you our kitchen."

"So because of your dietary laws, you can never come and eat pancakes at our place? What a shame!" I said.

"We only eat at the homes of Jewish people who respect our dietary laws. Or we go to a kosher restaurant. But Mummy says there are so few kosher restaurants in the city that she always sees the same people there. Mummy would like to go somewhere where she doesn't know anyone for a change. But Daddy's different. He likes people to know him, he enjoys it when people greet him *en public*, he's happy when someone comes to chat with him and he can tell a joke—he knows good jokes, really. Luckily Irma can cook well, and Mummy even better."

She laughed.

"Who's Irma?"

"She works at our house. You've seen her already. She often cooks."

"And your mummy?"

"She often cooks too."

"Are the women who work for you Jewish?" I asked. As far as I could make out, I'd seen three domestic staff. The children were friendly to them, but kept their distance more than from me.

"They're not Jewish. But they've learnt all our dietary laws. One of them, Krystina, used to work for the catering company that supplies El Al, the *ligne aérienne* of Israel. Krystina comes from Poland, just like Irma. Opris comes from Romania."

"My boyfriend Nima is a good cook. Suppose he were to cook for you one evening, using only kosher products and keeping to your laws? Would you come for a meal at our place?"

"The Eternal One is the most important thing for us," she announced, swallowing the last mouthful of her *pain au chocolat*. Her answer came out of the blue. The Schneiders excelled in this kind of *deus ex machina*.

"Is God more important than friendship?" I wouldn't be put off.

"He *is* friendship," she said, "and we never speak his name, out of respect for the Eternal One. Could you please never mention his name again?"

There I stood. Not believing in God or G*d or any kind of supreme being whatsoever. Seriously doubting the possibility of ever becoming friends with Elzira, or any other pious Orthodox Jewish child.

"But you can always come and eat with us. You don't have to keep any dietary laws. So you can keep ours," she said, without a trace of superiority. Adding that the best kosher chocolate was made by Callebaut, and that from now on we would get pastries at Kleinblatt's to take with us, or at Grosz, her favourite kosher supermarket, not far from their home.

By the time I helped her into the saddle, there was already more colour in her cheeks. Though it could have been my imagination.

Thirteen

Somewhere in Iran there are at least ten videotapes of films starring me.

Every few months, Nima would rent a portable 8mm Sony video camera and film scenes from our daily lives to send to his parents.

Many were recorded in our kitchen: dishes expressed more than we could say.

Nima prepared basmati rice the way his mother and grand-mother had taught him. He washed the grains in a fine sieve as I panned the camera from him to the tap and the sink, and then back again. As soon as the rinsing water was crystal clear he tipped the rice into boiling, salted water. I recorded him layering the bottom of the oven dish with thin slices of raw potato, then letting the rice, enriched with a big knob of butter and filaments of saffron, steam in the dish, which he'd covered with a clean tea towel. In the end, the potato layer was transformed into a crust patterned by the grains of rice. As I scraped out the delicious crust and gobbled it up, Nima zoomed in on my beaming face.

Flemish cuisine was demonstrated in the same way. While Nima trained the camera on me, I put large, peeled potatoes through a mechanical chip cutter. I dabbed the raw chips dry with kitchen paper, fried them once in lard, then fried them again. As Nima dipped the chips in—home-made!—mayonnaise and Andalouse sauce, I zoomed in on his greasy lips. We made shrimp croquettes, recording the whole procedure from A to Z. Even though we knew that pink shrimps weren't to be had in Iran. I made pancakes and spread them with pear syrup.

We gave his parents a tour of Antwerp. Guided them from the Royal Museum of Fine Arts to the cathedral, from the Rubens House to the Begijnhof, from the pedestrian tunnel under the Scheldt to the Middelheim sculpture park.

We wanted to show them the Jewish neighbourhood.

When we filmed a group of boys with sidelocks under the bridge by Van Den Nestlei, we were stopped by a police officer who said that we'd been under observation since we'd entered Mercatorstraat and Simonsstraat. In those streets we'd filmed three picturesque, typically Jewish shops: a bookshop, a baker's, a greengrocer's. At the synagogues, housed in ordinary town houses, Nima had filmed the faithful going in and out. The security guard standing at the entrance, his legs slightly apart, had nodded at us. When they saw our camera, the worshippers had turned their heads away angrily. A man dressed in civilian clothes, somewhat flustered, came to tell us to go away. Which we'd done without too much protest, walking in the direction of Belgiëlei, to the bridge where this officer had stopped us.

"You've been spotted," he said.

"Spotted?" Nima asked laconically. "Like celebrities, you mean? Or UFOs?"

"Can I see your identity document."

"Why?"

"You've been spotted."

"By whom?"

"By our colleagues at the places of worship."

I tugged at Nima's sleeve. He ignored me. He asked where it was written that you couldn't stand under a bridge or film in Simonsstraat. He wanted to see the law on paper; only then would he perhaps be prepared to admit that he'd committed an offence.

He asked the officer for his name and the names of his superiors. He suggested that we all go to the police station together. "Then we can get to the bottom of this case." I burst out laughing.

The policeman looked a bit at a loss, but he was sympathetic towards us and quite communicative. He told us that the Israeli embassy, in consultation with the local and federal police, deployed its own security patrols in Antwerp's Jewish neighbourhood. They were the ones who'd spotted us.

"I'd like to see the Iranian embassy try that," said Nima.

"Sir, I can't change the world," the officer replied. "And if there was no injustice in it, we'd be out of a job."

He noted down our personal details, but didn't impound the camera or the videotape. "In future, film more discreetly," he advised us, "and respect the wishes of those who don't want to be filmed." Deciding to celebrate this happy outcome within our budget, we went to Hoffy's, fairly new at the time, but which almost instantly became the best-known kosher restaurant and takeaway in the city. Run by photogenic Hasidic brothers, with a menu in Yiddish, it did the second-best takeout hummus in town.

Fourteen

Less than an hour into our practice session—I'd let go of the back wheel and given her bike an extra push—Elzira came a cropper on the cobblestones.

I saw it happen. At first she pedalled timidly. Then she grew bold, starting to go faster and faster. She was only about thirty metres away when she panicked and lost control of the handlebars. The bike collided with a Renault that was parked by the kerb. So did she.

I ran towards her. She struggled to her feet, holding her right hand with her left. With a grimace she started picking bits of gravel out of her glove, removing them carefully, finger by finger and centimetre by centimetre. Her skirt was dirty, her woollen tights were torn at one knee and there were dirty, wet patches on the right sleeve of her jacket. Her wrist was red and already quite swollen.

She tried to stand her bicycle upright. Again and again it fell over. The more she tried, the more awkward her movements became. It was as if a flame had been lit under her clumsiness, causing a host of slumbering frustrations to flare up. When I tried to help her, she pushed me away. *"Laisse-moi."* The white Renault, whose rear end was now scraped and disfigured by pink stripes, suffered fresh wounds.

I went to inspect her wrist. *"Non."* I asked where it hurt. *"Laisse-moi, je te dis!"* I said soothingly that everything was hard at first, and as I said it, I heard my mother, and knew how ludicrous these well-intentioned words must have sounded to Elzira. She pushed me away. I picked her bike up; the chain had come off. "Shall we put it back on together?" I asked her.

She started to punch me violently on the chest. Short blows punctuated by sobs. As she punched, she jumped up and down like someone trying to warm up as quickly as possible. She was saying something to me in French as she hit me. I didn't know what, couldn't follow it at all. Small and frail as she was, she was stronger than I'd thought.

"Look at me, Elzira," I commanded. I didn't dare grab her punching hands, she might have sprained her wrist.

She thumped me hard on the chest. It hurt. "Stop it, Elzira, look at me."

"I'm not coming back!" She ran off angrily.

When someone runs away, you should let them run, I knew from personal experience. Just then I didn't care about the trouble this would certainly cause. The Schneiders would sack me on the spot, I was sure. The very first time I'd taken their daughter somewhere they felt she shouldn't be, I'd abandoned her to her fate.

She'd never be able to find her way home. Unless she asked a passer-by for directions. But she wouldn't dare. She'd never done that in her life. All the activities organized by Aguda, the Jewish youth movement, took place in the Jewish neighbourhood. And the movement's summer and winter camps were held abroad, in places where the Jewish faith and all that went with it weren't threatened by outside influences. Once a year she went skiing with Aguda. Boys and girls separately. The ski slope was the only place where Elzira wore trousers, immediately changing into her long skirt and tights for the après-ski. I've seen photos of one of these camps; in her ski pants she looked strong and pretty.

She would probably hail a taxi, I thought. But hardly any taxis drove around this neighbourhood, especially on a Sunday morning.

The people who lived here used public transport or walked. She didn't have any money on her, I realized, but that wasn't necessarily a problem; her parents would pay the driver when he dropped her off at their door.

I replaced the bike chain and went and drank a cup of coffee in Entrepôt du Congo, a cafe where I regularly read the papers of an afternoon. There was a payphone near the toilets. Should I call Elzira's parents? Should I look for Elzira? Or would she come back, as I suspected she would?

I drank a cup of coffee, ordered a second.

Elzira came round the corner, dragging her feet, her hands pressed against her temples.

She saw me through the window and gave me a nod. I waved, gestured she should come inside. She shook her head. I pantomimed that I wanted to finish my coffee. She nodded.

When I went outside, she came and pressed her body against me. I felt her tense muscles—neck, shoulders, back—and wasn't quite sure what to do. I stroked her glossy, dark brown locks; they smelt so nice I wondered if she'd sprayed them with perfume.

"Your hair smells really nice," I said.

"Mummy taught me that," she said softly. "Mummy says, 'put a dab of *eau de toilette* on your hair, everyone's the better for it.'"

I laughed.

Her mother, she went on, had warned her to keep this tip to herself: a devout Jewish woman shouldn't wear alluring perfume.

"Mummy doesn't wear a wig either. Never. She told me and Sara that as a married woman you can be true to your religion, your tradition and your husband without a *perruque*. Mummy is very religious, but she is more *moderne* than most of us."

Once again, Elzira began to sob.

Were she to cry in public in her own neighbourhood, her outburst would instantly be public knowledge. Crying was a bit like eating: you couldn't do it outside the home—and certainly not on the street—without being noticed.

We went and sat on a bench. My bottom got wet and cold, and I made Elzira sit on my rucksack.

Elzira asked if she could tell me something in confidence. Her voice was hoarse and she was breathing quickly.

"Of course," I said.

"But you mustn't tell it to anyone. *À personne*. Not even Mummy and Daddy."

I reminded her that I was only eight years older than her, and told her that I'd once been an Elzira just like her. Also that all children have secrets they want to keep to themselves, stories their parents should never know.

"It's about Him, the Eternal One," she said.

"It can be about anyone," I said, "it'll stay between us."

She told me that when she was in primary school she prayed to God every day, asking Him to turn her into a bird. He could do that, she knew; every now and again He would grant a special wish to a girl who'd been good. She'd done her best to be good, always and to everyone, but she'd never become a bird, not even for a single instant, so she probably hadn't been good enough, because otherwise He'd have let her soar through the air just for a little while, with strong wings instead of trembling fingers. That's why she'd wanted to be a bird, because birds don't have hands, but they do have freedom, and she'd just wanted to experience that for a single day, she'd longed for that gift much more than the bicycle she got for her *bat mitzvah*.

After praying to be a bird, she'd often prayed for a friend. Still did, in fact. She was nice to all the girls in her class, and the other girls were nice to her, but not especially nice, whereas she would do *anything* for a friend if she had one, but she didn't, because no one chose to be her friend, just as, when picking teams in gym class when I was at school, no one picked the fat girls.

Sometimes, increasingly in fact, she couldn't sleep at night because she was thinking of her future. As she lay there in bed, she grew fearful. She had visions of future suitors leaving her in the lurch. If she couldn't make friends, she'd certainly never be able to find a husband. That, *le désintérêt des autres*, was her biggest nightmare.

"I hate my hands," she said. "I'd like to hack them off."

She pulled her sleeves down over her fingers. Like so many girls—I'd been one of them—she hunched her shoulders to make her budding breasts look smaller. A time-honoured method of concealment until their owner was more used to their curves.

Elzira pulled her sleeves over her fingers because her hands had become an obsession.

She said she often fantasized about having them surgically amputated. In that fantasy, her father had two prosthetic hands made for her. Of course, people would stare at her artificial hands, but less judgementally than at a healthy teenager who couldn't hold a fork, glass or pen properly. What's more, you could control prosthetic limbs, but not shaky hands.

She talked non-stop, holding my hand. She assured me her parents would buy me new gloves, because it was her fault that they'd got oily from the bike chain. She showed me her wrist: scraped and swollen, but certainly not broken, hopefully not sprained.

"We're going home," I said.

"No, please help me back onto the bike," she said.

Then she asked me to put a note under the windscreen wiper of the Renault with her parents' telephone number on it.

I did write a note. But the number I gave was made up.

Fifteen

Our training sessions were tough going. But after each fall she got up again, by the end often in fits of laughter.

Two months after that Sunday afternoon Elzira could cycle, even on quite busy roads, without losing her balance or panicking. In fact she seemed transformed as she pushed down on the pedals, radiating a new self-confidence.

One evening, after having seen his daughter cycling through the local streets, Mr Schneider came into the office, after having knocked on the door three times, and asked me if I knew the story about the girl and the spider.

I shook my head, bracing myself for another anecdote along the lines of Moshe and Abe. Once again Mr Schneider showed all the symptoms of a man about to tell a joke he thinks is very funny: a theatrical stance, twinkling eyes, anticipation of applause.

He did not tell a joke. He'd decided, he said, that from now on tutoring sessions wouldn't be held in the office but in the children's rooms. Everything we needed was there. It was warmer, too, in winter. "And the walls aren't so bare."

Then he told me about a girl who was terrified of spiders, and about the tests to which she'd been subjected by a group of psychologists and medical researchers. They put a big black spider in the middle of a room and encouraged the girl to walk towards it. Four metres was as close as she ever got; she didn't dare go any nearer. At that distance her heart rate would shoot up. She would start to sweat and shake, grow pale and hyper-ventilate.

For the next stage of the test, the researchers had invited about ten of the girl's friends to join her. They sat on a raised bench where they could see the spider.

Each time the girl began her assignment, her friends high-fived her. Backed by her team of supporters, the child managed to approach within two metres of the spider the very first time she tried. By the tenth time, all her physical fear responses (which were scientifically measured) had gone down to normal.

"You are like such a team for our Elzira," he said. And he turned to his daughter: *"N'est-ce pas, ma fille?"*

Sixteen

Jakov told me he had French and history tests coming up: could I help him prepare? He asked it as if it were the most natural thing in the world.

We used his bedroom as our workspace. All four children had their own bedrooms, even their own bathrooms. A washbasin, toilet and shower for the boys; the girls had a Jacuzzi as well. I was stunned by such luxury. At my home, we'd had to draw up a roster for the bathroom on Friday evenings. Otherwise there'd be a pile-up, especially if more than one of us hoped to score at a party. Our house didn't have a shower and we bathed only once a week. The same bathwater had to be used by at least two people, and you weren't allowed to top it up with hot water.

Jakov's room had been painted sky blue. The curtains were dark blue. On the bed lay a blue-and-white-striped coverlet. The carpet was yet another shade of blue. Everything in his room seemed to have been designed with care. His bed stood against the longest wall. At its foot was a little platform, with his desk at the centre, ornamented by five miniature sailboats. Sitting there, we could see the posters he'd hung on the wall by his bed.

Other boys his age brightened up their rooms with photos of footballers, pop singers or film stars. The more pretentious ones hung up pop-art prints by Andy Warhol; Jakov went to sleep under the stern gaze of eight chief rabbis.

The portraits were life-size and hung in two rows of four. All the rabbis had beards. All the pictures were black and white. Some of the faces seemed to date from antiquity.

"Are those Jewish ayatollahs?" I joked, still a bit nervous. I'd assumed by now that the Schneider boys weren't going to need my services, and found that comforting. I already had my hands full teaching Elzira, which took up several hours a day. As yet, Sara didn't need any help with her homework, but in a year or two I'd be tutoring her too.

"Eight ayatollahs next to your bed. Do you sleep easy, Jakov? They'd give me nightmares."

"Don't mock Maimonides, Judah the Prince and the other great Jewish minds," Jakov said drily. He got two ring binders out of his rucksack and threw them on his desk.

"Nima would be intrigued by these portraits," I went on.

"Who's Nima?"

"My boyfriend."

"Funny. Sounds like a woman's name."

"He's Persian."

We were sitting next to each other, but about three feet apart. Clutching onto the arm rests and pressing my bottom against the seat, I made a few frog leaps with the chair in his direction. Jakov didn't react.

"Can I see your history book?" I asked. "Where have you got to? What period are you learning about?"

He opened one of the ring binders.

"If I have to test you, I'd rather sit opposite you," I said, "like in an oral exam." Jakov looked uncomfortable at the idea.

"We don't have oral exams yet."

"But you do with me." I stood up and put my chair opposite his, on the other side of the desk.

"What's a Persian?" he asked, before I'd even sat down properly.

I looked at him in surprise. "Someone from Iran. Don't tell me you don't know that."

"*Un Persan?* A guy from Persia? Why didn't you say so? We learnt about Alexander the Great last year."

"It's not '*Persan*' but 'Persian'."

"Your boyfriend's from Iran? If my parents knew that…"

"Your parents *do* know that."

"No kidding?"

"Ask them."

"Do you see him often?"

"We live together."

He blushed. "Are you *hoteldebotel* about him?"

I was amazed that his Dutch extended to a word like *hoteldebotel*.

"It's Yiddish for 'madly in love'."

"I didn't know that. So you're teaching me now. Great! And yes, I am *hoteldebotel* about him."

"Dutch also gets the words *lef* and *mazzel* from us."

"From Hebrew, you mean."

"By a detour. They meandered from Hebrew to Yiddish, then from Yiddish to Dutch."

"Congratulations. What a lot you know."

"Are you married?" He averted his gaze.

"No, we're not married."

"Do my parents know that too?"

Now he *did* look me straight in the eye.

"Yes."

"But your boyfriend is Catholic…"

"No, Muslim."

"He's not!"

"He is!" I said. For once I found myself beaming from ear to ear as I said it.

"Mummy and Daddy don't know that."

"Yes they do."

Jakov looked at me, suspicious and curious. His gaze betrayed a strange mix of respect and censoriousness.

"But you'll soon marry and have children."

"I don't think I'll marry. And I'm not sure if I want children."

He took off his spectacles, polished them with a big checked handkerchief and replaced them, as if cleaner glasses would help him understand me more clearly. His blush had spread to behind his ears, even his earlobes glowed.

"We share a bed too, of course," I added, having found a way to get him back for all those as-you-knows. "If you know what I mean."

He saw that I was aware of his growing agitation and embarrassment. I feigned not to notice his blushes, turning slightly to face the posters. That, too, he saw.

"We're in the middle of the Second World War. The teacher is keeping the subject as general as possible."

"One minute we're talking about my bed, the next about the war?" I said. "Only joking."

"He's not asking us to tell our family history," he said.

"Were your relatives in concentration camps?" I asked, now serious again.

I'd often wanted to ask Elzira that question, but had always stopped myself in time. Now it popped out.

"We don't talk about that."

"Is your history teacher Jewish?"

"No, he's secular. This year we're going to Fort Breendonk. And the Anne Frank House."

"That's good."

"Breendonk is a terrible place."

"I've never been there."

"Lots of people were tortured and killed there, Jews and non-Jews. After the war, it was used as a prison for collaborators."

"You know more about it than I do."

"My grandfather, my father's father, died in Auschwitz. My grandmother survived the camp. Mummy lost nearly all her family... Daddy was born during the war. We children were all named after relatives who were rounded up in raids and never came back..."

I was silent.

"Who was Jakov?"

"Let's talk about something else."

His colour had returned to normal. "Yiddish is written in the Hebrew alphabet, did you know that?" he announced perkily.

"I find that hard to believe," I retorted. "Yiddish is an Indo-European language, and I happen to know a bit about Indo-European languages!"

"Bet you a hundred francs that the Yiddish and Hebrew alphabets are the same!"

I didn't take him up on it. Instead, I asked him if that meant that Isaac Bashevis Singer, whose books had been recommended to me by my German teacher, wrote his whole oeuvre in the Hebrew script. He asked me who Singer was.

"Don't you have a Yiddish newspaper here somewhere? That would settle the question."

"We don't take a Yiddish newspaper. There *is* one though: the *Forverts*, the *Jewish Daily Forward*. It's published in New York."

"The *Jewish Forward*! That must have a big circulation," I mocked.

"*Before* the Shoah there were quite a few Yiddish newspapers," Jakov said. "But the Yiddish-speaking Jews were almost exterminated during the war. Of the six million Jews who were killed, they were the biggest group." And he changed the subject once again. This time drastically: "Your boyfriend, is he circumcised?"

"Yes," I answered.

"And do Muslims also bury the foreskin, as a sign of the sanctity of the body?" he asked.

He couldn't have blushed any more hotly. And I no longer knew where to look.

Seventeen

J akov had to write a report on his trip to the Anne Frank House, and asked for my help.

He grumbled at the assignment, calling it a waste of time and effort. It was a museum for girls, he complained, though he did allow that Anne couldn't help being born a girl, of course, any more than she could help being born Jewish—"Some people have all the bad luck."

He'd counted on being able to write most of the report on the way back, on the train, but things didn't work out like that.

On the train journey from Antwerp to Amsterdam, one of the boys, David, had managed to catch his jacket on the arm of a seat, tearing it in the process. The conductor had witnessed this mishap. He told the boy and one of the three teachers accompanying the group that they could probably claim the damage on the insurance. "But it would be best if you reported it as soon as you arrived."

Later, as they stood at the counter of the railway office, his teacher, Mr V., had asked: "Why have you taken your *yarmulke* off to talk to the official?"

David hadn't understood what Mr V. meant. Until he saw his *yarmulke* in his hand. "But sir, when we're outside our community it's always better for us to keep a low profile. If I was on my own, I wouldn't even be doing this. Better a torn coat than be accused of being a thieving Jew."

On the journey back, in a separate carriage that had been reserved for the group, Mr V. had discussed this incident with the other boys. It became a much bigger topic of conversation than the history of Anne and Margot Frank, their betrayal and Bergen-Belsen.

They could all tell stories about their instinct not to stand out. They could all list instances of attempts to conceal religious identity, so strikingly advertised by certain dress codes.

Fathers who, when road rage threatened, ripped their *yarmulkes* from their heads for fear of being called a dirty Jew by other drivers. Relatives who, attending a Diamond High Council reception where non-Jews would be present, put on goyish suits just in case, or made sure to leave their coats and hats in the cloakroom—so that no one would complain about the long coat draped over the back of a chair. To do anything to avoid people saying or thinking, "Another Jew."

The boys were particularly on the alert at stations, it turned out. The previous winter, at Gare du Nord in Paris, two of them had been surrounded by a group of lads of about their age, perhaps even younger. The youths had forced them into a corner and pulled the *yarmulkes* from their heads. They'd even set fire to one in front of their eyes: holding a lighter underneath it, yelling *Allahu akbar*. The boys had bought new *yarmulkes* in the Marais. Ever since then, they'd pull the hoods of their jackets over their heads in stations, or hide their skullcaps under a cool baseball cap.

"You report these nasty incidents to the police, I hope," one of the teachers had ventured.

"There's no point," they'd answered. "The cops don't like us; some of them at least. They don't say that to our faces, but we can tell."

"Nima's told me similar stories," I told Jakov. "And he and his friends reacted the same way. They don't trust the police here either."

"Nima won't be hiding his *yarmulke*."

"There are Iranians who change their first names. As a precaution. Names that sound too foreign don't work to your advantage. Or they say they're Persian. *Un Persan* gets a different response to *un Iranien*, to put it in your words."

"After the war many Jews changed their surnames. For fear of getting targeted and arrested again."

After recounting their own experiences of anti-Semitism, Jakov said the boys had talked about other attacks on their personal and collective integrity. Not long before, a restaurant had been blown up in Paris, in Rue des Rosiers, at the centre of the Jewish neighbourhood. They talked about the attack on the synagogue in Rue Copernic, which they'd all heard about at home.

As the train crossed the Belgian border near Roosendaal, Mr V. had clapped his hands and concluded that the boys' self-confidence had got torn. He told them they needed to do something about it. After all, if you could mend a tear in your jacket, surely you could mend a tear in your self-confidence? He'd then wondered aloud whether observant Jews might just share some responsibility for these nails on which anti-Semites got caught. And then he really got started. Why did the boys, just when their values needed defending, retreat into the trenches of society? Why was this community as tightly closed as a fort? Why didn't they admit non-Jews to their world?

The pupils had discussed the issue until the train reached the outskirts of Antwerp, and as it rumbled towards Central Station, they'd pointed to the *shuls* and the diamond district, with a turnover worth billions, surrounded by run-down blocks of flats, the balconies full of junk, rubbish bins and black clothing hung out to dry.

By the time they got off they felt utterly drained. Never before, outside the *shul* or *yeshiva*, had they talked so long and so freely about their Jewishness.

*

But it meant that Jakov still had to write a report on his visit to the Anne Frank House.

"I can help you formulate your observations and conclusions," I told him. "But you'll need to tell me what you thought of the museum."

When I was young, I'd been blown away by *The Diary of Anne Frank*, just as I'd been blown away by *Christiane F.** I'd never visited the museum.

"I didn't like it at all," he answered.

It gradually became clear that he hadn't paid attention during the guided tour. He couldn't remember anything, in fact, apart from the cramped little attic room. He'd hardly been able to follow a word the guide said: "He spoke so quickly and indistinctly, even worse than a Fleming." He hadn't bought a book in the museum shop: "It's just a racket, I wasn't going to fall for it." He hadn't even brought back a brochure as a souvenir.

"So how do I write a report without any material?" he asked.

"We could go to the library."

"But then we'd lose even more time."

"Not really."

"We'll just have to manage with what we've got."

"We haven't got anything."

"That's why I'm asking you to help me."

"Suppose we join up the dots?" I suggested. "We'll link your personal stories from the train to Anne's experiences. We'll ask ourselves whether there's a connection between what happened to Anne and her people and your collective reflex to hide in certain situations."

"I can't imagine how you'd tackle that."

---

* An exposé of the Berlin drugs scene in the 1970s, based on the experiences of a teenage girl.

"We'll do it together."

"You're being too ambitious. It needs to be simpler. I'm no great shakes at this kind of thing, maths is more my line."

"Do you remember how you blushed, Jakov, the first time I sat next to you in this room?" I asked.

He looked me straight in the eye, again with raised eyebrows behind smeared spectacle lenses.

"When you're conscious of blushing, you feel horribly conspicuous: you want the earth to swallow you up. When it doesn't, you blush even more. But people who don't know they're blushing—or just don't care—don't have that problem. In other words, everything starts with that strong sense of self-consciousness."

He continued to stare at me: "I haven't the faintest idea what you're talking about. Could you please get to the point?"

"In your report, we're going to ask ourselves whether the contemporary Jewish fear of persecution has a historic explanation. Is your instinct to retreat into your own fortress the result of centuries of being persecuted? Perhaps the Jews are more self-conscious than anyone else in this country. With all the reflexes that go along with it."

"Like Elzira's hands?"

"What do you mean?"

"My sister's shaking gets worse as soon as she *knows* she's shaking."

"Exactly. And being ashamed of her condition only makes things worse."

"I'm not ashamed of being Jewish! And you can't compare my culture to a disorder!"

"There are times when you'd like to conceal your belief."

"Being a Jew is more than a belief. It's a way of life. My way of life! This is pointless. You don't get it at all."

"But even in a country where there's freedom of religion, you're frightened to profess your faith."

"Because I'm scared of the consequences, *tiens*, not because I'm ashamed! I'm proud to be Jewish!"

"Okay. Sorry. I should have put it differently. But you get my meaning."

"Mr V. would know I hadn't written a report like that by myself. He'd spot straight away that a goy had a hand in it."

"Not if we do it properly."

"That's to say, if he doesn't lose his job." And then Jakov mumbled something about the *rebbe* and how Mr V. had been given a dressing-down by the *yeshiva*'s board of directors for overstepping his bounds by insinuating to the children that, just by "being who they were", they perhaps helped to create a climate of anti-Semitism.

"So anyone who says something you don't like is sent packing?" I asked him. I wanted to defend this teacher, precisely because he'd had the guts to ask the boys some relevant questions.

Jakov pushed a pen and paper under my nose. "Let's get started."

Eighteen

" So you're going to work for those Jews, in your stretch pants and short skirts?" Milena asked. She was the girlfriend of Serge, a fellow student who was happy to let others copy his essays and beautifully clear lecture notes.

Milena worked in a boutique on Keyserlei that was so expensive I didn't even dare look in the window.

"I can't believe they don't chuck you out!" she went on.

I was surprised and irritated. It had never occurred to me not to wear my stretch pants, or a miniskirt and T-shirt. And it never seemed to bother the Schneiders.

"Elzira, the elder daughter, even copies me," I said. "She wears the same kind of clothes, the same brands."

Recently, Elzira had started wearing a black T-shirt with a white long-sleeved blouse underneath. If, despite the air con, it got too hot in her room, she'd roll the sleeves of her white blouse up to her elbows, never higher. She seemed proud of that T-shirt.

My favourite trousers were a pair of Jean-Paul Gaultier stretch pants I'd snapped up in a second-hand shop. I wore them until the seat almost wore away. They were light grey, with a print of dark-brown and yellow skulls. They could hardly have been more eye-catching.

One day, Elzira had casually asked what brand they were. A few weeks later, in her bathroom, she showed me her brand-new, burgundy Gaultier dress. Floor-length and close-fitting, it had a high neck and long sleeves. I encouraged her to put it on—which she did, after a lot of persuading. She looked stunning in it. You wouldn't have thought she was only twelve or thirteen.

She bought tights of the same brand I wore: Wolford, an Austrian brand that had just teamed up with some French fashion designers, and was fast becoming hip. Elzira went for plain dark-blue and black tights, not the patterned ones I preferred.

"Real Jewesses are the *worst* customers you can imagine," Milena said. She spoke the word "Jewess" as if it tasted really bad. The tone of her voice, the conviction with which she spoke and her look were familiar to me: the same as when people talked about Nima and his kind.

I never spoke of Jewesses. The word stuck in my throat. Made me think of the Holocaust. Seemed light years away from the confident, elegant Mrs Schneider, sweet Elzira and energetic little Sara.

"'Real' Jewesses?" I repeated. The use of the word "real" in this context was alas all too familiar. "But he's not a *real* Muslim", "You can't call him a *real* Iranian!" and "Nima isn't a *real* refugee": I'd lost count of the times I'd heard things like that. Mostly from people who didn't know a single Iranian besides Nima, people who'd never yet met a Muslim or refugee.

"The rich ultra-Orthodox ones," Milena said. "They're *terrible*. For one thing, they refuse to use the mirrors in the shop. Suppose a male customer were to come in and catch them twirling around in plain sight? So my boss—who bends over backwards to accommodate them—has even installed a special large changing room for these Jewesses."

"Aren't other women allowed in?"

"Yes. But he designed it for them."

"Well I like Elzira and her little sister, they're sweet girls," I said.

"And *Madame*?"

"Mrs Schneider is a very nice woman."

"Who knows, she might be one of our clients. All the rich Jewesses shop with us. Is she one of those haughty, English-speaking ones?"

"She speaks French and Dutch."

"Oh, the French-speaking ones are the *worst*."

"The family's well off, it's true. But they don't show off their wealth. The children aren't spoilt. They study all the time: their lives revolve around intellectual development. They don't go out at all, not even the oldest. My childhood was quite different. I was already partying at fourteen—going to dances at the church hall."

"And *Mijnheer* works in the diamond trade, I take it? That's what all Jews do."

Once again I thought of Nima and of the difficulty we'd had finding somewhere to live. The owner of a flat we viewed near Marnixplein was quick to air his opinions: "All Muslims are the same. Don't get me started. Before you know it they'll be slaughtering sheep on your balcony."

That had been two years ago. Soon afterwards we found a really nice apartment near Vlaamse Kaai. But I couldn't cycle past Marnixplein without those images coming back to me.

"Those rich *madammen* rarely come into our shop with their husbands. They're usually with other Jewesses. I shouldn't really say this, I know, but they're just like spiders spinning their webs. They plot together. They won't let you into their world. They'll gobble you up if you get too close."

"Please, Milena."

"Try working in our shop for a few weeks! Those real Jewesses try on all the clothes and never hang anything back. They like to make as much mess as possible. They like to see us work. The 'chosen ones' want us to be their slaves."

"Guess they don't try on any stretch pants," I kidded.

"Ha, don't you believe it! Young Jewesses try on *everything*. They want to know how they'd look in leggings or a miniskirt. Or in a skirt with a high split, and push-up panties. Our changing rooms are the only place they can do that! You can't teach me anything about Jewesses!"

"What time will Serge get home?"

"They accused our boss of anti-Semitism."

"Who?"

"Those supposedly chosen people, who *themselves* act in a *totally* racist way! Do you know how these superior beings interpret our returns policy? Officially, customers have three weeks to return an unworn item of clothing. If it's not damaged, they get their money back. Do you know what these real Jewesses do?"

I shrugged. I felt very tired.

"They make a sport of buying expensive clothes, wearing them at one of their many parties with the price tag tucked away, and then bringing them back, claiming: 'I haven't worn it so give me my money back.' If you have the nerve to point out signs of wear, those Jewesses call you an anti-Semite, and write to the manager *and* the city council. Like I said, they're the *worst*."

Nineteen

Every two months, Nima's mother would send us a food parcel from Tehran. Not because she feared her children would starve, but because she hoped that familiar delicacies would assuage their homesickness.

Amongst other things we received tins of the world's finest and costliest caviar, the roe of wild Beluga and Ossetra sturgeon from the Caspian Sea. When we were struggling to make ends meet we would sell the caviar to the chef of a famous Antwerp restaurant. The proprietor of a local delicatessen regularly bought Medjool dates from us, selling the fleshy fruits at ten times the price he paid us. The pistachio nuts and spices—saffron, baharat spice blend and whole sacks of dried dill—we kept, along with the basmati rice and the dried limes that Nima used in all kinds of sauces.

His mother always addressed the food parcels to us. Inside, the contents were usually divided into separate sections, the idea being that we'd deliver the things marked with Marjane's name to her. This we were almost never able to do. Nima had virtually no contact with his sister, who lived in Schaerbeek, just north of Brussels. Every now and again they rang each other, but that was it. In the years I'd been with Nima, he'd tried about five times to visit Marjane. But although he'd always arranged it with her in advance, she was never at home at the agreed time.

In her last telephone conversation with her son, Nima's mother had urged him to visit his sister. She'd tried many times to reach her daughter, but in vain. It seemed that Marjane's telephone had been cut off. The number no longer existed, and she and her husband were so worried they couldn't sleep.

So Nima set off on the train to Brussels, without a rendezvous but with caviar.

I went with him.

When his sister didn't open the door, we pressed all the doorbells of the building, which looked like an ordinary house but to judge by the names was home to at least thirty people.

An old man who spoke a language we didn't understand let us in. We asked to see Marjane and he pointed to a basement entrance at the back of the narrow hallway. The floor of the hallway was awash with post and flyers. Sifting through the huge pile we found around ten letters addressed to Marjane, almost all from utility companies. A few cards had been left by the postman: "A registered letter addressed to you could not be delivered. It can be collected from the nearest post office." Without speaking we went downstairs. Mould crept up the walls of the staircase. The steps were sticky with dirt.

The basement door was unlocked.

There was no light on in the first room—the kitchen—and the two vents that might have let in sunlight were covered with cobwebs and dust. The cooker looked as if it hadn't been cleaned in months, the porcelain sink was cracked and piled full of dirty pans and crockery. The only "view" of the outside world was of the pavement: through the grime you could just make out the feet of passers-by.

Wrappings from packets of Suzy waffles lay scattered everywhere. A grim pile of grey and crumpled washing was heaped in a corner. A couple of photos of Marjane and Nima, taken when they were infants, had been stuck up on the wall. We had the same ones at home: charming portraits taken in the same studio, with the same background and the same sheepskin rug that contrasted so nicely with their jet-black hair, their coal-dark eyes and their long eyelashes and dark eyebrows. Marjane's skin was darker than Nima's. She'd inherited her colouring from her father, Nima more from his mother.

Nima looked round the room. He chewed fiercely on the inside of his cheeks and bit his lip.

In the next room, separated from the kitchen by a thin piece of cloth, lay a grubby mattress. A bedside table made of wooden fruit crates was covered with glossy magazines. I bent down and found, amid a scattering of broken lipsticks and bottles of nail varnish, a folder with clippings of fashion models. Red and blue stripes had been drawn over their faces, sometimes delicately, sometimes savagely.

From the tone of Nima's voice when he called me into an adjacent room, I could hear something was wrong. I hurried in his direction. I'd heard it said that people don't age gradually. That when you're dealt a real blow—one that breaks your spirit—it can happen from one day to the next. In the space of a few seconds Nima looked a changed man.

We were standing in the bathroom. The shower was primitive: a yellowish plastic affair. A makeshift partition had been erected to screen the leaky toilet. The stench from the drain was overpowering. Behind the partition, in a damp corner, stood a table on which a round mirror had been placed. The table was brightly lit by a lamp with just a bare bulb. A woman was sitting at it. A woman who didn't seem real. Not sitting erect, but hunched up. Her face was covered with white powder, like a geisha's. Her bright-red lips were clown-like, made bigger with lipstick. Her eyes, under which dark circles showed, stared fixedly at the mirror.

Nima fell on his knees. The floorboards cracked under his unexpected weight, the table wobbled. He threw his arms around his sister, who remained as motionless as a plastic doll. The house was so silent that Nima's soft crying sounded loud. The hairs on my arms stood on end. "My little sister, my little sister," Nima sobbed, in Farsi, French and Dutch, "Marjane, Marjane, Marjane, what's happened to you Marjane, *pardonne-moi*, forgive me, *kheyli motasefam, khahare azizam…*" His tears wet her cheeks, which he kissed; he kissed her forehead too, but Marjane did not respond, not even when he put his head in her lap, held her hands and said that he would help her, that everything was going to be okay, that he would take care of her.

Bicycle bells tinkled from the street. A dog barked. I could hear a low ticking sound: pigeons pecking up food in the courtyard, I thought. I could see that Nima was scared.

He gestured with his chin at the walls. They were covered with photos of Western fashion models. I recognized Cindy Crawford, Claudia Schiffer and Linda Evangelista. In among their portraits, Marjane had stuck up daubed photos of herself.

Twenty

We took her to an Iranian doctor in Brussels. She didn't say a single word. Neither to us, nor the doctor. She was injected with a sedative and given a prescription for more tranquillizers. It was only when we were in the doctor's surgery that I saw her head was covered in bald patches. Marjane had been pulling out her hair.

I asked if she minded me wiping the make-up off her face. When she didn't answer, I took a tissue and bent over her. She pushed me away. I handed her a few tissues. She didn't respond.

We went to a hotel. I filled the bath and invited her to get in. She crawled to the very end of the bed and stayed there without moving.

I washed her jumper. She put it back on when it was still wet. I also washed the other clothes we'd taken from her flat, but she paid them no heed. She was emaciated: her jeans hung from her waist, several sizes too big. "This isn't my sister, this is a shadow of the Marjane I know," Nima said, more to himself than me.

While we were in the hotel he rang some friends.

They came to fetch us. We spent two nights at their place. A lot of telephone calls were made on Marjane's behalf. Everyone was kind to her. She wouldn't allow anyone near her, wouldn't communicate at all.

A psychiatrist came. She still wouldn't say anything; her eyes remained blank.

The psychiatrist, who knew a smattering of Farsi, talked to Nima. She prescribed yet more medication for his sister.

One of the friends drove us to Antwerp. My study was transformed into Marjane's bedroom.

In Antwerp we went to yet another doctor, who had her admitted to a psychiatric clinic. But Marjane refused to stay. She returned to our flat, sought out the far corner of our sofa and just sat there. She wouldn't eat anything. We bought Suzy waffles; those she did nibble at. She leafed through magazines, forever cutting and tearing out photos of white-skinned fashion models. The dark tint of her own skin obsessed her; she constantly tried to it wipe away or conceal it, using whatever came to hand. Next to her bed stood a packet of powdered sugar she'd taken from our larder. She'd sprinkled it on her face.

After a while she wanted to go out. If you went with her, she shook you off. If you followed her at a distance, worried that something might happen to her, muddled and dozy as she was, she would just stand stock still and not go another step.

In the end, we let her go alone. We no longer knew how to deal with her, or the whole situation.

We put notes in her jacket pocket with our address and telephone number.

Sometimes she'd disappear for a whole day and a night, and Nima, no longer able to contain his anxiety, would go looking for her. He would walk the streets of the old city, to which she fled time and again. She had a preference for the cathedral and for the church of St Paul's, stony bastions of religion and history.

One night Marjane was brought home by a police officer. He'd seen her wandering the streets around St Paul's for hours and was worried that, so near the red light district, she might get assaulted, or might walk to the river Scheldt and jump in.

He'd tried to get her to talk to him. She told him, in English, that she wanted to go back to Iran, that she wanted to be with her parents and the rest of the family. She'd allowed him to take her home. While the policeman drank a cup of tea in our flat, she rubbed her cheeks furiously, making them redder, not paler.

She gave off a peculiar smell: of something unhealthy.

"Something in her has died," Nima confirmed.

Twenty-One

"And this is my mother," Mr Schneider said. His wife and four children were lined up behind him in the dining room, which was furnished in a sparse, modern style. Only the sideboard struck a more old-fashioned note: it was crammed with framed family photos, at least fifty of them, all jumbled up together. "We'd like her to come and live with us, but she doesn't want that, *n'est-ce pas, maman?*"

Seated at the long table, which was covered in dishes, platters and bowls full of delicacies, a wiry, dignified woman nodded at me. She was dressed entirely in black, right down to her hair net.

Suddenly my red Champion tracksuit felt horribly garish. Sweat trickled down my back. I could smell the coconut-scented shampoo I'd washed my hair with the evening before. The scent emphasized my presence even more.

The idea had been to drop off a book for Elzira on my daily run. I thought it might be useful for the talk she was preparing for her Dutch class, on organic farming. I hadn't intended to stay, but to run straight back home.

Grandmother Schneider, who turned out to be called Gabriella Pappenheim—she'd taken her second husband's name—beckoned me over.

When I got to her chair, she gestured that she wanted to whisper something in my ear. Before I'd even bent over, she said, in anything but a whisper, that Elzira was full of praise for me and that Jakov, to her surprise, didn't seem to find me objectionable. Jakov heard this. He began to blush but recovered.

I hadn't realized I'd rung their doorbell on a Jewish holiday, and I didn't even know what holiday it was. But when the intercom didn't respond and when shortly afterwards Simon came and opened the door manually and then didn't take the lift—Schindler—but the stairs, I realized I'd violated their rules.

Might it be Pesach, perhaps? There were lighted candles and bowls of pickled cabbage and cranberries. Along with hummus, halved avocados, fried cauliflower florets and the creamy aubergine and sesame paste dip that Nima called baba ganoush but the Schneiders *salat hatzilim*. For all I knew they were celebrating Purim, Jewish carnival. Or did this dish featuring a gigantic carp flanked by bowls of pickled herring mean it was Sukkot, the Feast of Tabernacles?

Once I'd brought some caviar as a present. "Extremely kind and thoughtful of you," Mr Schneider had thanked me, "but most species of sturgeon don't comply with our dietary laws, so we can't take the risk of eating this roe, and we're not allowed to profit from the sale of non-kosher food either, so—and please don't take this the wrong way—I'd appreciate your taking that tin home again, because it would be a shame to leave it here."

Don't ask me if alcohol was drunk at their table that day. I can't even remember whether it was afternoon or evening when this family gathering took place, winter or summer. But there was a steaming pot of tea on the table that smelt of mint. And Jakov was opening a bottle of Coke, and if I hadn't whipped a platter away from under the bottle in time, the fizzy drink would have dripped onto the plaited loaf of bread.

His grandmother saw my quick, subtle intervention, and she smiled from me to Jakov. I smiled back and had the ridiculous feeling that no more was needed to create a bond between us.

She made a deep impression on me. The warmth of her voice seemed in keeping with her frail stature. Her eyes sparkled more brightly than the pearls around her neck, which, like her face, was deeply wrinkled. She radiated a kind of volcanic intensity, as if both death and life were contained in her.

Before I knew the Schneiders, I'd never met any Orthodox Jews. Now, for the first time, I was in the company of someone who'd been in a camp, who'd survived the Holocaust. I felt a deep longing to tell her all about Marjane. It seemed to me she'd be able to understand Marjane's pain, and perhaps know how we should deal with it.

Granny Pappenheim took my hand. Looking at her hand, it was impossible to conceive that less than fifty years ago, this imposing woman had been taken off to Auschwitz. That *that* hand had experienced the camp. She smiled at me, then looked at the chair next to her, which I took to be an invitation to sit down.

Carefully, with one hand, I pulled the chair back. "We must pack up some tasty things for you to take back home," she said. "I hear you have a husband. He must be waiting for you."

She continued to hold my hand for a while, squeezing it as children do, and lovers. Her warmth spilt over into me, but the sweat on my back felt cold.

Twenty-Two

M y meeting with grandmother Pappenheim must have had something to do with it; when Mr Schneider appeared in the doorway of Jakov's room, poised to tell the joke about the German, the Frenchman and the Israeli who were shipwrecked on a desert island for the umpteenth time, I interrupted his mock jollity: "Jakov has told me that your mother, Mrs Pappenheim, survived Auschwitz. What I don't understand, and what I keep wondering is: where were you born? In... the camp?"

Mr Schneider turned solemn. He came into the room and went and sat on Jakov's bed, under the gaze of the eight rabbis.

"Where's Jakov?" he asked.

"He's still in the kitchen," I answered.

"That boy is always hungry. He'll eat us out of house and home."

He looked at me, stroked his beard and said: "We Jews have always had a great feel for language. But all the words in the world would not suffice to describe what it was like in the camps or to comprehend the manifestation of so much evil. How could anyone who has not experienced these horrors talk about them? When even those who *have* gone through these things and survived are unable or unwilling to find words to describe them? Do you understand why we choose to be silent? Silence is the way of least betrayal."

"I'm sorry," I mumbled. "I was just wondering."

He was silent. We were silent. For a long time.

"Do you know that a few years ago my mother suffered a heart attack?" he began. "It happened at Knokke, on the seafront. She felt a sharp pain on the left side of her chest. Concluding that it must be a heart attack, she walked to the nearest taxi stand and had herself driven to the hospital emergency department. On arrival, they had to carry her out of the taxi on a stretcher. Yet she still had the presence of mind to give her name and age, and, just before she lost consciousness, told the medical staff that she should not be revived under any circumstances whatsoever, *n'est-ce pas*. An operation, okay. But resuscitation, no way. Do you understand the point of this story?"

"Yes," I said. But I hadn't the faintest.

"That her will to survive and her cool-headedness are a legacy of the camp," he enlightened me.

Jakov entered the room. He looked a bit surprised, but plopped down next to his father. His glasses were all smeared again.

"Our children know the general outline of their family history," Mr Schneider said, greeting his son with a nod. "If they want, we will tell them everything, *n'est-ce pas*. But for the time being they don't feel any need for this information, and as far as I'm concerned, that's fine. The general outline's bad enough. You have to stop somewhere."

There were three wraps on the plate in Jakov's hand, filled with home-made falafel. He stuffed the first roll into his mouth like a sausage and, as he chewed, gazed at his father, who continued his account.

"My father managed to evade the Nazis' clutches until late 1944," Mr Schneider said. "But then he and others were betrayed and arrested. Weakened by his ordeal, he died of typhus in Auschwitz-Birkenau."

Jakov stopped eating and put the half-eaten wrap back on the plate, which he placed on the edge of his desk. I loved the smell of pickled cabbage, it reminded me of my childhood. Now, though, it made me feel sick.

"I'm willing to answer your question," Mr Schneider said, "if from now on you promise to talk about the future. We know our past. It informs our present, from morning to evening, and it's one of the reasons why we cling so steadfastly to our traditions. Our parents were murdered for who they were. We have a moral duty to stand up for them. To defend their way of life, which is also ours."

I nodded.

Jakov looked at his father almost imploringly. It wasn't clear to me what the downturned corners of his mouth signified: "Daddy, stop it," or "Daddy, please go on."

"I was born at the beginning of the war, at a place where my parents were living in hiding. At my mother's insistence, I was immediately placed in the keeping of a non-Jewish farmer and his wife, in Wallonia, in the south of Belgium. Those people took good care of me. For the first five years of my life my name was Pierre—that was what they called me. After the war, my mother came to fetch me. That was painful for everyone, not least those brave people to whom I am eternally grateful… In those five years I had become their little son." He cleared his throat. "My mother didn't even want me to be circumcised, you know. She knew, even before the war had properly started, that being circumcised might mean my death. But my father could not bring himself to comply with her wish. He wished to carry out this rite on the eighth day after my birth as our religion prescribes, and so it came to pass."

There was no embarrassment in the room, only an attentive silence occasionally broken by noises from the kitchen: the rattle of plates, the clatter of cutlery. I'd never seen Jakov look so serious.

"Can you name one of the main characteristics of cool-headedness?" Mr Schneider asked. He turned to me and Jakov but didn't wait for an answer. "Cool-headedness is knowing when to speak and when to be silent. My mother knew that. She didn't have to know the names of all the SS officers in the camp. As long as those SS officers knew who *she* was. She understood very well that she had to distinguish herself from the faceless group, the group dismissed as 'dirty Jews'… Everyone in the camp knew my mother was called Gabriella and that, besides her sister, she also had two daughters with her—my sisters. She made sure of that: that in her inconspicuousness she became conspicuous."

Mr Schneider stood up. Because he wanted to end this conversation, I presumed, and I was relieved. I'd wanted to know where he was born. But I knew my question was disingenuous. I hadn't quite believed that he was born during the war. Now I'd heard enough. Had probably already gone too far.

Mr Schneider closed one of the curtains and sat down on the bed again.

"The history of our people is built on this cool-headedness," he went on. "We know what discrimination and inequality are. We know that above all we have to be smart to save our skins. Look at Abraham, the very first Jew on earth, father of Isaac, the boy who was nearly sacrificed to God. When in the power of the King of the Philistines, Abraham could only think of one way to survive: he pretended that his beautiful wife Sara—after whom our Sara is named—was his sister. The King saw Sara as a prize worth having. He took her into his harem, and so the couple was saved."

I nodded.

Despite being raised a Catholic, I didn't know much about Abraham, Sara or the Philistines. But I did know that refugees, whether political or economic, would go to great lengths to save their skins.

"Or take another example," he said, as if he could read my thoughts, "the mother of Moses, who placed her child in a basket on the river."

Once again I nodded. I knew *that* story.

"My mother always said she followed the example of Moses' mother, though it cost her great pain. I wasn't put in a basket. But I *was* shipped off to another place for my own safety."

That had also happened to Nima, of course, but I didn't think it appropriate to say so. Nevertheless, I was sorry it hadn't occurred to Mr Schneider to make that comparison.

"Yet that cool-headedness didn't help your people against the Nazis," I said.

"That's true. We hadn't appreciated how evil humans could be. No one had ever thought twentieth-century Europeans capable of such horrific acts."

"Did you ever go back to your foster family in Wallonia?" I couldn't help asking.

"Repudiation is part of the necessary silence," Mr Schneider answered softly, looking at me with eyes that had welled up with tears. "There are two kinds of sorrow, remember that. One that can bear being prodded. And one so great that you have to keep your distance from it, even when asked apparently innocent questions."

Twenty-Three

Elzira could be moody. Not just with those predecessors of mine who'd only lasted a few weeks. With me too.

Sometimes I'd arrive to find her just sitting there, in the office or in her room, her head propped on her hands, staring out of the window or into space. Immobile. Calm. Mysterious. Withdrawn.

She wouldn't respond to anything. Not to the books I put in front of her. Not to my greeting, which I sometimes repeated ten times. Not to any of the jokes that I came up with on the spot, hoping to break the ice. At most she'd grant me a distant, friendly little nod, without the least affectation. Sometimes she'd start singing, and seemed unable to stop. One song came back over and over again, a little tune full of *shalom aleichem*. I remember, too, how one evening she sat there imperturbably for hours, declining the verb *s'asseoir* in different tenses: present, past and simple future. She just couldn't master the last one, remarking drily that while most people wrestled with the past, she, young as she was, didn't even know how to cope with the future. At that, I burst out laughing, and then she did too, and it was as if our shared laughter brought something into being, a momentum that I could feel, and that she surely sensed too. Suddenly, though, her laugh was switched off like a light, and she went back to just staring into space. I tried teasing her about her stubbornness—it was more sinewy than the veins that ran like cables over her jaw and neck, I told her. She merely shrugged. But a little later she went and looked in the mirror.

I knew all about teenage pig-headedness. I knew that sometimes there was no way out. That you couldn't back down. That you sometimes even had to kick things up a notch. Because to back down was to surrender.

One night when I was young I came back from a party an hour later than agreed. My mother opened the front door: "You're an hour late. You can't come in any more." She shut the door behind her. Then locked it. All the lights in the house went out. Half an hour later, one of them came on again. She unlocked the front door but didn't open it—*I'd* have to do that. But I didn't. I stayed where I was, standing on the drive. When she didn't hear me come in, she came to look.

"You said I wasn't allowed to come in any more. So I won't." "Come in." "No, I'll do as you said. An hour ago I wasn't allowed in. So I'm obeying you." "Come in, I say." A curtain was pushed aside in one of the flats opposite. It was one of our neighbours in her nightie, eager to know what all the commotion was about. "Come in at once!" my mother said. "What will people think?" I didn't come in. I spent the night in the wheelbarrow in the garden shed. The next morning my father found dozens of inexpertly rolled cigarette butts underneath it, and stopped my pocket money.

Elzira was always calm, never bad-tempered, during these fits of obstinacy. Eventually I learnt to ignore them. I would read aloud from her textbooks. Or from any book I had with me—whether prose, poetry or an academic work. I would analyse newspaper articles or tell her about my life. Often she would start writing poetry during these introverted moods, scribbling a few pages full of words and phrases that she then rearranged in a kind of collage. I gave her tips. I tried to get her to look at words and things from different perspectives.

There were also evenings when I would just sit down next to her and study, or silently read a book.

"Are you coming back tomorrow?" she would ask after a while, and her voice always seemed to startle her, as if she was surprised that a sound was coming out of her mouth.

Twenty-Four

Would I come to Mr and Mrs Schneider's room?

Yes, of course. At first I was excited that they'd summoned me. Maybe I was getting a raise! But in the lift, whose mirror was stickered with sweet Post-its from Mrs Schneider to her children—*snacks dans le frigo, pappie et mammie vous aiment* (snacks in the fridge, Mummy and Daddy love you)—doubts began to creep in.

Had they decided to dispense with my services? Had I crossed a line, asking about Mr Schneider's childhood? Had I been wrong to encourage Elzira to write poetry? But it was so impressive, the way she sampled her complex feelings and observations in at least five languages—French, Dutch, Antwerp dialect, ancient and modern Hebrew—to create her very own modern verse. Was I wrong to have introduced her to the work of Andreas Burnier and Judith Herzberg, even though they were both Dutch Jewish women poets?

The third floor, which I'd never been to before, turned out to be a suite of rooms entirely furnished in yellow. The satiny, pale-yellow carpet felt like warm snow; here and there lay gold-coloured, hand-knotted rugs that might have been Persian or Armenian. The textured wallpaper featured yellow flamingos on a grey-black background. The sofas, made of carved, gilded wood and upholstered in ochre-coloured fabric, were in the style of Louis XIV, or maybe XV or XVI—what did I know?

As always, Mr Schneider wore a dark suit and white shirt. He did what most men do as soon as they come home from work: he loosened his tie.

"Come in, take a seat," he said, still fiddling with his tie. He led me to the second room, the walls lined with bookcases, where Mrs Schneider, whose elegant simplicity stood out even more in this baroque interior, turned out to be sitting in an armchair, waiting for me.

As soon as I sat down opposite her, I wondered whether I should have taken off my shoes, which looked scruffy and unpolished in this gleaming interior, rather than just wiping them on the front doormat. Was that it, I suddenly wondered? Was I going to be ticked off for wearing tight trousers and high heels?

Mr Schneider went and stood behind his wife, resting his hands on her shoulders. Posing as if for an aristocratic double portrait. Light fell into the room in shards through the blinds.

He said: "We need to talk about Jakov."

This opening statement took me completely unawares.

Mrs Schneider nodded; I felt her glance sweep over me.

"As you know, some time ago Jakov went to Amsterdam with his class," Mr Schneider continued.

Panic seized me; this had to be about our essay. It had earned Jakov, lazy but gifted, the highest score in his class. His Dutch teacher had even asked him to read it aloud and then devoted an entire lesson to it.

Anyone who knew Jakov, even slightly, would know he couldn't possibly have written something like that by himself. But why were they only raising this now? At least three months had passed since we'd written about Jewish self-consciousness and how it seemed to have warped. After that, I'd tutored Jakov on a number of occasions: had summarized certain lessons, helped him with a presentation on a book by Orwell. We'd analysed and discussed Hector Malot's novel *Sans Famille*, brilliantly translated as *Alone in the World*. Had I somehow, without realizing it, stepped on some toes?

"Jakov and two friends dropped out of the guided tour of the Anne Frank House halfway through, without their teachers noticing. The three boys then explored Amsterdam. And bought condoms."

Mr Schneider gave a short, hearty laugh. He was attractive when he laughed at something other than his own jokes. I grinned too, more from nervousness and relief than anything else. Mrs Schneider couldn't suppress a smile either: her mouth curled delicately at the corners, making her look even more aristocratic. Mr and Mrs Schneider were as different as chalk and cheese, but in many respects they seemed well matched. I didn't doubt that their marriage was a happy one.

"We're relieved to know our youngest son has a healthy interest in the opposite sex," Mr Schneider went on, giving his wife's shoulders a visible squeeze. "But we're not exactly over the moon about his scheme to get rich by selling Durex at a massive markup in the *yeshiva*."

Once again he laughed. Mrs Schneider looked up at him from her chair, silently amused. Seeing their merriment, I wondered how they could be so sure the condoms were bought with the opposite sex in mind. Antwerp's Stadspark, a well-known gay cruising area, was in the Jewish neighbourhood, wasn't it? When they strolled there on Shabbat, didn't they see all the used condoms in the shrubbery?

For the first time I pictured a youthful Mr Schneider, and tried to imagine what Jakov would look like in a few years' time.

Like other religious Jews, father and son tended to dress the same. They had the same overly long limbs. They even walked the same way—I hadn't noticed it before—each step seeming to start with the tips of their shoes. It was as if they couldn't plant their feet down without having first traced a route with their toes. When they laughed, they blossomed in the same way and radiated the same energy. Jakov's ambition—so painfully obvious—would go the same way as his spots, I felt. It was just a question of waiting for it to burst, for the breakthrough.

"You mustn't think that Jakov and his comrades actually *used* those condoms," Mr Schneider said, interrupting my thoughts. "Boys buy condoms to look cool. And when they're alone, to try out how they work."

I nodded.

"What do you want of me?" I asked. "What's this got to do with me?"

"What my spouse and I would like to know is this: has anything about Jakov struck you in recent months?"

"No," I answered honestly.

"Are you sure?"

"Why?" I asked, shocked and wary.

"We've been comparing your hourly schedules for the last months. We've got them here. Take a look yourself."

They showed me the exercise book that circulated in their house, in which I noted down the hours I spent per day per child: mostly with Jakov and Elzira, only very rarely with Simon and Sara. Next to that figure I described in keywords what we'd spent our time doing: Dutch, geography, revision, homework, preparation. There were no limits to my working hours. I could come as often and as long as the children deemed necessary. On Sundays, the day the Schneiders called Day One, I was paid as agreed. My fee was calculated per hour—or quarter hour, if the times didn't work out exactly. If they didn't have quite enough small change and I said "don't worry about it", they would shush me. The next day the outstanding amount was lying there on the table, right down to the last franc: "Fair's fair."

"I've no idea what you can conclude from my work schedule," I said, "except that we don't waste any time."

"A few days after Jakov's trip to Amsterdam, you started working with him. Since then, you and he have joint sessions every week, whereas before, he never requested your help."

"What are you insinuating?" I asked. I felt insulted.

"Were you aware of this little business? Those condoms—are they anything to do with you?"

Twenty-Five

Nima didn't dare tell his parents how things were with Marjane. He couldn't possibly let them know the state their daughter was in. He felt guilty; he'd failed as a brother. What had he been thinking, he reproached himself, assuming his sister could manage entirely on her own? That as long as he didn't hear anything from her, she was all right?

During those days and weeks I often found him in fits of tears, kneeling, sobbing, throwing his arms in the air.

He couldn't sleep any more. He ate hardly at all, but on the rare occasions he did sit down for a meal, he stuffed himself until he felt sick. He rang all his friends and acquaintances, mostly Iranians. In turn, all these people rang other people. A couple of times, his mother rang him.

He lied to her that she shouldn't worry about Marjane, that she was too busy with her work and evening courses to have time for friends and family, that all the delicacies from Tehran made her happy, that her telephone number had only been cut off because she didn't want to be disturbed, her girlfriends were forever calling her to chat, but she'd soon have a new phone number, a secret one, she'd already applied for it, secret numbers weren't just dished out like that, though, so she was in the middle of the process, but they mustn't let that upset them, they'd soon be able to ring their daughter again, it was just a question of time.

While Marjane was staying with us, Nima got into a fight with a guy outside De Volle Maan, a cafe in the centre of Antwerp. He'd been offensive, told Nima to fuck off back to his own country. The next place I saw my boyfriend was at the A & E department of Sint-Elisabethgasthuis, where they were sewing up a gash next to his eye that needed twelve stitches. We were told his face might turn all the colours of the rainbow over the next two weeks, a prediction that came true. In this same period he lost his identity papers, bank card and residence permit. He picked fights at work, too, even though he'd had this temporary job at a screen printing shop for months and really enjoyed it.

One Monday, Nima resolved to ring his parents later that week, to tell them exactly what was going on.

But the very next evening, his mother herself called, in a terrible state. Of all the telephone calls that had been made about Marjane, some had been made to Tehran.

Nima's parents had rung a couple of doctors in Brussels who'd examined Marjane. They knew more about her and her condition than we did.

In the three years she'd been in Belgium, his sister hadn't made a single friend. Contrary to what she'd told her parents and brother, it turned out that Marjane—who'd had a successful career as a secretary in Tehran and who'd rejected one marriage suitor after the other—had never found work in this new country. She'd got no further with her evening course in French than registering for it. She'd been living off benefits for a while, but hadn't cashed a cheque in months. As far as we could tell, no one from the social services had tried to contact her.

About four months after we'd found Marjane in her fusty basement, her parents paid for her to fly back home, armed with a medical certificate saying she needed urgent psychological care. This proof of mental incapacity meant she could be admitted to Iran. As soon as his sister was safely under his parents' guardianship Nima regained some of his equanimity. But he was never the same man again.

Twenty-Six

When Nima and I had been together for three years, we gave a party.

We did so in the summery green of a friend's garden, which bordered on a field overrun with buttercups, nettles and sorrel. At the end of the garden there was a large, ancient greenhouse, in which tomatoes hung heavy and ripe. Its windows were whitewashed; if you looked closely, you were supposed to be able to tell from the glass that it dated from before the war, but however closely I looked, I wasn't able to.

We sat—somewhere in Tehran there's a video of this—at wooden tables that we had placed end to end. The maize crop in the adjoining field was half grown. White cloths covered the tables, absorbing the bright sunlight.

There were about twenty-five guests: a mix of Nima's pals, friends I'd made at school and university, and some of my relatives. About half the guests were Flemish or Dutch. The rest came from all over, but mainly from the Middle East: Iran, Azerbaijan, Kurdistan.

Nima's chess-playing friend Khosrov was there too. Whenever we saw him, he was on his own; he never brought a friend. His sexual preference was never mentioned. He and Nima didn't joke about it. Not even about the irony of their fate.

The two had met at the Immigration Office in Brussels, where Nima regularly worked as an interpreter at hearings that, in the best-case scenario, led to a residence permit. After a couple of stints there he knew what refugees should and shouldn't say to increase their chances of asylum. "No one, no one at all, leaves their country for ever just on a whim. Every migration is an amputation. That alone causes enough pain." He knew where you could get hold of fake IDs or driving licences, and how much they cost, but usually it wasn't necessary to go to such lengths. Sometimes Nima didn't translate what asylum seekers said, but made up stories and traumas he felt would go down well with the officials.

One of his most successful tactics was to present young Iranians or Azerbaijanis as homosexuals who risked the death penalty in their own countries. Such applications were usually approved. But despite having secured the coveted residence permit, these men were very angry when they found out how Nima had done it: there was no greater insult than being called a homo. During his time as an interpreter, Nima had painted Khosrov, too, as a gay man whose life was threatened. Without knowing that his lie was in fact the truth.

Well away from the tables two charcoal fires blazed, tended by willing helpers, on which aubergines, onions, pumpkin and bell peppers were charring, along with lamb and chicken. Bowls and platters were set out on folding tables, full of vegetable and fruit salads: tabbouleh, watermelon with pistachio and goat's cheese, grapes with fennel, carrots with cumin—the last of these a recipe copied from Mrs Schneider.

Nima had started his engineering course; I was in my last year at the Institute of Interpreting and Translation Studies. We just had enough money to pay our bills.

For that reason, and because we liked cooking anyway, we'd made most of the dishes ourselves, with ingredients from the garden and products bought cheaply from market stalls at the end of the day. Wine was tapped from cardboard boxes. Beer and fruit juice flowed freely. Nima didn't drink alcohol, nor did some of his friends.

A few guests had brought desserts—from Iran and elsewhere

in the Middle East. The Caspian Sea caviar had been provided, as always, by Nima's parents, and was served with potato and a dollop of sour cream.

The story about the missing rib hooking up with the missing body was something Nima and I didn't believe. But we *did* believe with holy fervour that together we could take on the whole world, the future, and even eternity. The fact that our friends shared this conviction gave our love and togetherness an extra dimension.

The only "formal" element of the party consisted of the speech, ardently declaimed by an eloquent friend. Another friend simultaneously interpreted her words into English. A third guest tried to convey them in Persian.

I was allowed to be the icing on the cake.

Our friend Behrouz had written out a Persian love poem by the fourteenth-century bard Hafez. It was in Persian, but he'd done it phonetically, so I could recite it. Which I now did. I'd practised my pronunciation long and thoroughly, and it had paid off. It sounded as if I really spoke that language, with its melodic cadences.

While I was still reciting, part of my mind was asking itself how, in the long term, Nima and I would cope without a common native language. I couldn't repress these thoughts. It was as if my recitation had brought them to life. Would we, when it came down to it, be able to comfort each other or make each other laugh with the right words? Didn't a native language constitute a secret society to which an outsider would never be admitted?

We partied until deep into the night, under an unusually clear sky full of stars. We ate and drank, danced and sang, told stories and listened, laughed and cried, planned and dreamt. I felt wrapped in a blanket of affection.

Until the moment when a friend slung his arm around my neck and slurred: "Have I told you yet what I really think? Those foreigners pinch everything from us. Even our women!"

Twenty-Seven

Elzira begged and begged for a dog and was given a dachshund. She named the hairy little red sausage Monsieur, even though Jakov had argued passionately for him to be called Mazel Tov. Elzira had no objection, but Daddy didn't think it such a good idea.

Monsieur was a four-month-old puppy when he swapped his kennel for the Schneider residence. He smelt of the litter, of wet dog squared, which Elzira found delectable. She carried the animal around like a teddy bear, burying her nose in its coat.

She rang to tell me the good news.

"I thought dogs were unclean," I blurted out. Pious Muslims believed that, I knew, so I assumed that pious Jews thought no differently. After all, both religions had their own, similar slaughtering rites. Plus they both shunned sausages, chops and other pork dishes.

"Do you know what the Hebrew word for dog is?" she asked, knowing very well that I didn't speak Hebrew. "*Kélèv*. And do you know what *ké-lèv* literally means? *Comme le coeur*. Like the heart! We Jews love dogs, they are like our hearts; we have to look after them well, that's what it says in the Talmud and the Torah." The way she said the words Talmud and Torah, in her slight French accent, made it seem as if the books were walking on high heels.

During our phone call I shared her joy. But privately I was thinking: another pup that's destined for the dogs' home. The deep-pile white carpet alone! They really didn't know what they were letting themselves in for.

Elzira did well at school: her marks see-sawed above the class average. Whenever she did get a fail, it was because of her dyspraxia. There was some overlap with dyslexia, so she mixed up letters. And when she had to draw maths diagrams with a compass, the lines shot all over the place. But she did get full marks for biology, which, by the by, seemed very light on sex education. The illustrations in Jakov's textbooks, I discovered, were different from those in Elzira's: Jakov didn't get to see a front-on picture of the vagina.

"By loving a dog, she will learn to love herself more." This, or something of the kind, had been whispered to me one day by Mrs Schneider as she placed a cup of tea in front of me, along with some buttered matzos sprinkled with sugar.

Since Jakov's condom exploit, Mrs Schneider had got into the habit of coming up to the room each evening bearing a tasty snack: from matzos to half an avocado with olive oil and coarse salt from an enormous tub, from almond cookies to chocolate or cheesecake, from *asperges à la flamande* to vanilla ice cream with strawberries.

"But your lovely carpet?" I asked Elzira.

"I'll teach him to wipe his feet."

"I've never seen Jewish people walking a dog."

"That's true," she laughed, "Granny says, *dans son* Yiddish: '*Az a Jid hot a hunt, iz der Jid kejn Jid oder der hunt kein hunt.*' If a Jew has a dog, either the Jew isn't a Jew or the dog isn't a dog. *Je sais.* It's *une exception.* But then, so am I."

Hearing her speak Yiddish sparked a kind of homesickness in me, as if the sound, the rhythm, the music of the language took me back to long-gone times in Limburg, linked me to people of many generations ago.

"In Israel, certainly in Tel Aviv, a lot of Jews have dogs. Not in Antwerp, *je sais.* I'm an exception. I don't know why that is. Hasidic Jews aren't allowed to have a dog, I think, *je sais pas*; I think that hairy pets are unclean, and that Hasidic Jews are only allowed to keep goldfish. Or koi." Her mischievous smile really suited her.

The office on the ground floor became Monsieur's doghouse. After he arrived, the doors to the walled garden were kept open all year round, even though it took over six months before Monsieur, thanks to the loving patience of his little mistress, sought out the lawn of his own accord to do his business. Elzira always cleaned up after him, including his little accidents in the room. Opris, the Romanian home help, removed the dirty paw marks he left on the carpet. But Elzira trained Monsieur to frisk about on a special doggy doormat before dashing down the corridor. When Elzira was at school, Opris took charge of Monsieur, taking him on the bus to parks for long walks. If she had too much other work she would ask her daughter, who was about my age, to help out.

It was Elzira and no one else who, over the space of several months, taught the dachshund to stop chewing the legs of desks and chairs, and not to touch her insoles and shoelaces (her father had made her learn to tie laces, sometimes with a stopwatch ticking). One day Monsieur chewed all the corners off a holy book. How he managed to reach it was a mystery. That was the only day no one had a smile for him.

Elzira kept Monsieur fed and watered, dabbed the sleep crusts out of the corners of his eyes with lukewarm water, inspected his paws and belly for ticks and other insects, washed him when he needed it and, even when he didn't need it, deposited him in an oblong, plastic tub. After a while, on hot days, Monsieur would go and sit in his bath of his own accord; he enjoyed splashing around. The floor of the doghouse was littered with balls, and chewy toys lay everywhere. Many were shaped like shoes, with shoelaces and all.

Because Elzira was worried that one day Monsieur might tumble into the pond, she got her parents' permission to ask the odd-job man to cordon it off with terracotta flower pots. By that time the koi had all died, or been snapped up by a heron.

From the day that Monsieur entered her life, Elzira got up promptly three-quarters of an hour earlier than usual. In the afternoon she would cycle home, whatever the weather, as quickly as possible: *"O, comme je suis contente* that I can cycle!" She no longer ate her lunch at the kitchen table, but spent her lunch break in the garden with Monsieur. Mikaela, a classmate, would come along with Elzira during the break or after school, and became her best friend. The girls played together and chatted away. Mikaela and Elzira weren't allowed to go farther than two blocks away on their own. When they went for a longer walk, someone had to go with them: Opris, Opris's daughter or me.

After a few months, the dachshund was used to trotting next to his mistress on a lead. Elzira soon mastered the extendable lead: a real test of her motor skills. I'd never seen her so relaxed and happy throwing balls—the hand-eye coordination exercise she usually detested—as to her eager little companion, the first love of her life, Monsieur.

Twenty-Eight

Jakov's parents believed their son when he told them I had nothing to do with his condom enterprise.

The affair even had a positive effect on our relationship: he asked for my help more often. But we could never get started without him first making a song and dance about the Dutch language.

"Why do I have to spend my time and energy on a poxy language like Dutch?"

"I'm not making you do anything. But you're being educated in Dutch. If you hate Dutch so much, maybe you should have gone to Brussels, to a school that taught in French."

"How many people even speak Dutch?" He said it mockingly, fiddling with his *tallit katan*, which he allowed to poke out from under his jumper, seemingly nonchalantly.

A *tallit katan*, a small tallit, is—I can't think of a better way of describing it—a life vest for observant Jewish men. They wear it day in, day out. Whereas an inflatable life vest has an air nozzle hanging from one corner and a whistle from the other, from each of the four corners of the tallit hang *tzitzit*, eight threads knotted five times: thirty-two threads in total. A number of ritual significance, since nothing in Judaism is coincidental. According to the mystic teachings of the Kabbalah, the numerical value of the Hebrew word *leev*, heart, is thirty-two, and the numerical value of the word *tzitzit* is six hundred. Six hundred plus eight threads and five knots corresponds with the six hundred and thirteen commandments set out in the Torah, which is precisely what these ritual tassels are supposed to be a reminder of. Thanks to this life vest, which may never be worn right next to the skin, the pious will not drown in superficiality.

Jakov had already shown me the black leather phylacteries he put on for morning prayers, as all observant boys over the age of thirteen are required to do. One strap he wound many times round his left arm—from elbow to palm—the other he bound to his forehead in the prescribed way. A small black leather box—called *tefillin*—is attached to each strap. Just like the *mezuzahs* on the door posts, it contains a passage from the Torah. The box attached to the strap that's wound round the head must be affixed to the centre of the forehead, the one on the arm above the elbow. The texts in *tefillin* all over the world are more or less the same.

Whenever I saw Jakov busying himself with these items, I was always reminded of Ann Demeulemeester's fashion designs. The way the boy wound the black leather around his left arm: it could be one of her accessories. And it wasn't hard to imagine these straps on the catwalk. There was something about his religious garments that seemed both timeless and fashionable. They were powerful in a way no substitute could have been.

"Huh, you're really putting me on the spot, Jakov. How many people in the whole world speak Dutch? Including Flemish, right? A good twenty million, I think, but I could be wrong."

"*Aimes-tu raconter des blagues?* You like to joke, right? You call Flanders and the Netherlands 'the whole world'?"

"Suriname, Curaçao… Dutch is spoken there too."

"At least Yiddish is a world language. Yiddish is spoken on all continents! We Jews are an international people! It's always been like that. We were always spread all over the place."

Once again he put on that arrogant, superior look. Nima sometimes armed himself with the same fake toughness.

"Oh come on, Jakov. How many people speak Yiddish? Only a fraction of the Jewish community, right? And how many Jews are there, worldwide?"

"About twenty million too, I reckon. So the number of Jews and Dutch people in the world is the same! But like I said, we live all over the place. And you only hear Dutch in this little bit of Belgium, in the Netherlands and those two African countries you mentioned."

"Suriname and Curaçao aren't in Africa."

"Whatever."

"But how many of those twenty million Jews speak and write Yiddish? You don't even speak it yourself. Sure, the odd word or phrase. But you don't know the grammar. You don't speak it fluently, like your grandmother."

"Perhaps there aren't so many of us. But we're smart. We don't even make up half a per cent of the world population. But have you ever noticed how many Jews win Nobel prizes? Around twenty per cent of all prizes!"

"Congratulations."

"To say nothing of all the top jobs we hold in all kinds of sectors: banks, universities, the film industry, diamonds, art, literature... No one can deny we're more creative than any other minority—even than the majority."

"Yes, you are the elect," I said. He'd done it again. Provoked me into a remark like this. I didn't care.

"What would you know about electness?"

"Election. If you must delude yourself you're one of the elect, at least get the word right."

"Electness."

"Nothing, that's how much I know about election, Jakov. How would I know what special pact God made with you guys? *You're* the chosen people, not me and the other goys."

"Blessed art Thou, O Lord, who has chosen us from all nations."

"You guys are superior and we're the plebs."

"What does plebs mean?"

"Nothing that need concern one of the elect. Don't worry about it."

"Everyone is born with more or less the same brain. But *we* excel. No one can deny that."

"I write your essays and make your summaries."

"That alone proves I'm smarter than you."

We laughed. It felt good.

"Catholics don't believe in a Messiah," he went on, "but in a guy, *nota bene* a *Jew*, who was nailed to the cross. Now *that* is *ridicule*."

"I'm not religious; as I've told you before, there's a difference between someone who's a devout Catholic and someone who's just a cultural Catholic. Can we get started on your homework now?"

The challenging gaze he shot me was at odds with his spots and spectacles.

"We don't watch TV," he blurted out.

"I know," I said. "Come on, get your books out."

"Some of my friends have a TV at home. They watch TV like you guys do. Some of them can get Israeli channels via the European KingOfSat satellite, you know? *Dingue!* But not us. At most we go to the cinema when there's a film Mummy and Daddy think is okay for us to see."

"How often have you been to the cinema?"

"Three or four times. The last time to see *Rain Man*."

"Do you watch TV at your friends' places?"

"Sometimes."

"So what do you watch?"

He blushed. "You're annoying. Does your boyfriend never say that? That you're annoying?"

*

Jakov and I became proficient in writing essays, reports and presentations.

We followed a set method.

The first step involved analysing the topics his teachers had given him to choose from. We always picked the topic or book that tied in best with both our worlds: I had to be able to say something about it, he had to be happy with what I wrote.

For Dutch, for instance, Jakov was given the following three essay titles: "Life after Chernobyl", "Is a world without child labour a utopian dream?" and "The human voyages of discovery of today".

Television, video and the rise of mobile telephones were discoveries of the new age. But if we wrote about these technologies I'd be putting forward views alien to the pious Jakov, and I'd probably find it hard not to mock the painful contortions made by modern Orthodox Jews as they wrestled to fit their ancient traditions into a modern society. Like the religious Jew in the electric wheelchair who asked two senior Antwerp rabbis for advice: "Is it *treyf* if I press the buttons on the armrest on Shabbat or Pesach? Should I push myself forward manually on these days of rest?" Another wanted to know: "What about the lift? Am I keeping our commandments if I get into a lift on Shabbat and a goy presses the button? What's better: to programme lifts to stop on every floor, like they do in some skyscrapers in Manhattan, so Jewish residents can get in and out without having to break their laws? Or to have a goy press the button of the twenty-third floor, so that we, the faithful, needn't stop on every one of the twenty-three floors, thus wasting a lot of time?"

The story of the lifts had been told to me by Jakov himself. Other examples were plain to see.

Anyone who took the last train from Brussels to Antwerp on a Friday night—something Nima and I occasionally did—would see evidence of similar ambivalence. Between Berchem and Antwerp

Central, the lights in all the houses and flats inhabited by Hasidic Jews, many of them poor, would blaze all night long. Sabbath law prohibits Jews from making or creating anything, including electricity or fire. So in the days before home automation, the lights and even the cookers would be on the whole time, from the start to the end of Shabbat, on average twenty-four hours at a time.

Of the three subjects given by the teacher, I would have opted for the theme of child labour, but Jakov waved away that suggestion and lobbied for Chernobyl. First, because the explosion in the Ukrainian nuclear reactor would allow him to display his knowledge of physics, and second, because he just happened to find science more exciting than exploited children. So by the rules of our method, I had to go along with that.

The second step consisted of collecting material.

That meant a trip to the library for me. I would try to prod Jakov—who was usually given about ten days to write an essay—into going to the library himself; if not the big central one, then one of the smaller branches in the Jewish neighbourhood.

He didn't see the point, and said I should just add all the hours I spent looking things up to my work schedule, which I did without protest. If Jakov happened to come across a relevant article somewhere, he would tear it out and put it in the blue wicker basket under his desk, which was full of comic books. He had some *Tintin* books in Hebrew. When I asked whether Hergé's anti-Semitism wasn't a problem, he shrugged: *"J'aime Tintin."* "Is Tintin's name the same in Hebrew?" "Yes." "What about his dog Snowy?" "Zachi." "Do you know what Tintin's called in Persian?" *"Tintin, non?"* "Tan Tan."

Steps three and four were the most interesting, for him too: we would put together all the information that had been collected and discuss it for hours, trying to view the topic from different perspectives. Then we'd pick an angle. After that we'd sketch out a framework: beginning, middle, end.

From step five, it was all down to me.

I would try to blend all the elements into a consistent narrative. If necessary, I'd try and find more information. I would do this all at home. Alone.

I would write down all the hours I'd worked, including the ones typing out the essay on my first computer, an IBM with green letters on a black screen. I charged for it all, just as if I was teaching at the Schneiders' house. We'd go through the finished item carefully. Make changes where necessary.

As an approach it was pedagogically unsound. But that didn't bother me.

I could use the money. On top of that, I actually enjoyed doing these tasks. The more assignments I rounded off successfully for Jakov, the more I became aware of a new form of freedom—one that reminded me of the day when, having left home at last, I browsed a supermarket's aisles, pushing my own shopping trolley, *without a shopping list*. It was a first. I bought what I wanted to buy, including Granny Smiths ("We don't buy imported apples, Limburg has apples aplenty!"), giant bags of crisps, wine and cigarettes.

Twenty-Nine

Less than a year later, Jakov started a little business in essays, presentations and book reviews.

With my knowledge and support, he sold my work to other pupils in his year; he pocketed a third of the sales price, the rest went to me. I can't remember any more how much I charged per essay, or for writing a book review or presentation. But it was certainly a lucrative little number.

In practice, our partnership amounted to me writing six or seven different essays per assignment. The pupils signed up for my work in advance. Because they were given a choice of topics by their teacher, I never had to come up with six or seven versions of the same theme or book title. Usually I would do two versions per topic or book, making it less likely we'd be rumbled; I didn't find it too hard to vary them sufficiently but subtly.

The only thing I refused to do was to betray my beliefs. If the essay title was "For or against the death penalty" I'd be against it by definition, not so much because I wouldn't have been able to make a credible argument in its favour, but because I was dammed if I was going to preach a message that went against everything I stood for.

Book reviews followed the same lines. The reading list of Jakov's *yeshiva* was different from the lists I'd had at secondary school. It didn't include any novels about Flemish Catholicism, nor any books featuring sex. No Claus, Boon, Geeraerts or Wolkers. No Willem Frederik Hermans, with the sole exception of *The Darkroom of*

Damocles. And certainly no Gerard Reve, with his homoeroticism. The list did contain a couple of works by Elsschot: *Cheese* and *Will-o'-the-Wisp*, though some of the passages in which the main character speaks of ladies of pleasure had been censored with a big fat black marker. Mulisch was considered acceptable. Along with, if I remember correctly, Leon de Winter's *Kaplan*, *Mendel's Inheritance* by Marcel Möring, Frans Pointl's *The Chicken that Flew over the Soup*, Anton Koolhaas and Frederik van Eeden.

"How do you explain that, Jakov? That prominent Jewish writers are thick on the ground in the Netherlands, whereas Flanders, apart from our wonderful Eriek Verpale, has none, as far as I know? Where are you in our literature?"

"You Flemings don't love your language," he answered, without even having to pause for thought. "You don't love Dutch and therefore you don't love yourselves, so how could you love us, and we you?"

His words were like a blow. On a couple of occasions, Nima and his Iranian friends had reached the same linguistic conclusion. I thought this silly and simplistic. As if our language lay only in our camp, and those who spoke other languages didn't have the responsibility to get to know it too. So as to get to know our culture. To take part in it.

"In Argentina, Sweden, Moldavia, Australia—*everywhere*—someone is saying *gutn tog*," Jakov rubbed it in.

"*Gutn tog* sounds like the dialect of Limburg, Jakov, or West Flanders," I said, tired as always by debates like these.

"Anyone who speaks Yiddish loves that language."

"You keep saying the same thing, over and over. What *is* your native language, actually?" I asked.

"French perhaps. Hebrew, Ivrit, to an extent. But later my native language will be English or American. I'm going to get a master's in business administration. I'm not going to stay in Belgium."

"Your native language is the language of where you were born, you can't change it 'later'!"

"I was born in Judaism."

Our fraudulent business flourished.

And it remained a secret for years, as all our accomplices realized they'd be better off keeping this underground network to themselves.

My conscience knew no pangs, not even the teensiest.

"You're worse than we are," Jakov laughed.

"What do you mean?"

"You're always *shakhering*.* You're a dirty Jew."

---

*   Yiddish: wheeling and dealing

Thirty

I said: "Come on, let's take the tram to the city centre for once, and walk with Monsieur as far as the Scheldt."

But we didn't take the tram. Mrs Schneider dropped us—Elzira, Monsieur and me—off at the Steen castle, the oldest building in Antwerp, on the bank of the Scheldt, close to the historic town centre. She would pick us up an hour and a half later at the castle's gate. "Just to be clear: you are to walk *away* from the city, towards the bend in the river, not in the opposite direction, *n'est-ce pas.*"

Monsieur was excited to discover this new terrain. Snuffling up the smells of the quayside cobblestones, he kept lifting his head skywards, scenting the breeze blowing from the river.

A freighter with a Panamanian flag lay moored to the quay, its churning engines spreading the stink of diesel. A member of the crew vaulted gracefully over the gangplank: "I have just such a dog at home, my wife takes care of him—oh, he's so cute." Monsieur allowed himself to be petted.

We strolled northwards, past the old warehouses. Near what used to be the tollbooth, Elzira pointed out a cable strung high in the air.

"That's the *eruv*," she said.

"What?" I asked.

"Do you see that wire?"

"I see a cable."

"Hung at a height of six metres. That's the *eruv*."

"You might as well be talking Chinese," I said. "What on earth's an *eruv*?" She laughed, and picked up Monsieur. From the way she held him against her chest, I could already see how she would cherish her children later.

She explained to me that Antwerp was the only city in the world to form an *eruv* in its entirety. An *eruv* is a ritual enclosure of a specific domain. In cities like Paris, London, Amsterdam and New York, there were *eruvs* too, but not enclosing the whole city.

An *eruv*, she told me in fits and starts, could be created by walls, embankments, train rails and water. In places lacking these natural or architectural boundaries a holy wire was stretched at tree height, under rabbinical supervision.

"The *eruv* represents a house: an imaginary house, fictional, you understand?" She massaged Monsieur's little paws and put him back down again. He barked at a couple of screeching gulls. Curled his tail tensely.

I had no idea what she was talking about.

"Our laws allow us to do much more inside our homes than outside. The *eruv* turns *l'espace public* into our *espace privé*."

I burst out laughing. She was kidding me.

It took quite a while before I got it.

As always, it had to do with the five books of the Torah and with the Talmud. That was nothing new: I'd long got the message that there was no place for trivialities in the lives of observant Jews, and that everything they did was formalized by their religion.

"Six days shalt thou labour and do all thy work. But the seventh day is the Sabbath of the Lord thy God; in it thou shalt not do any work." Elzira quoted the Bible, going on to specify what this pronouncement meant: the Eternal One had pronounced a ban on thirty-nine forms of labour—including cooking, writing, travelling, building and making music.

Without knowing it, she was finally giving me an explanation for the transparent plastic bags that many married men and rabbis would put over their sable *shtreimels* summer or winter, before Shabbat began, even if it wasn't raining. You never knew—it *might* rain, and opening an umbrella is like putting a roof over your head: you can't do that on Shabbat. I told Elzira what I'd just realized. "But those hats cost a fortune, you know," she responded. "As much as 20,000 francs. And often they are *patrimoine familial*, handed down from father to son, so it's kind of *logique* that they use plastic to protect them against water. Do you now also understand why our synagogues have to be so close together?" Elzira asked. "On Shabbat we're not allowed to use any means of transport. Or take more than a certain number of steps. So all Orthodox Jews have to live within walking distance of the synagogue. Which is why we have so many *shuls*."

So within the *eruv*, the symbolic, imaginary wall that had been constructed around Antwerp, the city was transformed into an imaginary house. And within that imaginary house, in line with the Shabbat laws, certain strictly defined actions were permissible: carrying a baby, carrying shopping, pushing a pram... In cities without an *eruv*, none of that was allowed.

"Are you allowed to walk Monsieur on Shabbat?"

"We asked the rabbi that. Daddy rang him. The rabbi thought it strange we had a dog, but he said that walking him wouldn't be a problem. But I still don't take Monsieur outside on Saturdays. Mummy and Daddy think we shouldn't make a display of our *chien*. And Opris is at our house *toujours*. It is all right for Opris to show that we have a dog. Much more than for me."

"Don't you mind that?"

"*Pourquoi?*"

"Do you often ring the rabbi?"

"We ring if we don't know how to interpret a certain law. If we have a problem, or want advice. A rabbi is much more than a religious teacher, you already know that of course, he is very *sage*, wise: an authority. We consult him on domestic questions, but also on issues like my dyspraxia. Mummy and Daddy went to ask him for advice on that."

"Is it true the rabbi won't let you live in the same house as non-Jews?" I don't know why I asked her this. Milena—Milena who worked in a boutique and knew all there was to know about *real* Jews—had whispered this to me not so long ago. She added that modern Orthodox Jews made sure to move into apartment buildings occupied only by Jews with deep Belgian roots—"because those new ones from the Eastern Bloc aren't like us, they'll only cause us problems."

Elzira shook her head.

"So it isn't true?"

"It's a myth. Like so many other myths that exist about us."

I didn't know what to think of the *eruv*.

I didn't understand that need for biblical mores. I couldn't fathom why people had to make their lives so complicated. Who was kidding whom here? How could you live in the modern age and yet observe all the rules, laws and rituals of Jewish religion, Jewish culture and Jewish identity so strictly? In that respect, the Amish at least played the game more consistently: they still travelled about by horse and cart, cultivated crops rather than diamonds.

We walked along in silence for a while.

Monsieur created a diversion. He found a dead fish on the quayside and tried to gobble it whole. Pulling a face, Elzira dragged him away. In the grass behind the sheds, the dachshund discovered a frog. He nudged it with his nose and it jumped up, croaking. Teasing the frog amused him for a while, then he dashed off in hot pursuit of a fat bumblebee. Hampered by her long skirt, Elzira struggled to run after him elegantly. We laughed and laughed. A good hour and a half later we found the car waiting for us in the car park, with not

Mrs but Mr Schneider at the wheel. Elzira and Monsieur crawled into the passenger seat; I was invited to sit in the back.

"The *marit ayin* is very important to us," Elzira whispered.

"The *what*?" I asked.

"Appearances," Mr Schneider answered for her. "An Orthodox Jewish man will never allow a woman other than his spouse to sit in the passenger seat. It might be misinterpreted."

I mumbled something and fiddled with the white leather of the seat, which was torn in a couple of places.

Classical music boomed from the speakers.

"The opera *Lohengrin*, by Richard Wagner, is set here, at the Steen," Mr Schneider said.

"Oh," I said.

"Lohengrin is a knight. The opera is about Antwerp and the Duke of Brabant."

"Oh," I said, once again ignorant. "So this is Wagner's music we're listening to?"

"No, this is a composition by Daniel Sternefeld, an excellent Jewish composer from Antwerp who died only a few years ago. I don't listen to Wagner. He was Hitler's favourite composer. Worse, he was notoriously anti-Semitic."

"Oh," I said, completing my hat-trick of ignorance.

Thirty-One

"So you read left-wing propaganda?"

"What do you mean?"

"That's the magazine of the far-left Workers' Party of Belgium, isn't it?"

Elzira and I were working in her room. Before us lay French grammar exercises on the subjunctive. Mr Schneider was pointing at *Solidair*, a copy of which, featuring Arafat on the front page, stuck out of the side pocket of my rucksack.

I nodded. When Marjane urgently needed medical care, Nima had discovered the "people's doctors" of the PVDA, the Workers' Party, a Flemish party to the extreme left of its already left-wing Dutch sister organization. Without these doctors, the emergency assistance provided to his sister, who had lost all her asylum papers and no longer had a valid identity document—or at least none that we could find—would never have been so efficient and affordable. And without the unwavering support of a PVDA militant—Ludo, a helpful man who seemed to have been born with an Arafat scarf round his neck—Marjane might well have ended up in prison, or been dispatched to the Petit-Château, a former barracks in Brussels that was now the immigration detention centre.

Ludo spent countless afternoons in all kinds of bureaucratic institutions. Because Marjane's case was so complex, he was frequently sent from pillar to post. But he didn't give up until he'd sorted all the necessary papers.

Wherever he went, Ludo would peddle the party magazine. We bought one every now and again, out of gratitude for his efforts and because we were sympathetic to him. One day he managed to inveigle us into an annual subscription. That was in 1990, a turbulent year. The year when, in Nicaragua, the Sandinista leader Daniel Ortega was not re-elected, when the first intifada was still at its height and when Saddam Hussein invaded Kuwait.

For Iranians and other citizens of the Middle East, the first Gulf War, which we followed on the brand-new American channel CNN, wasn't a video game, but cruel reality close to home. They empathized with their region, and mistrusted Western motives.

Oil state Kuwait could count on the support of the West. The West also included Israel, apart from the Palestinians. Europe and the US supported the war against Iraq. Of course, Arafat styled himself even more strongly as the Palestinian leader. There was a very real fear that Iran and the whole of the Middle East would get sucked into the conflict.

Nearly all the political and economic migrants from the Gulf and the surrounding region followed CNN's live broadcasts and fulminated against the Americans and the Saudis. Every evening, Middle Eastern friends would join Nima at our television sessions. They even included an Iraqi. Neighbouring Iraq was regarded as Iran's enemy number one and vice versa, but in their battle against the Americans the two stood side by side, so on the same side as Arafat and the Palestinian Liberation Organization.

They saw how American troops and NATO armies shot Iraq to smithereens. They saw entire convoys of retreating Iraqi soldiers being bombed flat and President Bush proudly announcing the death toll. They became emotional and furious. They reached for the phone, constantly ringing the home front. They felt that the Americans had no business in their region.

"You even have a subscription, I see. Your name is on the magazine…"

"Er…"

"Those PVDA followers would like nothing better than to personally string up Rabin, our minister of defence. While at the same time lobbying for the abolition of the death penalty. I request you not to share such indoctrination with the children."

Mr Schneider had said "our" minister.

"I'll put the magazine in my rucksack."

"How should Rabin deal with the intifada?"

"I don't know. But the violence perpetrated by his army is out of all proportion with the violence of stone-throwing boys who, in the name of their people, are resisting occupation. There've already been a thousand deaths on the Palestinian side…" I stopped halfway through my sentence. Not because he interrupted me, but because I didn't want to get embroiled in discussions like these. Not here. Not with Elzira present. A silent Elzira. She was fifteen.

"If you lie down with dogs, you get up with fleas."

I was taken aback.

"Yes, I know that proverb. I know lots of Flemish proverbs," Mr Schneider said. When he said "Flemish", he often meant "Dutch".

I preferred his jokes to his proverbs. We'd never talked politics, apart from local issues. And the discussions we did have tended to be light-hearted and about trivial matters: the poor state of the city's roads, the exhibitions in the Diamond Museum or Silver Museum, the tram that rattled through the narrow Lange Leemstraat—a source of terror to mothers, whose little children often got their bike wheels stuck in the rails—the lack of places to park in the diamond district.

"I'm not here to teach politics, Mr Schneider, you know that." I nodded at Elzira, who seemed to be lost in thought. She'd just washed her hair; it was tied up in a pink towel that she'd learnt to knot elegantly.

"Jakov was harassed by some boys last week."

I was shocked. "I know nothing about that."

"No, you couldn't have known. We didn't tell you. I'm telling you now."

"What happened?"

"The thing that so often happens. Jakov was coming to my office—you've been there, so you know where it is. He took the taxi to the Stadspark, but just beyond, in the diamond district, there was a traffic jam, so he decided to walk the last stretch. Four boys, perhaps not even sixteen years old, started shouting at him. 'Dirty Jew', 'Shame your parents and grandparents didn't die in the gas chambers', 'Death to Israel and all Zionists'. They tried to surround him. He fled into a hotel. He called me from there."

"Did he also ring the police?"

"The boys had long since gone. After shouting that they'd avenge their Palestinian brothers."

"I'm so sorry. That's terrible…" I suddenly understood why he wasn't so happy with Arafat in my rucksack.

"You know that Simon is doing military service in Israel."

I nodded.

Simon was the last person you'd expect to sign up for the Israeli army after finishing school in Belgium. One of those young men that seem to be apologizing for their existence. Gangly, thin as a rake. I hadn't been able to picture him in combat. But now I'd seen photos of him in uniform, with a machine gun clamped to his chest, looking straight into the lens with a pride that straightened his hunched shoulders.

"We're afraid," Mr Schneider went on. "Afraid for Simon, for the other three, for ourselves, for all of us. Simon is in the Golan Heights, near Syria. For a year now, my spouse and I have hardly slept a wink. Sara says she wants to join the army too, later. I know Sara. She will go."

"Why are they going? Why aren't they staying here?"

"Nine years ago a bomb exploded in the diamond district. Three people were killed and a great many injured. I saw the victims with my own eyes, one from very close by."

I nodded silently, only vaguely remembering those attacks. I knew that security measures in the diamond district had since been drastically tightened up. There were now barriers in the main streets. Jewish schools and synagogues had extra protection. Elzira and Sara knew the police officers who stood outside their school and synagogues; they brought pretzels for them.

"A war is different, of course," he went on, "don't misunderstand me. It's just that we now feel that madness breathing down our necks. And I trust our intuition. We Jews are like the canaries in the coal mine. We have heightened senses. We smell social change *years* before the community at large. We know when danger is coming. That intuition is in our genes. How could it be otherwise, after a history full of persecution?"

"What are you trying to tell me?"

"Did you know that more and more Flemish Jews are considering voting Vlaams Blok in the local elections?"

I gazed at him in disbelief. Vlaams Blok—"Flemish Bloc"—was a fascist party. They wanted Flanders to break away from Belgium and become an independent state. Its adherents opposed all that was foreign. Several of its leaders didn't hide their admiration for National Socialism. Some of its representatives—and some of its voters—came from a background of wartime collaborators.

"I can't believe that," I said. Instead of putting *Solidair* in my rucksack, I took it right out.

"Once again, we smell hatred of Jews," Mr Schneider said, stroking his *yarmulke*. The patches of sweat under his armpits seemed bigger than usual. "You're too young to remember this, but that slip-up by Mayor Craeybeckx put an end to the tradition that Antwerp Jews largely voted Socialist."

What did he mean? I didn't even know Craeybeckx had been mayor. I only knew the tunnel that was named after him.

"One day, Mayor Craeybeckx—he was a Socialist, you know— was sitting outside a cafe on the main square, Den Engel or Den Bengel, I can't remember which. Some Orthodox Jews were crossing the square. He called out that it was a shame the Germans hadn't put more of their kind in the gas ovens..."

I was silent. Then asked, "Mightn't it have just been a tasteless joke?" What else could I say?

He plucked thoughtfully at his beard. "Only Jews are entitled to make jokes about Jews. Just as only blacks can make jokes about blacks. You have to know the suffering of a community from the inside before you're allowed to make fun of it."

"Are you frightened that anti-Semitism is on the rise?"

"Hatred of Jews—I use that term deliberately—hatred of Jews is a mutating virus. It pops up again and again, each time in a new guise. It's happening again now."

"This time because of Muslims?"

"Your friend knows why he fled his country."

"Nima would never vote Vlaams Blok," I said.

"You're a lefty. Well, when does your beloved political faction express views about us, the Jews? Right. Purely when it's about Israel and the Palestinians. And everything that's said is just one cliché after another. People don't know the country's history—or its antecedents. Do you *really* think that all Jews are happy about what's happening in Israel today: the hardening of attitudes, the shift to the right? Do you *really* think we all support the illegal settlements? Do you, like your left-wing friends, regard Zionism as a term of abuse? What do you know about Zionism? About the evolution of that concept? What do you know about the PLO? I'm prepared to bet that over three-quarters of all those who have an opinion about our country couldn't even find Israel on a map and haven't the faintest idea how it came into being. People don't know where the occupied areas are, but that doesn't make them any less eager to pontificate about them. Nobody talks to *us*. Talks, as in listens."

"America does."

"I'm talking about Belgium."

"You could sound the alarm and speak out as a community."

"What, to your left-wing friends? They already have their opinions. But they've no idea how dangerous their one-sided information will be in the long term. Their biased reporting is creating a climate—I've seen it happen over the past thirty years. I'm not saying that everyone has to be pro-Israel. But what I *would* like is for people not to present the Arab world as saintly. Not that the Arabs have a monopoly when it comes to hatred of Jews, mind you. It exists among the police. It exists among local officials, among people working in healthcare, people working for all kinds of institutions. It's timeless and universal: wherever there's a decline in prosperity, minorities are targeted. That doesn't just apply to Jews. Your Persian friend will experience the same thing here."

"So why do you say hatred of Jews, if it's essentially hatred of other people?"

"Hatred of Jews is the most acceptable form of hatred of other people."

There was a long silence. Elzira took the towel off her head and shook her hair free.

Mr Schneider was the first person to speak again: "My entire generation, the first after the Holocaust, served in the Belgian army. Of *course* we wanted to join the army. We felt Belgian, we were—we *are*—thankful to this country for all the opportunities it has given us. We also felt ourselves to be true Flemings! There was a kinship between Flemish Jews and non-Jews. I was proud to be a Fleming. Our children feel that bond much less…"

"But you speak French at home," I couldn't help saying.

"You are as ignorant as they," he sighed.

I looked at Elzira, hoped she would save me.

"Do you know why so many Antwerp Jews speak French?" Mr Schneider asked, and in one tired breath he continued. "Not just because some of them are members of the bourgeoisie, in case you thought that. And not just because many Jewish children were taken in by Walloon and French foster families during the war, so learnt French while they were in hiding. When the survivors of the Holocaust tried to get on with their lives in Antwerp, they no longer wanted to speak a minority language. They wanted always to be ready to move to another, distant country, if such horrors ever came to pass again. That's why they chose French. Though they'd have done better to have chosen English, of course. And that's why they always kept their passports up to date and had them ready in their homes. Just as we always have our passports ready. You will never find an Orthodox Jew in this country—perhaps not even a liberal Jew—whose passport has expired. We're always ready to leave at a moment's notice."

I nodded. I had goose pimples on my arms.

"Would you ever vote Vlaams Blok?" I asked.

"What does a person do when they're afraid and can no longer trust mainstream political parties?"

"Hides. Leaves. Bands together with others who feel the same fear. Revolts against that which makes them fearful."

"You know it all too well."

"But a Jew can't possibly vote for a far-right party!"

"History has taught us that nothing is impossible," he said.

Thirty-Two

The things a dog can tell you, part one.

It was a summer's day in July. I was jogging through the city park. That's to say, I ran once around the pond, lingered on the iron suspension bridge until the swans swam beneath me, then went and sat on a bench for half an hour, reading the paper, daydreaming, people-watching. Sometimes, if there was a lot to see, that half-hour turned into an hour.

That day, there was a lot to see.

On one of the lawns, under the wide canopy of ancient trees, a group of at least sixty Jewish girls were playing games. Drop the handkerchief. Sack races. And a version of tag whose rules I couldn't quite make out.

The girls were members of a youth group, or something of that kind. They were aged about six or seven, eight at most. All wearing long dark skirts and tights, and long-sleeved, dark or pastel-coloured blouses or shirts. Yet it wasn't just because of the stereotypical clothing that I knew they were Jewish. There was something else, I don't know what. Something to do with the group, I think. Together, they all looked alike. Had I seen the girls separately, I might not have thought them Jewish at all.

Apparently I couldn't suppress my tendency to seek to define a people. What about my own people? Why didn't I list *their* characteristics? Dutch people I could spot a mile off—and there were plenty of them in Antwerp. I could tell whether someone was Dutch just from their happy expression, height, hairstyle, the position of their collar, the colour of their scarf and lipstick. In fact I made a sport of it, betting with my friends for a coffee or an ice cream: ninety per cent of the time I was right.

Not all the Jewish girls belonged to the same social class. Some wore clothes that were clearly expensive. Others had skirts, dresses or shoes that looked to have come from a charity shop.

The girls were completely absorbed in their play. They giggled, huddled together in groups, had fun. Two of them tried to turn cartwheels. They were pretty good at it, actually. As they kicked their legs in the air I thought of Sara's gymnastic exercises and Mr Schneider's little homily about their undesirability, and was relieved that cartwheels apparently didn't fall under this prohibition. Not for girls of this age, at any rate.

Suddenly I spotted Elzira in the group. She was one of the leaders, in charge of the group doing sack races.

Just in time I managed to suppress the urge to leap up and wave at her. I didn't want to interrupt the game, least of all to embarrass her. She didn't notice me; she was entirely focused on the children. Peeking from behind my newspaper, I caught myself regarding her like a craftsman regards his work: with affectionate interest and an eye for improvement. Proudly. Mothers would call it maternal instinct.

Joggers panted past. On another lawn, a group of Indians were playing cricket. A man was meditating, sitting cross-legged. Locals were walking their dogs. Walkers and commuters hurried through the park, passing from the statue of King Albert to the playground on the edge of the diamond district. Three of them, Indians, did so barefoot. Park maintenance staff gathered under a tree, leaning on their spades.

A woman with a little dog crossed the lawn on which the girls were playing. She held the Maltese—a white ball of fluff on four diminutive legs—on a lead.

One of the leaders approached the woman, hands on hips.

"Go away, lady," she burst out, "we don't want you here!"

The woman looked at her indignantly.

The leader jerked her head in the direction of the little dog which, because its mistress had stopped, had sat down obediently next to her. The animal eyed the girls with innocent curiosity.

"What did you say?" the woman asked.

"You heard what I said. Go away!" the leader said. She must have been about the same age as Elzira. Her voice was shrill and angry—an anger reflected in her gestures and the rest of her body language. Once again, standing belligerently in front of the woman, she jerked her head at the dog. The little scene took place right in front of my nose.

Meanwhile some of the girls, including the ones that were doing sack races under Elzira's supervision, had stopped playing. They ran to the angry leader and stood behind her, forming a front against the lady with the little dog.

Hesitantly, Elzira joined the little group. I was sure she'd be able to defuse the situation, would discreetly correct her colleague. That would be typical of her. She loved dogs. We had ourselves walked across this lawn many times with Monsieur.

"I've got just as much right to be here as you," said the lady with the dog, looking flustered. "I'm not disturbing you. You're not disturbing me. I'm walking past. You're playing. And that's all allowed."

Some of the girls giggled. Others went up to the dog and then, pretending to be afraid, ran away, shrieking with laughter. Two girls were curious. They crouched down, looked from the lady to the dog and asked if they were allowed to stroke it, what it was called, whether it was a boy or a girl. If anyone here should feel scared, it seemed to me, it was this Maltese. Four of him could have fitted into one of their rucksacks, which lay piled up in the middle of the lawn.

The leader felt emboldened by the backup she was getting from the group. "Go away, lady, and take that animal with you! Dogs aren't allowed here. Your dog's dirty. We're playing here!"

The lady with the dog was dumbstruck.

The children's mood began to change. The girls were no longer laughing. Some of them looked cross—hostile, even. They no longer ran towards the dog. No longer wanted to pet him. They looked at their leader and some of them echoed her: "Go away!"

Elzira didn't do anything. She didn't crouch down, as I'd seen her do a thousand times with Monsieur, to talk to the dog. She didn't abuse the woman, like the other leader. She was silent.

Thirty-Three

The things a dog can tell you: part two.

It was winter, and Elzira and I were going for a little walk with Monsieur. When she was with me she was even allowed to cross the *leien*, the main boulevards, on condition that we gave advance notice of this outing and came home punctually at the agreed time.

Just for the record: I wasn't paid for these excursions. I enjoyed them. And Elzira and Monsieur enjoyed them too.

I've no idea what day of the week it was. Not Sunday, at any rate. Nor can it have been Saturday. It was probably just a weekday afternoon when the Jewish school was shut in preparation for a religious festival.

We walked, both of us bundled up from head to toe, from the Schneiders' to Belgiëlei and then along Lange Leemstraat, which is indeed as long as its name suggests, heading for the park. We were chatting. Elzira was holding Monsieur's lead; one minute he'd be scampering ahead of us, the next trotting obediently at her side.

Suddenly a woman came running up behind us. She tugged at Elzira's coat and grabbed me by my shoulder. I felt my heart miss a beat. The look in Elzira's eyes was one I'd never seen before.

"Hey, you, wait!" the woman snarled.

I turned round and pushed the woman away from us. She was wearing an apron with the name of a sandwich shop embroidered in yellow. It was a shop we'd just passed.

155

"Wait, I said!" she raged. "I'll bring you a bucket of water and bleach, so you can clear up your own mess. It's no good looking all innocent. I'm no mug. I know you people all too well. You think I should clear up after you. Well you can think again! For once, you can just do that yourselves. We're not your slaves!"

I had no idea what she was talking about.

Elzira, even paler than usual, gave me a poke: "*S'il te plaît*, please, let's run away, *on devrait déguerpir*, she scares me, *elle me fait peur, tout cela me fait peur.*"

"No," I said shortly, "we're staying." There was no way I was going to leave before I knew what was going on. "*Mevrouw*, please take your hands off us or I will call the police," I said, and I could tell from the sound of my own voice that I meant it.

All was soon revealed.

Monsieur had peed against the pavement sign advertising the sandwich shop. Without us noticing, he'd lifted his leg against the special offer: ham and cheese sandwich 20 francs, crab salad sandwich 25 francs.

Monsieur peed against every tree and post. It was actually more marking his territory than peeing. Often he produced only a single drop; dachshunds aren't exactly known for their giant bladders. Elzira took care that he didn't foul any buildings, or at least as few as possible. If he made as if to pee on the pavement, she would drag him to the nearest tree or lamp post. That's how she was brought up: cause as little disturbance as possible, be as unobtrusive as possible.

"*On y va,*" Elzira begged.

"No," I said, "not yet."

"Don't answer this woman. *Il vaut mieux se taire.*"

But I wasn't going to shut up. I addressed the woman calmly: "If our dog peed against your sign, we would like to apologize. We hadn't noticed. In future we'll take care he doesn't do it again."

Elzira squeezed my arm. Monsieur was about to jump up against the sandwich seller's calves. Elzira retracted the lead. I could feel how tense she was.

The woman didn't pay any attention to our apology: "Your kind thinks this is all perfectly normal. You'd really like us to bow down to you, to clear up your mess. But perish the thought you'd ever buy anything from us—that's never going to happen, you're far too snooty for that!"

The woman's frustration erupted like a boil. I was shocked by all the hate that flowed out of her, despite having witnessed plenty of ugly scenes since I'd been with Nima.

I told the woman we would lodge a complaint with the police.

"I should lodge a complaint against your kind," she shouted.

"Remember the name of the sandwich shop," I ordered Elzira loudly. And then, to the shopkeeper: "Are you the manager? What's your name, please?"

"Your kind looks down on us, day in, day out. What are you going to lodge a complaint about? Discrimination? But discrimination is your national sport!"

She wouldn't give her name. I went inside to ask. The boy behind the counter told me without hesitating.

We didn't lodge a complaint. Just as Nima had never lodged a complaint. You were only wasting your time going to the police. No one took discrimination on the grounds of nationality, religion, race, sexual preference or gender seriously.

Elzira and I discussed this incident at length. As well as the episode with the Maltese in the park. Elzira's decision to be silent. To blend in with the crowd. The difference between being silent and standing up for yourself and other people. Nevertheless, Elzira managed to distil an unexpectedly positive note from the bleach scene. The woman had taken me for a Jew, not a *goyte*. "So, wrapped up in dark winter clothing, one person can look like another."

Thirty-Four

Evening after evening I cancelled on the Schneiders. "My own study first" was the excuse I invented, by analogy with the Vlaams Blok slogan "Our own people first".

But there was more to it than that. My studies. My work at the Schneiders'. My relationship. The Gulf War. The Schneiders' religion, permeating every aspect of their daily lives. Their closed attitude to the outside world. Their suspicion of that world. Israel's stance on the Palestinians. The intifada. The impact of those tensions on Nima and his fellow exiles. The jitteriness sparked by the term "Muslim".

"*Trop bon, trop con,*" Jakov had said to me only recently. Too good, too dumb: a soft touch, in other words. He was only teasing, but I'd lost my temper, had told him to cut the crap and speak plainly. It soon emerged that he strongly disapproved of my lifestyle.

He couldn't understand that I was living with a man whose religion was different to my own. He called atheism an expression of cowardice. "These days it takes courage to be religious. Atheism is proof of lack of courage. It's nothing, neither fish nor fowl." I contradicted him. He let me speak, but didn't listen. It was water off a duck's back.

He couldn't understand that my parents not only knew I was living with a man, but allowed it. He couldn't understand that I'd chosen a man from an alien culture, someone whose family I'd never met, who no one had vouched for, and who didn't have a permanent job. How could I be satisfied with someone who was doing odd jobs and studying at the same time, who couldn't provide me with any security? Surely only because I was an idiot?

I called him a brat and told him to get lost. Said that *he*, with his narrow-minded, provincial outlook, *he* who'd never left his community, should perhaps take a long hard look at himself and his people. That not everybody chose to live in a straitjacket. That there was such a thing as emancipation, and that just learning by your mistakes was an education in itself. "You don't even *realize* you're in a straitjacket—how narrow-minded is *that*?"

Mr Schneider, too, annoyed me. How dare he take me to task about the newspapers I read? Or drag Nima into it? How did he have the nerve to censure my political views, which were by no means as radical as he claimed? What did he know about me? Wasn't this the same man who, three years ago, had asked for Nima's surname so he could have my boyfriend checked out? Wasn't *he* the one who should be criticized for his political leanings? For all I knew, Mr and Mrs Schneider voted Vlaams Blok. Voted indirectly against me.

After an overdose of Catholicism and all the hypocrisy that went with it, I'd deliberately chosen to study at a liberal university. Nima had fled a religious regime. Now I was up to my neck in the laws of Judaism.

Elzira wasn't allowed to swim in the same pool as boys. When she did risk a plunge, along with other Jewish girls in a hired swimming pool, she didn't wear a swimsuit or bikini, but an enveloping outfit worthy of Batwoman. Boys' and girls' schools opened at different times to prevent any hanky-panky at the school gates. Why, in the Schneider home, did I never hear any punk, pop or rock—not even Bob Dylan or Leonard Cohen, who were Jews after all? Didn't young Orthodox Jews, the modern ones at least, have a spark of anarchy in them? Elzira's bicycle and dachshund were the only subversive attributes in the rule-bound habitat into which she'd been born. These days I no longer had a soft spot even for Monsieur. Before, I would stroke him under his chin when he came eagerly to greet me. Now I turned away from him.

The differences between the Schneiders' world and my own had become sharper, like the taste of pickled fish, which—along with pickled onions, gherkins and horseradish—I suddenly no longer liked, not even on a poppy seed bagel prepared by Mrs Schneider.

And then there was Nima. In his sleep he muttered what sounded like prayers, but turned out to be snatches of songs he'd heard as a child. When he was studying, or even just sitting with me at the table, he would grow lost in thought.

"What are you fretting about?"

"Nothing, just leave me be."

Every now and again, in a roundabout way, he'd permit a glimpse of what was going on inside him. If my friends praised Mikhail Gorbachev, for instance, he couldn't restrain himself.

"You lot just can't understand that to all non-Westerners Gorbachev's a traitor," he would say tiredly. "That's the *real* wall separating the world, that's the *real* tragedy dividing us: that you guys refuse to grasp that not *everyone* sympathizes with the United States, which only has one goal: to wage war." He reacted just as hotly when the assassinated Egyptian president Sadat was painted as the Arab hero who'd shaken Menachem Begin's hand in 1981. "Sadat violated the independent, free spirit of Nasser and of all Egypt. You fete this puppet of the West—this man who sold the honour of his people, of North Africa and of the Middle East, down the river." If friends in our circle defended and supported the Gulf War: "Why should the *West* have a right to the oil of Iran, Iraq, Kuwait? The Americans never started a war unless it was in their own interests. And yet you lot believe the US should teach the whole world a lesson in morals, and you kowtow to them."

Fortunately, he spent more time than usual in a gym in Kammenstraat. The owner was called Benny or Eddie or something like that. A big muscly guy who knew all his customers' names and backgrounds. Benny's gym has long since disappeared from the corner of Kammenstraat, but the guy deserved a medal; at times of national and international crises he single-handedly managed to channel a lot of conscious and subconscious aggression into sport, endurance and fair play.

At home, we stuck up a poster in the window: "No to the Gulf War!"

Thirty-Five

For two months, I didn't go to the Schneiders'.

Then one evening, Mr Schneider appeared on our doorstep, under the window with the "No to the Gulf War!" poster.

Nima opened the door. "She isn't at home just now, she's still in the library. Would you like to come in?"

I was in my last year at the Institute of Interpreting and Translation Studies. Sitting tests. Resitting tests.

Nima took Mr Schneider's long coat and hat. He made fresh mint tea and spread out bowls of pistachios, almonds, figs, fresh fruit and nougat from Isfahan. Mr Schneider sampled it all, even the sickly-sweet, non-kosher nougat.

I never got to hear what they talked about. "All kinds of things," was the answer I got from both Nima and Mr Schneider when I asked.

"He's okay," my boyfriend said. "That father's okay." He also said he'd asked Mr Schneider what he'd done with the piece of paper on which I'd written down his name after my job interview. "I stuck it in the shredder," he'd answered. Nima said he found that hard to believe. Mr Schneider merely smiled and told a few jokes.

Mr Schneider left a letter for me, from Elzira.

It was the loveliest, most honest letter I'd ever received in my life, and thanks to three years of boarding school I had quite a pile of correspondence. After that two-month break, I went back to work for the Schneiders.

I'd missed them much more than I wanted to admit.

Thirty-Six

Then Elzira asked me if I wanted to help her prepare for Shabbat on Friday afternoon and whether we, Nima and I, would like to celebrate with them that evening.

"Of course," I said, excited and curious, without hesitating a second. But doubt immediately kicked in. "Is that allowed, then?"

"It's allowed if you do as I say," she answered resolutely. Her gaze was still soft, but had grown more self-confident over the years. Her movements were no longer clumsy. Her hand had become more stable, as had she herself.

"What time shall I come?" I asked. I knew of course that Jewish schoolchildren had Friday afternoons off, just like non-Jewish children had Wednesday afternoons off. But I had no idea what time her school finished.

"Come shortly after noon, if you can. Then we have *assez* time to cook and so on. Shabbat begins eighteen minutes before sunset on Hadlakat Nerot, when we light the candles. And the day of rest ends the next day, on Saturday evening, when there are three stars in the sky."

"Three stars in the sky? How do you know what time that is? Surely it depends where you are in the world?" This seemed to me yet another case of believing in one's own fairy tales.

"*Le calendrier!* The Jewish calendar hangs in all Jewish kitchens. Haven't you ever seen ours? It has all the Shabbat times on it. All our holidays. Everything we need to know and aren't allowed to *oubliëren*—to forget. We don't live in your time. We live in very different years."

The first thing Elzira showed me when I entered their L-shaped kitchen was their calendar, a thick exercise book with a purple cover, which lay at the far corner of the counter, next to the telephone.

For nearly four years I'd been coming to the Schneiders' house, on average five times a week. I'd grown accustomed to the holy carefulness that marked their lives and was more or less familiar with their festivals, mainly because they almost all translated into days off school, which meant I didn't have to come then. But no one had told me there was such a thing as a Jewish calendar. Nor had it ever occurred to me to that there might be—stupid, really, since Iranians, Kurds and Afghans had their own calendar. I saw it every day, in fact, stuck with magnets to our fridge door.

The Persian calendar wasn't remotely in sync with the Gregorian and Islamic calendars; it had often struck me as bizarre that the human race couldn't even agree about the era they lived in. I wondered whether that fact alone wasn't telling.

Nowruz, Persian New Year, is celebrated in spring, around 21st March. Rosh Hashanah, Jewish New Year, falls in autumn, in our September or October. Our own old year is shot down and replaced by a new one in the middle of winter. Islamic New Year, Muharram, is celebrated on a different date and using a different calendar. "We're already living in 5752," Jakov bragged. He dug around in the fridge and bumped his shoulder playfully against mine, a friendly gesture he'd never have made in the old days, certainly not in the presence of his mother, whose gentle dark-eyed gaze seemed to pierce all the relationships in the kitchen.

"Yes, you're way ahead of us," I joked. Mrs Schneider smiled. She was sitting at the far end of the kitchen, in a kind of bay window overlooking the garden. Sara, next to her, was busy clearing her plate. The kitchen was white: window frames, walls, floor, cupboards, sinks, cookers, table, chairs, the modern leather benches around the table—all white, white, white.

Krystina filled a bucket with soapy water. Her job was to make sure that everything was spic and span. She was wearing plastic gloves—even those were white.

Elzira helped me put on a white, freshly starched apron, then tied another round her own slim frame. (At home I never wore an apron, students like me shunning such bourgeois trappings.) Her hair was kept in place by a black velvet headband. She was wearing ballet pumps, and in my high-heeled shoes I towered above her: her head came up to my breasts. When we sat at her desk this difference in height hadn't been so obvious. And when we took Monsieur out for a walk, we didn't notice it either: we were so busy with the frisky dachshund. But here in the kitchen it was a little awkward, and Elzira must have realized that. Without saying anything she disappeared into her room and came back with some gym shoes that fitted me.

"This is the side for all the meat we can eat, meat from *mammifères* with shoes that are cloven."

"Shoes?"

"Like those of a cow."

"With split hooves?"

"And they must be ruminants. We only eat *mammifères* that are ruminants. And here on this side we put everything that has to do with *produits laitiers*," Elzira said.

"Mammals and dairy products," I corrected, in a whisper. I didn't want to play the role of teacher in the kitchen, too. Elzira was busy with pots and pans. She dropped a pan lid. "Don't take any notice," she laughed. "Lady Dyspraxia is assisting me."

It was the first time I was "really" in their kitchen. Really in the sense of beyond the doorway where I'd often stood waiting for Elzira and Jakov and sometimes Sara as they had a quick bite, or when they were preparing a snack for me, or having it prepared.

"Blue is for dairy products. Red for meat." Elzira was explaining the chopping boards, the dishcloths, the tea towels, scourers and kitchen knives: everything in both red and blue. All the ingredients were kosher, she said, in conformity with the dietary laws. She showed me the rabbinical certificate on the packaging of certain products, right down to the dishwasher detergent and sponges. The rabbi had declared their kitchen kosher, she knew. He had "kashered" certain utensils: purged them, it seemed, blessed them, cleansed them, immersed them in a special bath of boiling water, buried them in the ground, all so that they, as observant Jews, could cook and eat in a way that was kosher. It occurred to me that "rabid" and "rabbinate" sounded awfully similar, but I didn't share the joke. Jews, sometimes described as the world's first capitalists, clearly maintained their own protectionist economy, amongst other things, through their dietary laws. It was the umpteenth balancing act I'd come across in their lifestyle: on the one hand their mercantile spirit, on the other their own protected industry, economy, commerce.

"It's not for nothing that our fridge has two doors, you know," Jakov said, his mouth full. Since getting new spectacles he not only looked better, but could also see better. It turned out that for years he'd been wearing glasses that corrected his far-sightedness, but did nothing for his astigmatism.

"Don't forget to explain that to her, Elzira."

Their fridge was a two-door American model, with a tap in the middle and a machine that spat out ice cubes. The left half was for meat, the right for dairy products. Only when I saw the fridge did I get the full picture: the long side of the L-shaped room was a double kitchen: one side of the wall was the mirror image of the other. The Schneiders had two cookers, two sinks, two dishwashers and two kitchen worktops. Just as Elzira had once told me.

"If someone hasn't got two sinks they use two bowls, red and blue for instance. And if their fridge isn't a double one, they can divide it up, with *planches* or *tiroirs*, shelves or drawers for meat and dairy products. But nothing may leak: meat may not drip onto cheese, milk may not drip onto turkey, etc. And you must never put anything warm into a single fridge: everything that is warm breathes, and the hot air can make the whole fridge un-kosher."

Each side of the kitchen had its own crockery, cutlery, cookware, mixers, table linen and everything else that needed to be kept separate. Utensils that didn't feature red or blue in their design were marked with coloured stickers. Meat and pancakes were cooked in different frying pans. And steaks and *asperges à la flamande*—asparagus in cheese sauce—were eaten from different plates. You couldn't even eat tournedos and cheese from the same tablecloth or placemat.

"So what do you fry your chicken in, then?" I asked, since I, like Nima, tended to fry poultry in butter—it brought out the flavour of the meat.

"In goose fat, *bien sûr*," Elzira answered, and I felt I'd asked a dumb question.

"What about a cheese course after dinner?"

"Religious Jews would never order cheese after a meal. Or coffee or tea with milk. We can't do that if we've eaten meat. Or rather, we can, but then we have to wait at least six hours. Or three hours. Religious Jews in the Netherlands, the realm of dairy products, only wait one hour. *Tout est relatif,* I can't help it. But the other way round is fine. After milk we can eat meat without waiting. It's to do with chewing. It's complicated, *je sais*."

We would not only prepare the Friday evening meal, I gathered, but also certain dishes for Saturday breakfast and lunch. "We have a hot meal on Saturdays. We programme our cookers; at a set time they switch off automatically. But not everybody does that. In many traditional families the ovens and hobs are lit before the start of Shabbat and go on burning till Saturday evening. Do you know the typical Jewish dish *cholent*?"

"*Chaud lent?*" I asked.

"*Cholent*. It's a traditional stew that simmers from Friday to Saturday afternoon, and its main ingredients, in our version, are potatoes, *de l'orge, os à moelle* and beans."

"Barley. Marrow bone. Do you like marrow bone?"

"*Os à moelle?* No, I don't. But Daddy does. His mother made really yummy *cholent*. And grated potato, stuffed intestines, *saucisson*."

"Beef?"

"Of course. Never something from a pig. That's why we don't eat many of the sweets that you can eat. And why we only buy *confiture* that a rabbi has approved. Yours has gelatine, which is extracted from animal bones. Including pig bones."

"And fish?"

"Fish is *pareve*. It is neither meat nor dairy. The right fish can be eaten with both."

"What do you do if you can only afford *one* cooker?"

"You build a little wall between the hobs. Not a real one, of course! One made of aluminium foil, for instance. The best thing is never to cook meat and dairy on a single hob at the same time. But if you don't have a choice, you have to make sure that nothing splatters from one pan to the other. And if you lift up a lid, no *gouttes* may drip from one pan into the other."

"Good grief, Elzira," I joked, worn out before I'd even touched anything, or before we'd begun to prepare a single dish, not even "Jewish penicillin": chicken soup with matzo balls. "I'm unclean. This afternoon I ate a pizza with salami and melted cheese!"

Clearly in her element, she shoved a red-handled whisk into my hand. The bowl was full of egg whites. "Please beat those for the matzo balls. We make a lighter, more modern version than the traditional recipe."

Thirty-Seven

At around eight o'clock, Nima and I cycled to the Schneiders'.

The pavements, usually bustling with Jewish pedestrians, looked deserted. So did the streets: there was hardly any traffic. The synagogue service had already finished. In houses that permitted a glimpse of the interior, you could see people gathered together, and lighted oil lamps and candles, not just those of the *menorah*.

We'd been asked not to ring the bell—not to activate an electrical circuit. The front door stood ajar and, once we were inside, Nima and I shut and bolted the door behind us, as we'd been instructed to do—there were three bolts in all.

Once inside we were allowed to take the lift—"goys can do anything, even on Shabbat"—but we didn't. With our shoes in our hands, we climbed the stairs noiselessly.

I'd imagined that Shabbat would be observed in solemn silence: a bit like in church, where all sound and action happened near the altar, and people were only allowed to speak or sing when the leader gave permission. That turned out to be a misconception. Even before we got to the top of the stairs, we could hear a catchy melody being sung in deep, cheerful male voices, followed by loud laughter, including from women.

Mr and Mrs Schneider were waiting for us at the top of the stairs. They greeted us warmly; Mr Schneider embraced my boyfriend in the manner of Middle Eastern men: chin on each other's shoulder, each thumping the other on the back with both hands.

Mrs Schneider and I looked at each other. She kissed me twice. Never before had she kissed me. I held out the bouquet of flowers we'd bought for the occasion. She took it appreciatively, almost shyly. She nodded to Nima; her expression was sweet and friendly.

"Hadn't we told you not to bring anything, except your spouse!" exclaimed Mr Schneider. He laughed very hard, and we laughed along with him, somewhat less hard.

Mini-Sara, who'd meanwhile overtaken her big sister, was running busily between the kitchen, living room and the stairwell, waving and calling out *"Shabbat shalom"* without looking at us.

Jakov—the oldest now that Simon was serving in the Israeli army—had joined his father in the stairwell. He scrutinized Nima from behind his new spectacles. As the two shook hands, he checked out my boyfriend in the way of parents all over the world sizing up their future son- or daughter-in-law: critically, nervously, curiously. He nodded at me: "Oh, so this is him."

Nima gave Jakov a couple of manly thumps on the back, a friendly gesture that took Jakov by surprise. To hide his blushes, he put his arm over his face and felt his *yarmulke*, as if he suddenly needed to check whether it still was in place.

Elzira, subtly made up and wearing a slightly fitted, dark-blue dress with a lace collar, looked like a very young mix of Cindy Crawford and Julia Roberts. She wasn't afraid to meet Nima's eye and when he held out a hand—despite me repeatedly having told him *not* to—took it cordially: *"Enchantée de vous connaître,* pleased to meet you."

I experienced this Shabbat celebration in a daze. I could recall everything that happened before the dinner much more clearly than the dinner itself which, after various solemn blessings, morphed into a boisterous, Mediterranean-style family celebration in which the children, big and small, were the focal point—not just the children of the Schneiders themselves, but also the four belonging to another family. They crawled under the table. They played hide and seek. They were allowed to eat with their elbows on the table.

The dining table's leaves had been pulled out to extend it at both ends; it looked gigantic. Seated at it were lots of people in Orthodox Jewish dress, none of whom I knew. When we came in, the faces of at least three of them suddenly stopped, like clocks. I'd looked forward to seeing grandmother Schneider, but it turned out she wasn't there. "My honoured mother is visiting her sister in Amsterdam."

The table was spread with all kinds of special dishes whose name I didn't know or had forgotten. I couldn't even remember whether I'd helped prepare them, or seen them prepared. The plaited loaves that Elzira and Irma had baked that afternoon waited in a silver bowl, flanked by a pot of honey and a salt cellar. Where were the maids? Were they in the kitchen, washing up? Where did all these tasty-looking dishes keep coming from?

These are the things I *do* remember.

That in their loud conversations, which sometimes sounded more like arguments, the men spoke a mishmash of languages: Hebrew, Yiddish, Dutch, English, French.

That we were asked hardly any questions. Everyone interrupted everyone else; the dinner was an incredible cacophony. Not only words, but also gestures were echoed. If one person gesticulated, the other would gesticulate even more strongly. Everyone reached across the table, passing dishes. During the meal, people took children onto their laps.

That Mr Schneider and Jakov read aloud from the *siddur*, a Jewish prayer book that father and son often read together, an act that strengthens their bond. That they were assisted by a six-year-old nephew who could read Hebrew with amazing speed and who, as he followed the words with his tiny index finger, kept pinching the leg of his little sister, who was sitting next to him. That—and this is how I remember it, but I could be wrong—Mr Schneider didn't use his index finger as a reading aid, but followed the text with a silver pen whose end, shaped like a hand with an outstretched index finger, slid under the letters.

That Nima occasionally nudged me under the table. When Mr Schneider launched into the joke about the dying man and his business partner. When Elzira dropped her fork. When Mrs Schneider eyed him secretly from under her lashes. When I gazed too long at one of the children's aunts and didn't realize I was staring.

That the dinner must have been delicious, though afterwards I could only recall the sweetish, nutty taste of the chicken soup. Even the matzo balls that I'd rolled were a blank; I couldn't recollect their taste or texture.

That the men sang *zemirot*, Shabbat hymns, at the tops of their voices, and that I lowered my eyes during their rousing singing, I think because the exuberance and the intimacy overwhelmed me. I peeped sideways at them, feeling like a voyeur.

That I was envious of the naturalness with which they sang together, and not immune to their belief in the need for communal singing. That I envied the unity expressed in their hymns. Together, the men seemed to be spontaneously writing a story that greatly transcended their own individual histories. Strength of that kind was new to me, and sitting there I believed that people and peoples who sang together had a stronger bond than people who didn't, and for my own part I felt this lack.

I was reminded of the birthday parties of my childhood.

On my birthday, I would invite my school friends to a party at my home. My Moroccan, Turkish and Greek friends from Meulenberg wouldn't accept these invitations. Their parents weren't familiar with the birthday party tradition and, not knowing the language and rituals of their host country, didn't feel confident enough to send their daughters to a Flemish family, least of all a family where the mother was a teacher. A kind of shame seemed always to separate our different worlds. The one immigrant girl who *was* allowed to come to such parties always felt too uncomfortable to join in properly: because Dutch was the only language spoken, because she felt everyone was looking at her, because she didn't know the customs, because we had more money than her family did, because she knew her parents would never throw such a party. The girl would stand on the sidelines. Just as I was standing on the sidelines here at this Shabbat celebration. I'd been flattered to have been invited. But in the Schneiders' living room I couldn't shake off the feeling that Nima and I had stepped into an ancient painting, a *tableau vivant* in which we didn't belong. And in which we perhaps had no business to be.

Thirty-Eight

I n 1991 everything went wrong.
  One:

For the first time in Belgian history, the far-right party Vlaams Blok blew away all the mainstream parties in the federal elections. The city of Antwerp turned out to be the breeding ground of this extremist party. That Sunday couldn't have seemed blacker.

Two:

Jakov and his best friend Jack smashed up Jack's father's car. The boys had reached the age when you can legally drive in the United States, and they didn't want to be outdone by American teenagers. Neither of them had ever driven a car before, neither knew how to change gear or where the accelerator and brake pedals were. But one day, when his father was away on business, Jack had pocketed the car keys and they'd set off for a spin. A very short one as it turned out: reversing out of the drive at top speed, they'd shot straight into the garage door of the neighbour opposite, crumpling up the back of Jack's father's Jaguar like a concertina. The neighbour in question, a non-Jew, was absolutely beside himself and called the police.

In their panic, all the boys could come up with was to tell the police officer that Jack had been driving. They'd thought it would make things simpler for the insurance. But Jack's father's insurance policy didn't cover this kind of stupid stunt. Mr Schneider was asked to help foot the bill. He refused. As far as he was concerned, his son had merely been a passenger.

Jack was the first to crack. He confessed to his father that Jakov had been driving the car. Jakov accused his best friend of lying. The tension between fathers and sons got worse. To say nothing of the owner of the smashed garage door, who grew angrier by the day.

I was the only one to whom Jakov confessed his lie. It had caused him sleepless nights, and he didn't know what to do. I advised him to tell his father the truth. He did so—two weeks after the event. By which time, besides car and door, a lot of collateral damage had been caused.

The third piece of bad news, in June of that *annus horribilis*, also had to do with Jakov.

Jakov was doing his final Dutch exam, for which he wanted to write a really good essay. As good as the ones he and his friends had been handing in these last few years.

The essay had to be written on the spot, in the exam room. The pupils were given five titles to choose from. They had three hours—from nine to twelve—in which to write a well-argued piece.

Jakov overreached himself. Neither he nor two of his mates, who'd been buying my compositions for years, wanted to take the slightest risk. And so they took a risk that was their undoing. One afternoon they managed to sneak into the staffroom. They searched for the Dutch teacher's exam papers. They found them. They photocopied them. In their nervous haste they left the originals under the lid of the photocopier. The teacher realized what had happened. The class was called to account. Under pressure from the others, the three owned up. Fortunately they were smart enough and scared enough not to confess to their years of deception. At least not to the school. To his father, who demanded an explanation, Jakov confessed all. He told him all about our little sideline.

"*T'es un con!*" Mr Schneider exclaimed. "How could you be so stupid?"

Mr Schneider, it turned out, wasn't so much angry that his youngest son, with my connivance, had been hoodwinking the school authorities. Above all, he was incensed by Jakov's carelessness, by his son's amateurishness. "If you want to cheat, do it properly or don't do it at all!"

The whole time this affair raged, no member of the family ever questioned my integrity as a tutor. At least, no one ever took me to task about it.

Jakov and his friends were severely reprimanded by the headmaster and the Dutch teacher, but they weren't expelled.

They made a complete mess of the exam essay.

Four:

As if the sky of 1991 wasn't already dark enough, one evening, as Elzira and I were bent over her books, she mentioned casually that the *shadchan* had paid a visit.

"What's a *shadchan*?"

"She's a matchmaker."

"What does she do?"

"She arranges marriages."

She told me that the *shadchan* was a greatly respected figure in the Orthodox community, that she knew all the Jewish families in the world and had everyone's particulars in her card filing system. All the necessary data on their genealogy, family background, character and genetic particulars.

"Doesn't that bother you?"

"What?"

"Her knowing so much about you?"

"It's our custom."

"Are you being married off?"

"There's someone who wants to marry me."

"Are you being married off?" I repeated. My heart was beating very fast.

"Men who are interested in me introduce themselves to me and my family via the matchmaker."

"So you *are* being married off."

"No, I'm allowed to choose."

"Choose between two men?"

"Yes. No. I'm allowed to put forward candidates myself. So are my brothers. Anyone can."

"And if you don't like a candidate you can send him packing?"

"Yes."

"Time after time? A thousand times, if you want?"

"That won't happen."

"And what if you fall in love with some other man? Someone you meet by chance."

"That won't happen."

And then came the fifth uppercut. That blow struck in my own circle.

Marjane was admitted to a psychiatric clinic in Tehran. Initially it was thought that a stay of a few months would get her back on the rails. In the end it took more than a year before she felt remotely human again.

During her therapy sessions it emerged that Marjane had been raped in Brussels, more than once.

When Nima heard that he didn't say a word, but smashed the bathroom mirror to smithereens with his bare fist and stalked through the flat, letting the blood drip on the floor.

The same Nima who was responsible for the good news of this dark year.

"I must do better than her," he resolved.

"Better than she," I corrected.

He passed his second-year engineering exams and got a temporary job as a sound technician.

I, having meanwhile got my degree, continued to combine one part-time job after another with working for the Schneiders. The jobs rarely if ever made me happy.

Thirty-Nine

Jakov went abroad to study. First in Israel, then in New York and Boston, then in Israel again. Having tried his hand at business as a schoolboy, it was time to make it official: he wanted to get an MBA.

In the first years after leaving home, he would regularly send me postcards: "See, I can still write Dutch" and "This month I even read a literary novel, by a Jewish writer, too, Philip Roth, I didn't think much of it."

So, not counting Monsieur, that left just the three of us.

Sara. Elzira. Me.

Sometimes I helped Sara prepare for tests. But we never really developed the bond that I'd built up with Jakov and Elzira. Sara got excellent marks, so everything went swimmingly.

I saw Elzira even more than before.

We weren't friends, exactly, but we certainly grew closer together. She talked to me about things she'd never have mentioned when Jakov and Simon were still at home. Perhaps she was just more open because she was older.

"On Tuesday after school Mummy drove me to Brussels."

"Oh. To go shopping?"

"I had make-up put on."

"You what?" I asked, stunned.

"Je me suis fait maquiller."

"But you haven't got it on now?"

"On Tuesday evening, before I went to sleep, I washed all the make-up off my face."

"Did you have to go to a party?"

"It was for practice. Before long we're going to a cousin's wedding. She's getting married in Amsterdam. She's marrying a Dutchman. She will live in the Netherlands."

"Did you look pretty?"

"Mummy thought I looked very pretty. So did Daddy. But Sara said I looked prettier without all that *peinture*." She looked at me enquiringly.

"I'm sure you looked beautiful," I said, studying her face, trying to picture how she'd looked, professionally made up.

"Have you got any photos?"

"They're not ready yet. We went to Maison Roger. And we'll go back there on the day of the wedding."

"Who is Roger?"

"Don't you know Maison Roger? On Avenue Louise in Brussels?"

I knew Avenue Louise all right. The most expensive shopping street in Brussels, full of exclusive boutiques. The average dress cost the equivalent of ten months' rent.

"Queen Fabiola goes there. And all the princesses. It's the best hairdressing and beauty salon in the country. Sometimes Mummy has her hair done there. Mummy doesn't wear a wig..."

"Have you ever seen Queen Fabiola's hairdo?" I joked.

"I know. But Roger is very good."

"Will you wear a wig later?"

"I'll wear a wig if my husband wants me to. There are some very nice wigs."

"But you've got such lovely hair. Why would you hide it under a wig? Can you imagine me wearing a wig...?"

"You are not a *juive*. You don't have to." She burst out laughing.

Still smiling, she said: "The gentleman who did my make-up was like a girl."

There was a short silence.

Amused, I waited for her to go on.

"If you know what I mean," she ventured, looking at me questioningly, as if expecting a long answer or explanation.

"Was he a homosexual?" I asked.

"Shhhhhh," she whispered, covering her mouth with her hands in shock and glancing at the bedroom door. "Shhh…"

"What? Is 'homosexual' a forbidden word?" I teased.

"Shhhh."

"What should I say, then?"

She hesitated. "Yes, I think you may use that word."

"Do you know what a homosexual is?"

"Shhh! I think I know, *oui*. A man who wants to be a woman."

"That's not quite right. A homosexual is a man who falls in love with other men, and who has sex with those men."

The S-word made her jump. Her hands started to shake a little, and when I saw that I was happy in a strange, possessive way, the way it makes you happy to realize that two things you always felt went together apparently still do, even many years later. Elzira's eyes gleamed, her raised eyebrows testifying both to her prudishness and her curiosity.

"Was he nice?" I asked.

"Yes, very," she said. "And he had *des mains très fines*, very delicate hands."

"Why do you think he was a homosexual?"

"He made movements that *les hommes de chez nous* don't make. He moved his hands in a funny way. And when he walked it was just as if he… *comme s'il faisait du patin à glace, quoi*."

I grinned. Her image of the ice-skating man was both funny and apt. Yet I also had to think of *My Own Private Idaho*, a film Nima and I had just seen in Cartoons Cinema, in which the two main characters—played by River Phoenix and Keanu Reeves—confront the issue of desire between men. Halfway through the film, Nima had walked out.

"But he makes people up very well," she said. "*Il comprend les femmes*, Mummy says, and that's true. That's why it's so good that he works there. And that he isn't a Jew. I believe that there are Jewish men of that kind. But not in our community. Among religious Jews there aren't any such men."

"I've got friends who are gay," I said. "And there are girls, too, who are homosexual. Girls who fall in love with other girls. Do you know what they're called?"

I thought: she has no TV and rarely if ever goes to the cinema, and the Disney films she's seen don't feature any gays. She has no access to any reading matter that could educate her in these things—novels, newspapers, magazines—though I'd once seen a copy of *Paris Match* lying around their house. So from whom would she learn anything about the diversity and complexity of human sexuality if not from me?

"Lesbians," she said. She pronounced the word in the Dutch rather than the French way. The existence of lesbian relationships didn't seem to bother her, however. At least, she didn't go into the matter further. Of course, I'd already introduced her to Andreas Burnier (the pen name of Catharina Irma Dessaur, a Jewish author from Holland who wrote about her homosexuality).

I said: "My gay friends daren't tell their parents they're attracted to men. Their parents expect them to marry and have children. These parents, too, are quite sure that there aren't any homosexuals in their family."

"I don't mind that a gentleman who resembles a girl touched my face," was her response.

"But you should listen to what I'm saying," I said.

"*J'écoute!*"

"Being silent about something doesn't mean it doesn't exist."

"It's not a problem that the make-up man touched me."

"Why would it be a problem? You just said he made you up beautifully."

"I heard about it."

"What did you hear?"

"I heard about it."

"What, Elzira? You're talking in riddles!"

"About that disease."

For a moment I was perplexed. Then light began to dawn. But just to check I asked: "What disease?"

"Two. Both with names that are shorted."

"Shortened."

"You know what diseases I mean. *Tu me taquines.*"

"I'm not teasing. You mean HIV or AIDS?"

She looked down at the floor and nodded.

"They say all these men are sick," she said. "But Mummy says that isn't true."

"Your mummy is right."

"Could I get sick?"

"You don't catch HIV and AIDS just by someone touching you, Elzira. Only by having sex with someone who's infected."

"Tssst."

"Or through a blood transfusion. And by no means all homosexuals are sick! So you shouldn't talk like that…"

"In Antwerp there are hairdressers who guarantee that all the equipment in their salons is sterilized after each use: the scissors, the combs, everything. So the clients won't become sick."

"Where are these salons, then?"

"I don't know. I heard Mummy talking about it. It's on a sign in their window: we sterilize all instruments."

"I'd like to see that. I've never heard of such a thing—it's ridiculous! You can't get infected through a haircut! I'll bring you some information about the disease as soon as I can. Scientific information. And personal accounts. I can recommend a few books for you."

"They can't be hairdressers from our community."

"Why not?"

"We don't have homosexuals."

I sighed. So she'd managed to get the word over her lips. In the plural, even.

Forty

"Which one is the prettiest, do you think?"

I was waiting for Elzira in her room when Mrs Schneider came in with a carrier bag from The Short Way, an Antwerp lingerie store on Mechelsesteenweg. I knew its window, just as I knew the windows of many unaffordable shops.

She spread out four diaphanous garments on the desk. Two bodysuits with sleeves and two without, made of silk or satin with insets of see-through lace. Lingerie of the most exquisite, luxurious kind.

"I would like to choose two. They are for Elzira. She will soon turn seventeen."

I was in my mid-twenties at the time. Never in my life had I worn such sexy underwear, of such an expensive brand. Just regular bras were expensive enough; I'd grown up with Damart. In my family, underwear and nightwear had only to be robust and practical. Even though I'd left home years ago, I still slept in stripy cotton or flannel pyjamas of the kind favoured by old men. If I wanted to look sexy at the breakfast table I unbuttoned the top. That had to do. If it was really hot, I wore a tank top.

"You prefer which one? Is the white the most pretty, do you favour the grey or is the salmon pink more to your taste?"

She picked the bodies up carefully one by one and held them out in front of her, moving with typical measured elegance. Each had a matching robe, as silky-smooth as a kimono. She draped the precious garments—Chantal Thomass, La Perla—over the desk and stepped back a few paces to study both the result and my expression.

"The white one's really pretty."

"Preferably white than salmon-pink?"

"The salmon-pink one's pretty too."

"Which you would choose?"

"The black sleeveless one with the zip or the long-sleeved white one," I answered firmly. She nodded, rewrapped them all slowly, then asked when I was planning to become a mother, "because to wait long is not good".

Not put out by her sudden question, I said that for now I had no wish to have children.

"That time will come."

"I'm not so sure. If it does, I'll give it careful thought. But I won't let anyone talk me into parenthood. I think I'll be happier without children."

She stared at me, her eyes wide.

"You have a problem?" she asked. There was a hint of suspicion in her voice. A reaction I'd seen before when young women said that motherhood wasn't for them.

"A gynaecological problem, you mean? Not that I know of."

"That you do not want children I do not understand. I think you will be a good mother. And your husband, Nima?"

It was unusual for her to say his name. I was touched.

"Nima thinks the same way."

"It is that he is far from his family, perhaps," she said after a while. "But for that very reason he should start his own family here. That is better for everyone. *We* know that. Over the course of history we, the Jews, have often had our families torn apart. But we have gone on with our lives, *notre existence. Nous avons résisté, toujours.* We build new families, we uphold our values and way of life, even during those times when we were obliged *à nous convertir,* to convert, yes, *siècle après siècle*, century after century, and *still* we choose for new families."

One thing led to another.

Suddenly she was telling me about the times she gave birth and about the gynaecologist who had delivered her four children. They'd all been normal births, without complications. Simon had been very overdue, but oh, how great was their joy when their first child turned out to be a son, and their second too, and they were eternally grateful to this gynaecologist, because Judaism requires you to be eternally grateful to anyone who is good to children.

The gynaecologist wasn't Jewish, which surprised me once again, this modern note in their orthodoxy, the fact that the Bible or the rabbi allowed a doctor with *treyf* hands to touch the most intimate parts of a married, religious Jewish woman.

She gave me his name and the address of his consultancy: "For when it comes time for you."

A week after this conversation, Elzira handed me a present that felt very soft, and was wrapped in many layers of white, crackling, tissue-thin paper, tied with a white ribbon.

That evening at home I wore the sleeveless black bodysuit with the zip. Mrs Schneider had guessed my size correctly. Just in case, a card was enclosed, explaining how to exchange the gift. On another card, tucked between the folds of the packaged garment, was the message: "With many thanks for what you do for Elzira." Signed: Aaron and Moriel Schneider.

Mrs Schneider's gynaecologist—these days the son has taken over his father's practice—is now mine.

Forty-One

O ne day grandmother Pappenheim fell over, no one knew why, on the corner of Simonsstraat and Mercatorstraat, where she'd just bought her meat, vegetables and French crossword puzzles.

The lady who ran the bed linen shop outside which she collapsed ran to her straight away, and when Gabriella Pappenheim couldn't get up, even with the help of some passers-by, she immediately rang for an ambulance, then called the Schneiders' home telephone number and Mr Schneider's office, because that was one clear advantage of living in this small, closed community, which also had its drawbacks: everyone knew everyone, and everyone knew to which family people belonged. Hatzalah, the volunteer emergency medical service set up by Jewish communities in many places in the world—including latterly in Antwerp— did not yet exist, otherwise the poor lady could certainly have been able to count on lightning-quick assistance from young, Jewish emergency responders. These backpacked paramedics leap onto their fluorescent yellow motor scooters for anyone in need, of course, but you mainly see them weaving through the busy traffic of the Jewish neighbourhood—"we'll be there in four minutes".

Gabriella Pappenheim had to wait a quarter of an hour before the regular ambulance took her to Sint Vincentius, a Catholic hospital right in the middle of the Jewish neighbourhood.

I heard this all from Jakov. I don't know if that was the same hospital where he and his brother were circumcised when they were eight days old by a *mohel*, an official circumciser. The fact the Schneider boys had had their foreskins removed in a special suite of an Antwerp clinic was something I'd learnt from Mr Schneider, who passed on this glad tiding after telling me a "hilarious" joke. The one about the tax inspector going through the books of a synagogue, alert for Jewish skulduggery. "He says to the rabbi, 'I notice you buy a lot of candles. What do you do with the wax drippings?' 'We send them back to the candle makers, and every now and then they send us a free box of candles,' answered the rabbi. 'Oh,' replies the auditor. 'What about all the matzos you buy? What do you do with the crumbs?' 'We send them to the manufacturers, and every now and then they send us a free box of matzos.' 'I see,' the auditor says. 'And what, rabbi,' he goes on, 'do you do with all the foreskins left over from the circumcisions you perform?' 'Ah,' says the rabbi. 'We send them to the tax office, and about once a year they send us a complete *schmuck*.'"

Gabriella Pappenheim had broken her right hip, and was given an artificial replacement. Her rehabilitation took months, and for a while, on walks with Monsieur, Elzira would push her grandmother's wheelchair through the streets of the Jewish neighbourhood, accompanied by a housekeeper or Sara.

Granny Pappenheim temporarily moved in with her son's family. After his voluntary stint in the army, Simon was now studying medicine. His room had been redecorated in the meantime, in cheerful yellows and greens.

Despite her living on the premises, I saw Mrs Pappenheim so rarely that I asked Elzira if she was all right. Elzira told me not to worry, she was slowly but surely getting better.

"Doesn't your granny get lonely sometimes?" I asked.

"There's always someone with her, in the kitchen, in her room or at the physiotherapist. When we're not there, the nurse is. Granny doesn't like to talk very much. When I take her out for a walk she hums songs and tunes, and I hum along with her, because I know the songs and melodies from when I was small. And Monsieur loves it, I can see it by his tail, he wags it *comme une pendule qui a perdu le sens du temps*."

One Wednesday afternoon, grandmother Pappenheim entered the house in her wheelchair just as I was leaving.

"Good afternoon, *Madame*," I said.

"*Shalom*," she said.

"I was glad to hear that you're doing well."

"At my age, doing well is an extremely relative concept," she laughed bitterly.

"Only a few more months and you'll be walking about again," I said, trying to cheer her up.

"A long time ago, during the war, I was skin and bone. Now I'm just skin," she said.

I was shaken by the hardness of her words, by the vision they conjured up of a very different world. She saw that.

"Don't look so shocked, young lady. I have advanced osteoporosis—bone loss. I have almost no bones left."

"You must eat well and drink lots of milk," I said in my brash innocence.

"Children must eat and drink well, because children must grow," she answered. With her sinewy right index finger she toyed with the satin bow at the neck of her dress, over which she wore a pearl necklace. "Just because the nurse treats me like a child, doesn't mean I am a child. 'So how's *Madame* today?' and 'Was Mrs Gabriella a naughty girl last night?' To die decently is the only task I have left."

She took my hand and studied my fingers. "Why don't you wear a ring?"

"I don't wear jewellery."

"None at all?"

"I'm allergic to certain substances."

"Allergic to gold?"

"To all metals."

"Then you must wear diamonds," she said, her chin uplifted. She regarded me sternly, this woman whom I'd compared to a volcano. Now, injury and a major operation seemed to have tempered her fire. Or had Mrs Pappenheim broken more than her hip? Was she insinuating that her will to live had been crushed too?

"I must go, *Madame*," I said, at a loss to know what to say.

"Come up to my room," she commanded. "Drink a cup of tea with me." Her wheelchair just fitted in the lift, with me squeezed next to her.

Forty-Two

From Simon's room, Mrs Pappenheim rang the kitchen. "*A yid hot lib dem geshmak fun a yidish vort in zayn moyl,*" she said after she'd hung up, and when Krystina came up shortly afterwards to serve us tea and cake, she repeated this sentence twice, and Krystina, as she left the room, nodded in agreement.

Mrs Pappenheim asked me what she had said. I had to confess I didn't know, but assumed it was an old saying, some piece of folk wisdom. She wrote down the sentence phonetically, in the Roman alphabet, on an old *Paris Match*. Her ornate handwriting was at odds with her sober appearance. For that very reason, it suited her.

"Come on, translate it. You studied translation, didn't you?" I went and stood next to her. She shoved the sentence under my nose. I didn't talk back, didn't say anything about Germanic and Romance languages, didn't mention Jakov's similar inability to get to the point without first playing some linguistic game. It took me ages to come up with a remotely plausible translation. I felt uncomfortable.

"A Jew loves the taste of a Yiddish word in his mouth," grandmother Pappenheim cried out at last, as if she had won the lottery.

Relieved, I told her that I felt the same way about the Limburg dialect as she did about Yiddish. It was more than a language. It was a home.

Then she grew serious: "Yiddish was forbidden in the camps. Everyone had to speak German. If you were caught speaking

Yiddish, you'd go straight to the bath and disinfection building, that's to say, the gas chambers…"

I fidgeted on my chair. I nodded. I assumed, indeed hoped, she'd start telling me about the war, but at the same time I felt it would be inappropriate to encourage her, so I said that the weather was quite mild for the time of year, which happened to be true.

Out of the corner of my eye I looked at Mrs Pappenheim. The only Jewish person most non-Jews in my country knew was Anne Frank, and they only knew her posthumously, from the diary, from the secret annexe, from all the stories later concocted about her, perhaps from the horse chestnut tree in her garden.

The woman I was sitting next to had been such a girl during the war. Gabriella. A little older than Anne. Her maiden name might be Frank for all I knew.

"My daughter-in-law is a wonderful cook," the grandmother continued, having already forgotten the gas chambers, or perhaps trying to change the subject. She gestured with her chin at the cheese and apple turnovers that had been served with the tea. "Savour the pastries as I savour Yiddish," she said. "Eat. I like to watch people eating."

I didn't need telling twice.

Mrs Pappenheim only talked about one subject: her second husband, who'd apparently died three years earlier, a fact that confronted me once again with the closed nature of the Schneiders, because no one had told me back then that there'd been a death in the family. I hadn't been aware of it at all.

Although there'd always been this selective openness and closedness between us, I felt hurt. At the same time I took myself to task: why hadn't I seen any signs that the family was grieving, how could I not have noticed Elzira's sorrow?

Mrs Pappenheim told me how her beloved husband had got sick: cancer it was, first just in his bowels, then everywhere. How she'd looked after him as best she could, right up to his death, also afterwards. How she'd got to know him, no, how he'd got to know *her*. How he, Levi Pappenheim, had introduced himself to her through his family. How the rabbis had sanctioned the marriage and how both families—the few members that had survived the Holocaust—had approved their engagement.

The marriage of Gabriella and Levi Pappenheim had lasted forty-two years and produced three children, and according to her their love had matured like a good, full-bodied red wine, a Château Mouton Rothschild, if she were allowed to choose the vintage herself. "My husband had to travel a lot for his work. Back and forth to India, Israel and the US. Sometimes he was away for months. This time he's on a trip that will take a few years. That's how I try to think of it. It's the only way I can cope with his absence."

She talked about her apartment. How she missed him there. How she missed the very things that used to annoy her. Him slurping his coffee. Leaving the door open when he went to the toilet. Letting his beard trail in her home-made chicken soup with matzo balls. "My daughter-in-law now uses my recipe." His crooked, skinny back as, when praying, he turned to face Jerusalem.

Every now and then I nodded. I didn't know how to respond to these confessions. I wanted to hear about the war, not this run-of-the-mill love story: all widows were sad and all widowers wanted to remarry.

I said: "You survived the hell of Auschwitz."

"Yes," she said. Her voice was low, and her grimace betrayed that her hip was hurting. My experience of Marjane had taught me that physical pain manifests itself in recognizable ways, while mental suffering can take every conceivable form.

Resuming her thread, she told me how she missed the sound of his singing, as he led prayers at dinner. How he sang out of tune, but that now she longed to hear that tone-deaf voice.

How she missed the guests that he brought home from *shul* on Friday evenings. Missed the silence she'd shared with her husband, a silence that—so unlike the soundlessness of the last few years—had been brimming with mutual understanding and shared thoughts; nothing could surpass such wordless communication. She sometimes still talked to him, she said. She knew he could hear her, and that he was silently responding.

She told me how their three children resembled him, and how even Aaron and his sisters, who weren't her late husband's biological children, had acquired Pappenheim traits. "Like their love of telling jokes, they can't get enough of it."

Every now and again she would start to cry. She dabbed her tears with the tissues on her lap, the same brand as the box that my mother always kept on the dashboard in the car—you never knew when you might need them. She wadded the tear-soaked hankies into little balls which she hid between her thigh and the wheelchair, like a little girl. Sometimes she rocked back and forth silently, her eyes cast down, or gazing at her teacup.

"Shall we visit his grave together? Would you like that?" I asked. I knew that my own grandmother was comforted by her visits to the cemetery. She cleaned her husband's grave every week as if it were their house, scrubbing every inch of the headstone.

"My dear husband was buried in the Netherlands."

"We could go to the Netherlands."

"Can you drive?"

"Not yet."

"The trains don't stop in Putte."

"Where's Putte?"

"On the Belgian border. If the traffic isn't too bad, you can be there in forty minutes."

"So your husband came from Putte."

"No."

"But he's buried there."

"Many Belgian Jews are buried in Putte. Others buy their last one-way ticket to Israel with the assistance of a *chevra kadisha*, a voluntary association that helps repatriate Jews after their death. Antwerp doesn't have a Jewish cemetery."

I was baffled. She explained, but I still didn't get it. How could it be that members of Antwerp's Orthodox Jewish community, probably the largest in Europe, were welcome in Belgium while alive and prosperous, but that once they had the temerity to die, they were deported?

"Only a few liberal Jews, like the Tolkowskys, are buried in the Jewish section of Hoboken cemetery. What's it called again? Schoonhof."

I nodded. It was called Schoonselhof, but what did it matter? Famous writers lay there: Elsschot, Conscience, Van Ostaijen, many others.

"Do you know who the Tolkowskys were?"

I shook my head.

"They came from Poland, originally. Generations ago they made Antwerp the diamond capital it is today. Aaron owes his livelihood to them."

I wasn't listening. "Can't you, the Jewish community, buy some land in Antwerp and make it into a Jewish cemetery? What makes a cemetery Jewish? Does it have to be blessed by a rabbi?"

"You ask far too many questions. I don't know all the answers. But Belgium and the Netherlands have different laws about concession rights. We, the Jews, never want to be dug up. Our remains must lie undisturbed until the coming of the Messiah."

I only knew one Jewish cemetery: the old one in Prague where, in my youthful ignorance, I believed Kafka to be buried.

"So the people who died in the camps…" I said, a little nervously.

"That must make it even worse for their surviving relatives. They weren't buried, they were incin—" I was silent.

She pinched the bridge of her nose between her liver-spotted thumb and index finger. Only then did I realize that she didn't wear spectacles, that I'd never seen her with glasses on.

"After our first anniversary, my husband and I resolved never again to speak of the war and the camps," she said. "Only if the children asked us about it. Then we would answer their questions. But they rarely if ever did."

"Perhaps you'd like to talk to me about it?"

"*Like* to talk about it?" Her indignation almost propelled her out of her wheelchair. "You won't find anybody who *likes* to talk about the war! And if you did, you should immediately be suspicious of them! Silence is the best medicine. So I, too, am silent." From under her dress she pulled out a medallion on a chain. She carried her Orthodox husbands in duplicate on her chest: one photo in black and white and one in colour, which, given the nature of their clothing, amounted to the same thing. She caressed their faces with her wrinkled fingers.

I could have sunk through the floor.

Forty-Three

E lzira passed her final exams with flying colours. The end of her secondary school also meant the end of our partnership. And because Sara continued to manage perfectly well by herself, Elzira's school-leaving diploma put an end to six years of almost daily visits to the Schneiders'.

Elzira insisted I attend the diploma award ceremony.

I'd never been to the Yavne school before, at least not inside; I'd waited for Elzira a few times at the gate, along with Monsieur, who would jump up on her excitedly as soon as he spotted her and, folding himself round her neck like a fur stole as she bent to greet him, would give a fond squeak, a display of love exclusive to his little mistress, I knew, because I never heard him utter it for anyone else.

Elzira had told me that the school would probably soon have to move to smaller premises. Mr Schneider had also mentioned this concern a few times: the number of modern Orthodox Jews in Antwerp was declining, while more and more ultra-Orthodox Hasidic Jews were settling in the city. "It would be sad if we, modern Orthodox Jews, were eventually to become a minority in Antwerp's Jewish community," Mr Schneider said. "But I fear the worst. Our children won't want to stay here, you will already have some idea why. But we're also losing our position in the city's economy. In the last five or six years the cards of the diamond sector have been thoroughly shuffled. Indians, Lebanese and people from the former Soviet Union are now our competitors. They're very good at their profession, *n'est-ce pas*, but they practise it without respect for the craft's tradition or for the history of Antwerp. I don't blame them. But it's a regrettable development. You know what the worst thing is? The beginning of the end? That the expertise of our Antwerp cutting specialists, the best in the world, is being lost. No new cutters or polishers are being trained. Within a few generations, there will no longer be a Jewish middle class. Which means that the good schools and the modern Orthodox Jews will also disappear."

The diploma award ceremony was like diploma award ceremonies all over the world: pretty dull. The playground was decorated with streamers and balloons. A big Israeli flag hung on the far wall of the stage and when the Israeli national anthem was sung, everyone looked very serious. Mr and Mrs Schneider were sitting in the front row, along with the members of the parents' committee and the school board. They gave me a quick wave, signalling that they'd meet me after the official ceremony.

A couple of the mothers had a non-standard hairdo: not quite short, not quite shoulder-length. Some of the men were talking on their mobile phones: huge, clunky devices with protruding antennas. People constantly took photos: say "cheese".

To divert myself during the speechmaking, I tried to spot the little ways in which one child distinguished itself from another, just as pupils in Catholic schools manage to do, despite all wearing the same uniform. Though their clothing choice was very limited, my schoolmates had found ways of expressing themselves individually; you could tell just from the brand of socks they wore what class and clan they belonged to. I didn't know the codes of Jewish dress. Though I had grasped from Jakov that *yarmulkes* and hats had their own fashions and codes: Jews could tell from the make of a *shtreimel* where its wearer came from, and to what branch and community he belonged. One Hasidic Jew would let his sidelocks dangle in front of his ears, another would tuck them behind. Each detail had meaning. Black or white socks under the breeches of ultra-Orthodox men: the choice spoke volumes about their lifestyles and beliefs. The size of the *yarmulke* told you what political party the wearer identified with. Recently, someone had even invented a *yarmulke* made of synthetic hair. Resembling a toupee, it allows religious Jews to cover their heads in a way that doesn't advertise their faith to the outside world—a world where anti-Semitism is an ever-present threat. "A mini wig like that could only have been invented by a Jew," Elzira giggled, when she told me about this latest thing.

"*Shalom*," said the woman who sat down next to me. "*Shalom*," I answered.

She asked me something in Hebrew. It sounded like *ata bishvil shelcha*.

"I'm sorry. I don't speak Ivrit," I said.

At that the woman turned to look at me. "Oh, of course, I can see that now," she said. At which I laughed—I just couldn't help it—and she laughed too, somewhat apologetically.

"My daughter just finished school," she said a little later, in Dutch. Unusually, she didn't speak it with a French accent. "In a week's time she's going to Israel for a working holiday at a kibbutz. Then she's going to study in England." She mentioned an institute in Newcastle, and said something about *frum* girls.

I nodded. *Frum* meant pious in Yiddish; a *frum* girl would observe the religious laws much more strictly than Elzira. There were no Hasidic girls at this school.

Sara came up to me and handed me a bottle of mineral water: "*Shalom, erev tov*, you must be thirsty, I always have *soif... à tantôt*, my friends are waiting for me."

"Do you know the Schneiders?" the woman next to me asked, after greeting Sara.

I nodded. "They're friends."

"Elzira is going to England with my daughter." I looked at her. "On holiday?"

"No, to study at the institute I mentioned. A two-year course." She craned to get a better view of the rabbi on the platform. It must have been funny, whatever he was saying in Hebrew, because the audience occasionally burst out laughing. He'd come over from Israel for a temporary placement at the school. Religious leaders were replaced every two years so they wouldn't get too used to the liberal ways of Antwerp. Just as the mullahs in Meulenberg were, when I went to school there. I'd gathered from Elzira that some rabbis were stricter than others. A particularly stern one had taken offence at the clothing worn by a few mothers at the school gates. There were some mothers, even in the modern Orthodox community, who felt it was okay to wear long, loose-fitting trousers. When the rabbi took them to task about these garments they protested, but they did listen to him. The next day they'd appeared at the school gates in skirts that revealed their bare knees.

"Elzira Schneider is going to an institute for girls?" I asked. I couldn't believe my ears.

The woman nodded.

"She wants to train as a teacher," I said, telling her what Elzira had told me. "She's going to study biology. In Antwerp."

The woman was no longer looking at me. She was clapping. Everyone was clapping. The girls were called up on stage one by one and given their diplomas. When it was Elzira's turn I clapped too, filled with proprietorial pride. Her hands did not shake at all as she clasped her diploma. The little girl had disappeared, replaced by a confident young woman.

I urgently needed to speak to Mr and Mrs Schneider.

Forty-Four

The woman at the award ceremony had got it wrong: Elzira went, not to Newcastle or London, but to Israel to study, though the Schneiders had nearly registered her at an exclusive college for Jewish girls in Stamford Hill. But: "Too religious and too Yiddish for us."

Elzira left for a women's seminary in Israel, an institute where Orthodox girls could not only receive a general education but also be instructed on their role in Jewish life. "It's a lot cheaper than the one in the UK, too," said a relieved-sounding Mr Schneider, segueing into the joke about the hotel porter holding the door open for a guest with wet hair who's just leaving. "You took a bath?" asks the chatty porter. "No, why?" the Jew answers. "Are you missing one?"

A few weeks before Elzira left, I went to say goodbye to her.

"Monsieur is at Opris's house," said Elzira. We were sitting in her room, which looked even more immaculate than usual. "Monsieur is going to live with Opris and her daughter." In one hand she held a handkerchief, in the other a little dark-blue ball that squeaked when you squeezed it: the dog's favourite toy. Her father had had it made into a key ring.

"Daddy and Mummy can't keep Monsieur. I'll be away for at least two years. And Sara doesn't have time to look after him. Monsieur will be happy with Opris and *sa fille* Leila, *n'est-ce pas?*"

"Of course he will, Elzira," I said, "Opris and Leila are very kind to Monsieur. They know his little ways, they know what he likes to eat, where he likes to walk, what other dogs he likes to play with. He'll soon feel at home with them, though he'll miss you very much, I'm sure!"

As I comforted her, though, I felt a few stabs of pain. It was a shame that Monsieur and his little mistress were being separated. Apparently Mr and Mrs Schneider weren't attached enough to the creature to provide it with a loving home until Elzira's return. What was the Hebrew word for "dog" again? Okay, I realized the Schneiders weren't the kind of people who'd walk the dog several times a day. But given its importance to their daughter, I couldn't understand that they didn't feel obliged to care for it. With the help of Opris and her daughter that would have been feasible, surely? They had a garden, too. And there was Sara.

The sharpest stab, however, was this: no one in the family, not even Elzira, had thought of me when they were looking for a new home for the dachshund. After all, I'd known him since he was a puppy, and he me. How many hours had we spent together on our walks? Three a week? Five solid years? A hundred and fifty times five?

I'd fantasized about a sort of shared custody. Monsieur would remain the Schneiders' dog, but would spend half the week at our place, until Elzira came back to Antwerp after her stint in Israel. "Supposing…" I'd suggested to Nima. "Monsieur can stay with us," he'd answered resolutely. So we were already somewhat prepared for a four-legged house guest.

I gave Elzira a cookbook: *La cuisine juive à travers le monde* (The Jewish Cookbook: Recipes from Around the World) by somebody called Sylvie Jouffa. I'd snapped it up at De Slegte, a shop that sold remaindered books, and wrapped it in a black apron that said "I love Antwerp". But not before I'd copied a few recipes out of it. Latkes. Levivot. Pancakes with almonds. Carp stuffed with couscous. Shakshuka. Chicken sofrito.

Living with Nima had brought home to me how important a mother's cooking can be for someone who—whether or not by choice—is separated from home and family. It works like a poultice on homesickness. Sitting at a table full of the smells and tastes of your past, your present becomes tinged with warmth.

"You'll visit me, won't you?" Elzira asked hopefully. "We will see us there, surely?"

"We will see 'each other' there, Elzira, not see 'us'."

"Will you come to Jerusalem?"

"Perhaps," I answered. "But in the meantime you'll often come back to Belgium, right? For festivals and that kind of thing? Let me know, and we can meet up."

She knitted her brows; her hair was combed back off her forehead and tied in a ponytail with a clip in the shape of a blue-velvet bow.

"Do you think I'll be all right?" she asked. "Do you think I can do it? I mean: live with other girls? Cook with them? Study in Israel? Be away from my family?" It was only then that I realized how nervous and unsure she was. I'd been too focused on her growing self-confidence, and the slight self-pity at Monsieur's fate being placed in Opris's hands. "Shall we write to each other?" I suggested.

She reached under her pillow and, with that gentle smile of hers I'd miss so much, pulled out a gift: a set of wafer-thin sheets of writing paper and envelopes. For airmail.

PART II

1994–2000

One

After a long holiday travelling around Cuba, Nima and I decided to go our separate ways.

Neither Cuba nor Castro—both disappointing—were to blame for this decision. Nor did our break-up have anything to do with the fact that when we landed back at Zaventem airport, Nima was marched off by Belgian border officials and questioned for hours (while no one would explain to me what was going on). An Iranian political refugee who'd made a laughing stock of the Belgian national security services by refusing to work with them, and who then rubbed salt in the wound by travelling to the only Communist-run island in the world could hardly expect any other kind of treatment.

We made a few desperate attempts to save the relationship, but the spark had simply gone: the seven-year itch proved too powerful. Nima, who was leaving Antwerp for Brussels, suggested that I stay on in our flat. I thought it would be better to leave a building where the memories creaked as loudly as the wooden floor.

Not far from our old place I came across a nice-looking little apartment, light and airy, with high ceilings. And from the roof— which the landlord had declared forbidden territory—you could even see a sliver of the Scheldt. If a big container ship sailed past, you might just catch sight of the top of its bridge. The long and short blasts on the ship's horns sounded like melodies.

I signed the rental contract, knowing full well I didn't have the money for the deposit. Every cent of my and Nima's savings had been blown on the Cuba trip. Though we did manage to recoup some of the outgoings: we sold our haul of thirty Cohiba cigars, straight from the factory, to a well-known restaurant for a sum that lifted our spirits sky high. I wasn't worried about my precarious financial situation. My friends and family had always been better off than me; it shouldn't be hard to get a loan from someone. When push came to shove, though, I couldn't face the well-meant but tiresome opinions they'd surely trot out, ranging from "but you were such a lovely couple" to "well, you should have known, mixed marriages never work". Someone was bound to quote that old Dutch proverb *"twee geloven op een kussen, daar slaapt de duivel tussen"*: where two religions share a bed, the devil sleeps in the middle. In fact a third religion entered the fray in this sea of opinions: Hollywood.

The movie *Not Without My Daughter* had just been a box office hit. A cliché-ridden film about an American woman trapped in Iran by her brutish Iranian husband, trying to flee the country with her child. A romantic dream that turns into an ayatollah-filled nightmare. Everyone had seen it. Very few questioned the way it caricatured Iranian culture, peddled prejudice and stereotypes. A few people in my circle expressed relief that we'd split up. I could see them thinking: Nima might seem open and friendly, but I bet that's just a pose. And someone said to me: "So that goes to show: you just never know with Iranians."

Two years after I'd said goodbye to the Schneiders, I rang them up. They were far enough away from me, I thought, to be able to judge matters from a distance. But close enough to do so all the better. And: "If we can ever be of any assistance to you, you only need ask. Don't ever forget that." That was what Mr Schneider had said when he bid me farewell the evening Elzira got her diploma. I was touched by his words, but also struck by his ironic tone. I knew of course, just as he did, that I would never appeal to them for help. How could they, in their world, ever help me, in mine?

"How much do you need?" Mr Schneider asked when, seated at their round kitchen table a few days after our phone conversation, I outlined my situation. His hair had gone greyer. Six prints hung on the wall: colourful works by Chagall and Modigliani. They were new, and I thought: these paintings do what the children used to do, they fill the white room, cheer the place up.

"Fifteen thousand."*

"When do you need it?"

"Right now, preferably," I answered frankly.

"When do you think you can pay it back?"

I thought for a moment. "How about I pay you fifteen hundred on the first of the month, for ten months in a row?"

"Oh." He banged his fist on the table. "So you think you can borrow from us interest free! I see that after all these years, you really don't know us!" The loud guffaw that followed made me feel uncomfortable.

A little while later he slipped me an envelope. The kind of envelope I'd seen around their house before. The first time I'd noticed one was after Jakov crashed the car. Opris got given them. I'd received a few myself in my six years at the Schneiders': at the end of every school year; after Elzira had cycled to school effortlessly for the first time; after I'd helped her through a few difficult days, and on at least fifteen other occasions.

"Could you recommend my services to a family you're friendly with?" I asked Mr Schneider, finally, before leaving. "Now that I'm single again extra income is always welcome, and I'd like to do some more tutoring—after my time here I think I know how," I laughed. He nodded. The laugh was a poor attempt to disguise the longing behind my question. A longing that seemed to hang in the air. Did he sense it too? Whatever the case, I was embarrassed.

---

*   Around £250

Although I'd got my degree several years earlier, I still regularly went to the Institute of Interpreting and Translation Studies to look at the noticeboard advertising student jobs.

Once I saw that a Mr Schwarz was looking for a reliable, experienced female tutor for his son. I got in touch. He turned out to be a divorced Jewish man with one son, Benjamin. That was unusual: divorces were rare in the Orthodox community. Benjamin lived with his father. His mother had moved to Israel. Benjamin turned out to be a likeable, funny fifteen-year-old with light-brown curls and green eyes that didn't dare look at me directly, but peeked at me from under their lashes. He and his father were modern Orthodox, like the Schneiders, but at the more liberal end of the spectrum. They lived on the edge of the Jewish neighbourhood, more between non-Jews than Jews. Yet Benjamin went to a religious school.

We, Benjamin and I, did our best. But unfortunately we just couldn't click. I couldn't connect with him, nor he with me, and because his father was never home I, and even more so the boy, fell into a vacuum. After three weeks, not without a wrench, I gave up on the job.

I'd tried a similar job with children living in an Antwerp suburb. After a mere two visits I concluded they were even more annoying and time-consuming than the bus trip to get to them, so I soon gave up on this job too, without a wrench this time. Very briefly, I tutored a girl who lived near me. She was an only child and hideously spoilt. After only three sessions I'd grown to loathe her.

"I miss Jakov and Elzira," I admitted to Mr Schneider.

He nodded. "Of course you miss them," he said. "We miss them even more." He looked at me searchingly. I returned his gaze. The old familiar setting overwhelmed me. My place in it was different, all of a sudden. Sometimes you have to push something away to see it better. This house wasn't a place in which I'd been employed: it was where I'd spent time, shared life with a new family.

On a side note: the repayment of the loan went according to plan. Or rather, not entirely, because Mr Schneider let me off the interest. He drove to my apartment in his old Volvo, bringing me some bits of furniture he and his wife didn't need any more. "Now the children have left home, we're making a bit of space." My question about whether he could recommend me as a tutor to another family never got a response: children weren't passed around as easily as cash.

Two

S he wrote to me. Thin sheets of lined paper containing thirty or so sentences.

About the weather, her letters told me, about the dust in Jerusalem, the city sticky with sweat and tourists, how it could easily be thirty-five degrees in summer, and especially hot at the Wailing Wall, where the white stone remains of the temple blazed in the sun, hurting her eyes. She wrote how she'd discovered public transport and how, unlike in Belgium, she *did* feel safe; people sometimes lugged entire washing machines into the bus: *incroyable mais vrai*, I really must come and see Jerusalem one day, I wouldn't believe my eyes! She and some of her friends had tried a few of the recipes from the cookbook: *délicieux!* She hoped that one day, when she'd started a little family of her own, I'd come and eat at her house. She'd travelled to the north coast, Haifa, where she'd picked oranges from the trees and seen dates hanging from branches along the road.

About her new friends, she wrote: they came from all over the world, they understood one another despite their different backgrounds, and she loved it; that was new for her, to meet young people who knew nothing about her and Lady Dyspraxia.

About the school: that the lessons were mainly in modern Hebrew and English. About Israel, where she would live for ever, she'd never been so happy, didn't know you *could* be so happy, *everyone* was happy. Sure, the country had its drawbacks, the traffic for one thing, and the dust, but that was precisely what was so great, the fact that everyone was working hard to improve things. Never before had she let herself to be carried along by that kind of dynamism—that was the word she used. "And mazel tov to you, *j'espère que tu vas aussi bien que moi*, hope you're doing just as well as me!" She even wrote to me about a recurring ear infection, probably picked up from one of the other girls, she thought, because they were in such close contact, unlike what she was used to in Antwerp.

Now and then she scribbled a silly little made-up poem at the bottom of the letter. She'd discovered rhyme and gone into overdrive. PS: *Tu me manques, pétanque*, I miss you, a-tishoo. With the speed of a quick-change artist she veered from the formal to the informal, switching from *vous* to *tu*, from *u* to *jij*.

I wrote to her. Thin, crackling sheets of pale-blue airmail paper.

I updated her on Belgian politics. Told her about my work, the books I was reading and that I thought she should read too, though I suspected she never would.

We both knew that we were protecting our friendship by avoiding certain subjects. I don't know if that balance was as difficult for her as it was for me. Sometimes I struggled: how elastic was tact? Was it tactful or hypocritical not to point out to Elzira that in her ode to Israel she overlooked the Palestinian population entirely? She had found happiness in Jerusalem. Was that something she could share with a Palestinian girl of her age? Why didn't I tell her how cross it made me that, because of those dietary laws, I could never invite *her* over for a meal? She looked forward to cooking for me—why should I be deprived of the same enjoyment? Shouldn't hospitality be a two-way process? Or was that the whole point of *kashrut*: to strengthen one's own identity by excluding the other? Why didn't I ask her to have a good think about this issue?

I wrote to her about Nima's grandmother, who used to live next door to him in Tehran. When little Nima or his sister had an ear infection, she would light her opium pipe and blow the fumes into their ears. It made them better, and they loved it. Nima spoke nostalgically about his grandmother's home remedies. Mrs Pappenheim no doubt had some of her own. Come to think of it, why didn't Elzira consult her brother Simon about her earache? He was training as an ear, nose and throat specialist, after all.

I wrote about myself, about my doubts and ambitions, the struggle to turn dreams into reality. I even wrote about the lie that adulthood seemed to me to entail: from the outside you looked grown-up, but inside you didn't know whether you were tackling life the right way, hadn't even the faintest idea what the "right way" was—you saw so many different forms and possibilities around you, yet at the same time you were trapped in your own pre-programmed form.

On paper I was more open than in real life. Paper allowed more reflection—what you say is what you are, but what you write can be thrown in the wastepaper bin. Inadvertently, the correspondence with Elzira helped me to see more clearly the things I knew about myself, but had never considered properly. In one of my letters I sighed that above all I wanted to write: "Because when I'm constructing sentences, that's when I feel freest."

Her answer: "You always told me I should believe in myself. So why don't you believe in *yourself?*"

Three

Did you pack those bags yourself? Has anyone asked you to take anything onto the aircraft for them? What are you going to do in Israel? Who booked your trip? Where are you staying, for how long? What's in your hand luggage?

Standing at the El Al check-in desk at Zaventem airport I answered all the security questions. At the invitation of the Schneiders I was flying to see three of their four children who lived, worked and studied in Israel. Elzira had been the driving force behind the trip. I would also visit or meet Jakov. And Simon was having me to stay for a few days. He lived near Tel Aviv. According to Mr Schneider, Tel Aviv was a great place to be based for day trips to Jerusalem, where Elzira was studying. The bus journey to the Holy City only took an hour, he said, and there were more buses going there, round the clock, than there were stars in the sky, and only when I'd seen the stars above the Promised Land would I understand what he meant.

Elzira had extended her stay in Israel by a year. About three years had passed since I'd last been to the Schneider home. Since my request for a loan, I hadn't set foot in the Jewish neighbourhood. Not to visit friends. Not even to go to Kleinblatt's, the famous bakery, with its window full of sweet temptation—I just cycled straight past. And, now there was a flourishing falafel place in my own neighbourhood, I no longer had to go to Beni in Lange Leemstraat for my favourite fast food.

It seemed that a lot of Hasidic Jews were flying to Tel Aviv and, to judge by the awed respect of their hangers-on, they must have included *ravs* and *rebbetzins*: rabbis and their wives. Both at the check-in desk and at the gate I was swallowed up in a sea of black and white. Men with beards talked at one another, shouted into big telephones, swayed back and forth as they read their prayer books. Mothers, their hair swaddled in a kerchief, grouped their offspring and buggies around them and barred the way with their pregnant bellies, their gaggles of children and all their paraphernalia without the least consciousness of causing a problem. Whenever an agitated, non-Jewish traveller asked them to make way, they looked at him as if he, not they, was behaving antisocially. Which only made the other person more agitated. Boys shook their sidelocks; some of them looked cheeky. The floor was littered with plastic water bottles and biscuit wrappings.

My reaction was the same as when I started at the Schneiders': uneasiness at the surreal sight of this queue, a mix of mothers with their large broods and men in strict religious garb. Who on earth allowed their complex identity to be so publicly reduced to the level of hand luggage? Who was helping to foster this unflattering stereotype?

I was annoyed by their conspicuousness, by the way they drew attention to themselves. Did I harbour ill will towards these Jews? No. Did I, right now, harbour goodwill towards these Hasidim? No. I wished the world wouldn't make things so difficult for itself.

My thoughts drifted off to the two gay friends who'd brought me to the airport and would pick me up again in ten days' time. Since the day Thomas came out, his father had wanted nothing more to do with him. On the way to the airport Thomas told me that his parents had suddenly split up after thirty years of marriage. His mother had filed for divorce after finding out that, for decades, his father had been leading a double life. He was attracted to men. "Car park sex would be his speciality," Thomas had said sourly.

That was what I was thinking about, besieged by Hasidim, listening to an airport voice announcing that our flight would be delayed by at least two hours. Thomas's father had hated his son because he carried within him the same thing that he did, but whose existence he'd never openly acknowledged or wanted to admit. Perhaps he and I shared something. Who knows, perhaps I admired the courage of these Hasidim more than I wanted to admit. Who knows, maybe I was jealous that they had the guts to just do their own thing.

Inside the Boeing, the Hasidic hullabaloo that had raged at the gate continued unabated. People constantly swapped seats like a game of musical chairs. Men climbed over men, women joined other women. The Hasidim and the less religious Jews argued about the use of the cabin baggage space. Hasidim shoved their suitcases, bags and coats into every available space, grumblingly moved people's belongings to other lockers without asking permission, summoned stewardesses, pushed unwanted luggage into their hands "so we can put our hats here". They handled their hats as carefully as if they'd been cream cakes. Noisy children of all ages blocked the aisle. "They think this is Gaza," Nima would have said if he'd been there, but he wasn't. Even so, I couldn't help getting angry about the hoops we'd have had to jump through to get him a visa for Israel. Assuming he was actually granted one. Israel was Israel, just as Iran was Iran: Jewish Israelis could likewise forget about going *there*.

I sat by the window, next to a Hasidic woman with an attractive but suspicious face, and hands as pale as milk. I tried to start a conversation with her, but she didn't seem to want to talk, which was fine by me, as it meant I could concentrate on the travel books I'd borrowed from the city library. What a hope! The buttons to call cabin crew were in constant use. I couldn't read three sentences without one of the faithful summoning a steward or stewardess. They bloody well think they're God Almighty, shot through my head.

My neighbour did tell me, though, that El Al didn't just stand for Every Landing Always Late, but meant "skywards" in Hebrew. And that I must pay a visit to Eilat: "The best place in the world for diving."

Four

Mr Schneider had warned me: as soon as my feet touched Israeli soil at Ben Gurion airport, I'd never be the same again. Which was true, but not in the way he meant.

He was alluding to the intense joy and pride that fills every Jew when they set foot on the soil of the young Jewish state. To the deep-seated emotions that overwhelmed him and his fellow Jews when they "came home" again: really came home, to the roots of the tree of their history, to their origins. To the significance of the Holy Land, the country where Jews are allowed to be "just Jewish". Israel, that narrow, elongated plaster on the many wounds of his people; Israel, the decisive answer to a history of persecution and isolation; Israel, home base in a history without *Heimat*. To Mr Schneider, whose patriotic fervour for Belgium was such that he'd hung up official portraits of the Belgian King and Queen in his office, Israel was a home country of a completely different order. Israel was the father and mother country in one. It was a homecoming in the true sense of the word. *Medinat Yisrael*: the only country in the world where taxi drivers spoke Hebrew, he said: if that fact alone didn't make you feel right at home, well…!

I made the acquaintance of such a taxi driver. He came running up to me as I, bent double under the weight of my rucksack, scanned the terminal. I was to stay three of the nine nights at Simon's place. The rest of the time, including my first night in Tel Aviv, was my own to fill in.

I'd planned to go to the tourist office on arrival at Ben Gurion. But there was no one at the desk. It was already growing dark outside. I didn't know the city; I wouldn't be able to see where to get out or where I was. Though excited to have arrived, I also felt tired. And hungry: I longed for some tasty hummus. Counting the drive to Zaventem airport, I'd been travelling for ten hours.

So when the man called out "Taxi, taxi", I didn't wave him away. He, persistent but friendly, said something to me in Hebrew, but even before he'd decoded the message of my raised eyebrows he'd switched to English: where was I going, could he take me, did I know where I was staying the night? If not he could help me, he knew what young people like me wanted, he drove them to basic, clean hotels in the city every day of the week.

"Could you take me to a youth hostel?" I asked. By now I was pushing thirty, but since becoming single again I'd started acting younger out of sheer survival instinct.

"*Better* than a youth hostel," he said. I nodded cautiously in approval, by which time he'd already grabbed my rucksack.

"For the same price as a youth hostel?" I wanted to know.

"Of course! You have money on you?"

"Preferably a hotel by the sea," I instructed him. I felt in the front pocket of my bag for the envelope with shekels the Schneiders had given me.

"No problem. Welcome to Israel!"

I'd travelled enough to know that you always paid dearly for blind faith in a taxi driver. But I stifled that thought. Just go for it, I reasoned with myself: at worst you'll pay over the odds for the journey, if you don't like the hotel you can get him to take you to another, there'll be plenty around, it's late, you still need to eat, tomorrow is another day.

The blast of heat outside Ben Gurion's automatic doors was fiercer than I'd expected. "God is a woman and she's drying her long hair," Nima had said, as we entered the steamy hothouse that was Cuba.

The taxi driver was a tall man with a big nose and brilliantine in his hair, which grew abundantly, not just on his head. He didn't wear a *yarmulke*. The taxi was an official one—with air con—and he set the meter properly. That last fact, especially, reassured me. I couldn't say the same for his driving: he drove like a maniac, the violent jerks and screech of brakes bringing back long-forgotten childhood memories of bumper cars. Yet he seemed to know what he was doing.

From the signs and the increasingly crowded neon-lit streets and pavements it looked as if we were nearing the centre. I was struck by the near total absence of Jewish people like the ones in Antwerp. I couldn't spot a single man with a *yarmulke*; there were no hats, beards, or long coats to be seen. Instead, the men were mostly dressed in shorts or jeans. The women were like their counterparts in the West: they wore short skirts, little tops, looked fashionable and self-confident. Where had all the Hasidic Jews from the airport gone?

I was almost disappointed by this vision of modernity. But straight away my brain's autocorrect kicked in: if anything, I should be disappointed at seeing almost no *Muslim* men or women. Where were they? It was their country too, wasn't it? Why did I see almost no street signs in Arabic, while signs in Hebrew were everywhere? Had all the airport signs been bilingual? I couldn't remember, and that shocked me.

The sea was fringed with tall, ugly hotel blocks. There were a few classy buildings, but many had a dilapidated look: walls full of cracks; wires and cables dangling from the facades; whitewashed balconies streaked yellow and brown. The Malecón esplanade in Havana was a thousand times prettier. Was *this* what so charmed Elzira?

The shops were still open. The hubbub from packed pavement terraces wafted into the taxi. "This city never sleeps," the driver called over his shoulder. That's what every taxi driver says, in every metropolis, I thought, but I nodded and went on staring out of the window to signal that I didn't feel like talking, especially if it meant shouting to make ourselves heard; he'd switched from playing schmaltzy hits to some kind of klezmer music at ear-bleeding volume.

At bars and restaurants people queued, glass in hand, waiting for a table. I hadn't yet set foot in the centre, but I could already feel the city's positive, infectious vibe. The young soldiers—men and women with M16s—slightly dampened my excitement, but even they appeared good-humoured. Was Israel one gigantic *eruv*, I wondered. Was the whole country surrounded by this symbolic enclosure that made Shabbat more bearable? Were soldiers allowed to carry weapons on Shabbat? Allowed to use them?

The driver suddenly turned off down a side road, then another and another. The roads got narrower and narrower, though they were still quite busy. Just as I was about to tap the man on the shoulder to ask why we'd left the esplanade, he stopped unexpectedly in front of a terraced house, flanked left and right by a brightly lit, antiquated furniture store. Its window displays clearly hadn't changed in decades, its wares dated from a bygone age.

"One moment," he said. He leapt out of the car, opened the garage door of the house, switched on a light, retrieved my rucksack from the boot and opened the car door for me.

Bemused, my bag clenched under my arm, I got out.

"This is your hotel," he announced, pointing to the open garage. "You can spend the night here for 50 shekels."

Only now did I see it. On the concrete floor lay a neatly made mattress; in the corner there was a makeshift shower cabin.

"I live upstairs. You won't find anything cheaper and safer. A lot of backpackers sleep here. They sleep well here."

*

I didn't hesitate a second before ordering him to drive me back to the coast. On the way to this dingy neighbourhood we'd passed a Mercure hotel. For a while I'd worked as a translator for the Accor hotel group. Mercure was part of Accor, as were Ibis and Sofitel. After six months of employment, all permanent members of Accor staff were issued a card entitling them to a considerable discount on any of the group's hotels. I didn't have such a discount card as I'd only been a freelancer. But that wasn't how I approached the check-in desk. I told the receptionist that I headed the group's Brussels office but had unfortunately mislaid my card—"probably stolen on the way here, because when I left I still had it, I can't imagine how my pocket was picked, no idea where, hope I haven't lost anything else, I'll check that in a minute, just want to do this first."

I reeled off the names of all the big cheeses I could remember from my Accor days, and when I saw that the receptionist was impressed I laid it on even thicker: advised him to ring these ladies and gentlemen—mainly gentlemen—the very next day; they would certainly express their gratitude for the way he'd helped me. I said I'd ask my office to fax a copy of the discount card to him. I had the receptionist copy my passport and my identity card.

For a sum only slightly higher than the one charged by the taxi driver for his garage I was given a luxurious room, breakfast included.

So did I, from the moment that my feet touched Israeli soil, feel like a different person? Indeed I did: until that moment I'd never known I possessed such *chutzpah*.

Five

I took the bus to Bnei Brak, where Simon and his wife lived. Simon, the elder Schneider boy, was by now not only a doctor—an ear, nose and throat specialist, no less—but also the husband of Abigail, his brand-new wife. At the end of the year the young couple would move to the Netherlands, where Simon had got a job lined up in a hospital. At the moment he was still working in a clinic in Tel Aviv.

When I boarded the bus, I showed the driver the address Mrs Schneider had written down for me on a piece of paper: "Could you please tell me when to get out?"

The man, who was eating an orange, looked me over from head to foot and nodded. When I went to sit down across the aisle just behind him, so as to make communication easier, he shook his head and gestured that I should sit at the back of the bus.

Only from my seat on the back row—and it took a while before the reality dawned on me—did I see that all the men were sitting in the front half of the bus, and all the women in the back half. At the stops, the women got in and out of the rear door; the men used the door at the front.

As far as I could tell, the passengers covered the entire spectrum of Judaism, from secular to ultra-Orthodox. To judge by the sidelocks and *tzitzits*, the wigs and tights, the latter were in the majority.

Maybe my mood was distorting things, but throughout the

journey I felt I could sense the tension between these poles of Judaism, as if a nerve lay exposed.

It appalled me that this system of segregation was apparently openly applied on a regular bus. It was 1997; hadn't apartheid been abolished seven years earlier? How could the government of a country that called itself democratic not only tolerate a measure that discriminated on the basis of gender but officially introduce such a rule? Or was public transport in this country in the hands of a private company, and if so, weren't they obliged to comply with basic human rights?

My outrage about this state of affairs was the first thing that burst out when I greeted Simon at the door of his apartment. He was happy to see me, but taken aback by my tirade.

"Buses like these were introduced—after vocal protests from more modern Jews—at the request of the ultra-Orthodox community of Bnei Brak. A lot of Haredi Jews live here, a splinter group of Hasidic Judaism. Haredim are so strict that sitting under a tree without a religious book in your hand is regarded as disobedience to the Almighty. They have one single task on earth: to pray and study. Don't get so het up, there are very few such buses. You could have come in an ordinary bus, where you could have sat wherever you liked. You were just unlucky that you ended up in one of those apartheid affairs." He laughed. I couldn't quite gauge his laugh. I didn't know Simon like I knew Jakov.

"Did I understand that correctly? Do you live in an ultra-Orthodox neighbourhood?"

"City: Bnei Brak isn't a neighbourhood but a city. And you'll certainly see how Orthodox it is here tomorrow and the day after: Friday and Saturday. But let me show you our home and your room. And I'll introduce you to Abigail. At the moment she's at a heavily pregnant friend's place, helping her with the housework. She'll be back about nine. Have a shower. Freshen up. Relax."

It wasn't till then that my heart rate slowed down and I was able to study Simon properly. There were only a few years between us. The man standing before me was muscular, serious and self-assured. He looked more grown-up than me. He already knew what he wanted from life, it seemed, and usually I found that kind of self-confidence suspect, but in Simon's case there was something encouraging about it. There wasn't a hint of the macho posturing that Jakov sometimes went in for, or the evasive way he'd fob me off in our conversations. Simon, whose still waters ran deep, had served in the Israeli army. Jakov, the bigmouth, would probably never dare do anything that put his life at risk.

Outwardly, I now saw that Simon took more after his mother than his father. He possessed her refinement, her aristocratic way of moving and talking, her intriguing glance, which seemed to see everything and which I'd so often vainly tried to fathom. I thought: if he's not already about to become a father, it won't be long. Yet I couldn't imagine him as a soldier.

Their apartment was on the ground floor of a yellowish, four-storey building halfway up a sloping street. It was small, neat and comfortable, with low ceilings. The furniture looked both new and cheap, a random collection of items—no particular style.

"Don't you have IKEA here?" I couldn't help asking.

"No, not yet. But if there was, I wouldn't go there if I could help it. The founder of IKEA is an anti-Semite," Simon answered. "During the war he raised funds for the Swedish fascist movement. But nobody knows that. IKEA sells everything, except the truth about its founder."

I looked at him suspiciously.

"When the truth about his wartime past came to light, the Swede did apologize. He wrote a letter to every single Jewish member of staff, calling his involvement with fascism 'youthful stupidity'.

Could have happened to anyone." He grinned. "And before you ask: our things are in a container, waiting until we settle in Amsterdam. There wasn't any point in shipping all that nice stuff over here. It'd only get damaged."

The bathroom—with a shower, but no bath—looked immaculate. There was only one sink and one cooker in the kitchen. From the open bedroom door I could see that the couple slept in a double bed next to which, behind a screen, stood a made-up single bed: for the nights when Abigail had her period and, in that unclean capacity, wasn't allowed to sleep with her husband.

The guestroom contained two single beds, separated by a bedside table, as well as a clothes rack and a dresser that could serve as a table. Three light-blue towels lay folded in a neat pile on one of the beds. On a tray in the middle of the other bed there was a bottle of water, a glass and silver-coloured platter with pretzels. Next to a bowl filled with water I recognized the square shape of a bar of Sunlight soap.

Simon put my rucksack carefully in the corner of the guest room. He felt in his back pocket and proudly showed me a photo of "my dearest Abigail": an attractive, rather heavily made-up brunette with full lips and eyes like black olives. She looked modern and fashionable, even in her little hairnet and pretty, long-sleeved blouse, buttoned up to her slim neck. I poked him in the ribs: "Wow, you did well!" He grinned and took a step away from me.

"If you need anything from the kitchen, we'd rather you ask us," he said. "You can have anything you like. It's just that our kitchen is entirely kosher, and we'd like to keep it that way. We're happy to make breakfast for you, and other meals too. Abigail and I are usually around. Just in case, I've written the number of my office on a note stuck to the inside of your bedroom door. Don't hesitate to call me, any time, except on Shabbat. You are our guest, welcome!"

I thanked him for everything. "I think I'll take a shower."

He nodded. "Feel free. But please don't forget to lock the bathroom door behind you. I wouldn't want to walk in on you by accident."

Six

"You packed a long skirt and tights, I hope?"

Abigail and I were sitting at the breakfast table. She'd squeezed oranges for me and baked *poffertjes*—little pancakes. Abigail had a British father and a Dutch mother, which explained the *poffertjes*. She was even prettier than the photo that Simon carried with him.

We were alone in the house. Simon left home early every morning: a quarter to seven. He did his praying in the *shul* or with the requisite *minyan*—a quorum of at least ten adult Jewish men—in the clinic. Abigail only had one appointment that day. She worked as a lawyer in a big firm in Tel Aviv. Although she'd only recently got her degree, she already specialized in international trade law. In the bookcase in the living room, which also served as a study, law books stood next to leather-bound volumes of the Talmud, surrounded by textbooks that looked well thumbed. Loose pages headed "Gas contract between Israel and Qatar" lay on the dining table. On some of them, passages were marked in fluorescent pink and yellow.

"Yes," I answered. "I have got a long skirt, but not tights, they're much too hot in this weather, and I'm not Jewish, you know."

She chuckled. "I get that, gal. But I'm going to give you some of mine for the next few days. For Shabbat, especcially. How does my father-in-law put it again? *Wat niet kan, kan ook*. 'What can't be done can also be done.' So please put on a pair of tights. If not for

yourself, then for us. We don't want to offend or upset our neighbours. A long-sleeved blouse isn't a problem, I take it?"

I wanted to visit Bnei Brak, but hadn't intended to enter a synagogue or any other holy place. I just wanted to stroll round the
centre. See what there was to see. Sit on a cafe terrace with a glass
of something cool. "Do I really have to?"

"Yes," she said.

"Okay," I said. But not without wondering why I was deferring to
the dress code of the Hasidim in this country, while they continued
to wear their traditional garb in modern Antwerp.

When Abigail saw me coming out of their guestroom a little
later, she clapped a hand over her mouth in shock. "Good grief, you
can't go out like that! I can see your legs from top to bottom. Your
skirt's see-through. Not a problem in Antwerp, and in Amsterdam
you could jog through the Vondelpark nude if you felt like it. But
you're in Bnei Brak now, kiddo. Come on, let's go to the bathroom
and I'll show you how to dress up like an Orthodox Jewish woman."

The brisk friendliness with which she treated me after only a
day reminded me of the familiar directness of Dutch students and
colleagues. I liked their plain-spoken way of dealing with people,
leaving no room for subtexts.

"Here, put on this skirt of mine, and hurry up a bit. I've still
got to prepare some stuff for work. And it's going to be very busy.
All the mothers will be doing their shopping for Shabbat." She said
"all the mothers" and not "all the women". In Bnei Brak, which I'd
renamed BB, the two were synonymous.

Wearing her black skirt with matching long-sleeved top I felt
like a nun, and in my flat shoes and much-too-thick, warm tights I
looked like one too. The mirror in their hall was confrontational.
I never wore make-up, but if this was the natural look, it needed
banning pronto. In this moment it dawned on me that the more you
had to cover up your body with fabric the more important subtle

make-up, discreet jewellery and wigs became: otherwise how could Elzira and Abigail always look so pretty, dressed in the same garb?

After opening the front door for me, Abigail quickly shoved my hair into a grey, stretchy turban to give my outfit the finishing touch. "Have a nice day," she said, "and make sure you catch the bus back on time otherwise you won't get home—there's no way we can come and pick you up!"

I didn't have to wait long at the shared taxi stand before a *sherut*, a minibus taxi, arrived. I didn't mind where I ended up, as long as I could just look around.

I got in at the front and wanted to pay the driver, but when I held out a banknote he didn't take it. Instead, without looking at me, he held out a cap. Like a robot I placed the money in it. He threw the change into the same cap, which he pushed towards me across his folding table. I went and sat at the back. When drivers didn't want to take money from a woman in case they touched her hand, you could expect gender apartheid at all kinds of other levels. Not that my indifference meant I was resigned to reality. At most I was resigned to the impossibility of changing it there, by myself. And the muggy atmosphere was making me sluggish.

The separation of men and women in the minibus proved less strict than I'd anticipated. And Bnei Brak reminded me of the neighbourhood around Mercatorstraat and Simonsstraat. The houses, not as tall as the ones in Antwerp, were poky and basic-looking, the built-up streets monotonous in their lack of display. I couldn't even spot a nice garden, or a car bought for any other reason than functionality. Among the buildings were the odd *yeshiva* and *kollel*—institutes where unmarried and married men respectively studied the Torah and Talmud—which surely explained something about the landscape going past the window: those who study don't earn money. Simon and Jakov had spent one or two years here at a renowned institute where the language of instruction was English and the ethos strict.

Along the route, I saw a group of men *davening*. The way their upper bodies rocked back and forth and their almost ecstatic concentration made me think of dervishes; Nima had taken me to several dance performances. I was beginning to understand why the Jewish Israelis I'd spoken with in Tel Aviv—the receptionist at the Mercure, the flower seller who'd put together a bouquet of flowers for Simon and Abigail, the woman in the hummus bar, the young man who'd tried to sell me Ecstasy on the beach—had goggled at me when I told them I was going to Bnei Brak. The minivan had taken me, not to another neighbourhood or city, but to another planet: Ultra-Orthodoxia.

Wherever we went, ultra-Orthodox Jews set the tone. I could only see Haredim, with whom the Schneiders, if I'd understood correctly, felt no religious and cultural bond, but in whose midst they were nevertheless nestling. Haredi boys devote around forty hours a week to Bible study throughout their entire school careers. After finishing school they continue to read, interpret and study. They couldn't give a fig for subjects like maths, sociology or chemistry, and they never play football or tennis or any other form of sport. "Everything a person needs to know is in the Talmud and the Torah." Haredi women don't drive. They don't even ascend stairs in public if they can help it, I'd been told—someone might see under their skirts. They cross the street to avoid encountering a man other than their husband coming around the corner. They interpret the command to multiply very strictly.

"Why are those real Jewesses always so ugly?" Milena, my friend from the clothes shop, had once remarked, and several people around us had nodded in agreement.

"They're not!" I'd answered, stung. Later, I'd asked Elzira for her take on this comment.

"Beauty is relative," had been her answer, or something to that effect. She'd also said that Judaism gave clear guidelines to women on how they could remain attractive to their husbands. *Should* remain attractive. Did I know that, according to the Talmud, a devout Jewish woman could even forbid her spouse to go on a business trip if she felt a need for "intimacy in bed"?

I remember gazing at her in disbelief, tempted to laugh.

The same feelings overwhelmed me here; I couldn't say that most of the women I was seeing numbered personal attractiveness amongst their accomplishments. I wondered what the Talmud guidelines actually dictated.

"You're not an Orthodox Jew." The woman next to me addressed me in English.

Like everyone else, she was wearing the same clothes as me, though instead of a turban she sported a nightcap. "What brings you to Bnei Brak, if I may ask?" she went on.

"I'm visiting friends."

"Haredim?"

"Modern Orthodox."

"Oh Zionists. Yes, they live here too. Though far fewer than a few years ago. More and more Haredim are settling here in Bnei Brak. What do you think of them?"

"Of Haredi Jews?... Interesting."

"Interesting? That's a politically correct way of saying 'weird', 'incomprehensible', 'outlandish' or 'dangerous'."

"Aren't these Haredim Zionists, then?" I asked. I couldn't imagine this sect not being attached to the state of Israel.

"You're clearly not from around here," she answered.

"I'm from Belgium. Antwerp."

"Antwerp? The city of fashion? I've heard a lot about it." She stared at me in amazement, as if she couldn't believe her eyes. I became yet more conscious of my nun's uniform and that hot thing on my head. Even in Tel Aviv, people would look at me weirdly. "Three-quarters of the Jewish population of Israel aren't Orthodox or ultra-Orthodox," she said, "so you can imagine that Haredim are super critical of the state of Israel as it is now. They don't want a secular nation. Better not to have a nation at all than a heathen one. No, they're not Zionists. In fact, they're anti-Zionists."

"And yet they live here?"

"It's the best alternative. An enclave in an enclave."

I didn't want Jakov, Elzira and Simon to have their young adulthood formed in this suffocating environment. In the hustle and bustle of Tel Aviv, I hadn't seen a single *yarmulke*, beard, hat or *kaftan*. Here, I didn't see a single man without. Why didn't Bnei Brak have a beach? A beach—sand, sea, sun and bikinis—would do the people here good.

"They wouldn't hurt a fly," the woman said, "and they're very, very friendly. Talk to one of the women, you'll see. They're okay with how you are. They won't impose anything on you. They let you do what you want."

"They won't impose anything on me? But I'm not allowed to talk to men. And I'm dressed like a frump."

"That's your own choice. And who's stopping you talking to men? One will answer you politely. The other will turn his head away. No religion without rules."

"Have you ever eaten goose liver?" The question spurted out, to my own surprise, like venom.

"I beg your pardon?"

"Foie gras. Jews like to eat liver. Do they also eat goose liver?"

"Yes of course. We *invented* foie gras!" She rolled the French name around her tongue as if savouring it. "Religious Jews aren't allowed to eat lard. But they eat every part of the goose. Ever heard of tournedos Rossini? Steak with goose liver, a dish that must have been devised by Jews. It's my father's favourite. You don't need real butter for it!"

"To get foie gras, geese are force-fed!" I exclaimed. "The grain's rammed down their gullets. The birds can't stop eating, even when they're full. They lack a natural inhibitory system, a valve that says: 'Enough'. It seems to me that Haredim are like these geese. The Torah and the Talmud are rammed down their throats. They can't escape it. It's unethical and criminal!"

I was shocked by my pent-up anger: why didn't Simon live in Tel Aviv, that lively city I couldn't wait to get back to? Why had he and his wife come to this *shtetl*, this open-air museum for Jews? Why had the Schneider sons studied here?

The woman next to me ignored my outburst. She didn't even ask about my friends, or about my reason for visiting this place. "I'm a Jew who lives in Washington DC and doesn't give a hoot about Shabbat," she said with a twinkle, "and I'm here for work."

"Do you understand what I meant by this comparison?" I insisted.

"Western men and women are just as oppressed," she said. "The men have to work. Earn a living. And the women have to be thin, young and pretty. Spirituality and a quest for meaning are confined to an hour of yoga a week. So who's oppressing whom? And who's better than whom?"

Her sermon reminded me of Jehovah's Witnesses. They rambled on in the same way. The main difference between them and ultra-Orthodox Jews seemed to be an urge to proselytize. Jews didn't feel the need to convert others, whereas Jehovah's Witnesses wanted to convert as many as possible.

"We have choices. You can't say that about these men and women," I tried.

"Says who?"

"What kind of work do you do?" It was pointless trying to discuss this.

"Consultancy."

"What kind? Who do you work for?"

"A consortium focusing on projects for Haredim. They hired me because I'm an outsider. The fact that I'm Jewish but have a very different frame of reference gives me a good take on their traditions, customs and needs. I'm more or less familiar with Haredi rules. And because I'm American, they cut me a lot of slack, see? I'm allowed to makes mistakes, ask stupid questions. 'They' let me."

"So tell me about one of these projects that are specifically targeting Haredim."

"At the moment we're looking into building a new shopping centre in the centre of Bnei Brak."

Her use of the word "we" when talking about a corporation was alienating. I'd never felt a "we" when it came to any employer I'd ever had. And words like "project" made me feel itchy all over.

"A shopping centre?" I was keeping the conversation going.

"Rechov Rabbi Akiva is the cheapest shopping street in Israel. Haredim don't shop like we do. Everything that's sold here has to do with children, the household and religion. Nowhere in the world are so many food containers sold as in Bnei Brak. If you want sensible underwear or sheets, you won't find them cheaper anywhere else. You'll pay a lot more for exactly the same product in Tel Aviv or Haifa. But you won't find fashion items here."

"And the firm that's hiring you wants to build a shopping mall *here*?"

"They want to build a women-only shopping centre. No men will be allowed in it, whether as customers, staff or security guards..."

I told her about the apartheid bus I'd stumbled into the previous day. How shocked I'd been by the segregation. Once again she didn't react. Didn't even shrug.

"Where can I buy a Yiddish newspaper?" I asked. I wanted to take one home as a souvenir.

"You won't find one," she assured me. "No one reads newspapers here. Only holy books. By the way, I'm Hannah, nice to meet you."

We drove past a Coca-Cola factory. The name of the drink appeared in Hebrew letters in the famous logo, but it took me a while to realize that; the familiar image was so anchored in my mind that I believed I could read "Coca-Cola".

"If you had to rank brands symbolizing modern, decadent Western life, Coca-Cola would be top of the list. I'm amazed to find this factory of all factories in the midst of the Haredim," I said.

"Everyone drinks Coke," she said.

"Haredim too?" I asked.

"Of course. And they only drink Coke from this factory. You'll almost never see them drinking imported coke. Not even at an airport."

"Why?"

"Only in Israel can you be a hundred per cent sure that the drink is kosher. You don't know that about any other Coke producers in the world."

"You're joking, right?"

"No. At Pesach, the least little trace of yeast must have been removed from your home. Even in the homes of your modern Orthodox friends. Not a single crumb of bread must remain. But how can a religious Jew be sure that one of the Coca-Cola workers wasn't eating a sandwich just as he was cleaning the bottling machine? They can never know that for certain. Unless the drink was imported from Bnei Brak. Around Passover, export here peaks."

"That's too crazy to be true."

"Ask the manager of the Coca-Cola factory."

"It's a good job the drink's black—it'll always match their clothes," I mumbled, and laid my cheek against the cool window of the bus.

Hannah looked at me in amazement. "Wow, how observant of you," she said, "I'd never thought of that. I must tell my bosses. Maybe there's a new project in it for us. Because perhaps you're right. Maybe it's not just the taste of Coke that makes it popular here. Who knows, perhaps the colour plays a role too."

I decided to get out. To visit the factory.

"Where can I find somewhere to sit outside and have a drink?" I asked Hannah.

"In Bnei Brak? There won't even be a coffee bar," she answered.

"A restaurant?"

"Here you don't eat in the same room as people you don't know. Nowhere."

"What do you advise me to do?"

"Take another *sherut* to Rechov Rabbi Akiva. Go to Konditorei Katz, one of the best bakers in the city. There are two little tables there. You can order coffee with your cheesecake or *challah*. And maybe the old lady even serves Coca-Cola."

"How could you spot so quickly that I'm not Orthodox?" I asked, just before getting out.

"You've rolled the sleeves of your blouse up above your elbows and you look at men."

Seven

What a nice evening! What a lovely Shabbat!

We were eating in the garden of Simon's and Abigail's apartment, not much bigger than the canopy of the tree under which we were dining, from which two bright light bulbs hung that attracted mosquitoes and would burn until the next evening. The candle flames of the *menorah* flickered under the awning between kitchen and garden, we clinked glasses of water and white wine—*l'chaim*—toasting the good life, and I felt great and thought: look at us sitting here now, we're all in our twenties, time has already caught up with us, we're getting closer and closer together, my grandmother was right.

Yet initially the reunion had been a little awkward.

Elzira had been the first to arrive that afternoon. She was happy, in her quiet way, to see me, and the happiness was entirely mutual. As was the feeling of strangeness: it was odd to be seeing each other again after so many years. And in this environment, too. In Israel. In Bnei Brak. In the house of her brother and his wife.

Our letters had brought us closer together, but at the same time they'd created a distance. Now we were face to face, the intimacy with which we'd written to each other made way for awkwardness, perhaps even a little embarrassment and guilt. In our conversations we circled around our paper confessions.

But didn't she look terrific! Her face. Her aura. Her whole being. Before I'd thought her naturally melancholic: a trait she'd been born with, along with her dark eyes. Now I saw I'd been wrong. She'd shaken off her seriousness; now she radiated energy and charm. She had an air of emancipation about her, of autonomy. At the age of twenty-one, she'd transcended her life in Antwerp. I was touched by her.

Jakov didn't show up till a good three hours later. He nearly didn't make it at all. A friend had given him a lift and the two had got stuck in a traffic jam on the motorway. On a Friday afternoon, an overturned truck can have serious consequences for observant Jews, given that they can't travel after sunset, even by bus. I'd heard incredible tales about this religious law. About people who stopped their journey halfway, parked by the side of the road and continued on foot, in search of a hotel or some other place to sleep, because even on foot there were limits as to how far they were allowed to go. Some slept in their cars, only resuming their journey after Shabbat. Even if it was only a ten-kilometre trip. Even if they were in a city like New York, London or Paris. Telephones were left untouched: ringing to tell someone you were delayed was also prohibited on Shabbat. Though many could think of ways to get round this rule.

It was long past seven when Jakov and his friend reached Bnei Brak. They could no longer drive into the city: during Shabbat, devout Jews blocked the access roads with crash barriers. Jakov had completed the last stage of the journey on foot.

He stormed in, hurled his Kipling rucksack into a corner of the hall, strode to the kitchen and downed a glass of water in a single gulp, acting as if he visited his brother and sister-in-law every week. First he greeted his family, then me. He kissed me on the cheeks. "That's allowed after so many years," he laughed, without blushing. Elzira laughed too. Simon looked away. Abigail appeared amused and troubled at the same time. I felt like the odd man out.

"How's Nima?" Jakov asked before we'd even sat down to dinner in the garden. He was tanned; you could see a pale band of skin as he fiddled with his watch strap. His red Swatch wasn't the only thing about him that had remained unchanged.

"He's fine. But we're no longer together," I answered. He looked startled and sad. I gave Elzira a grateful nod; so she didn't talk to Jakov about me, which I was glad of—I'd written to tell her about our break-up in one of my letters, and she'd touched on it in her reply.

"A shame that you split up, *ou non*?" Jakov ventured.

"Yes, a shame, very much so."

"Why didn't you try?"

"We did try."

"You didn't try hard enough."

He ran up to the next storey, which turned out to belong to the flat. He and Elzira were sleeping there. During the week it was home to two students from the *yeshiva*. They would take up residence again on Sunday, the first day of the Jewish week.

Jakov was the ingredient that made us all relax. From the moment he arrived, one word started to pry another loose, and gradually sentences wove themselves together, stories bubbled up. Jokes. Memories. Dreams of the future. We talked and feasted, let down certain, but not all, barriers. I was the only one who, after the aperitif, drank wine: kosher wine from the Carmel Winery, founded by the Rothschilds and certified by the rabbinate.

I lingered longest in the garden, with Elzira, until after two in the morning.

When I paid a quick visit to the bathroom before going to bed, I found a pile of toilet paper sheets, pre-emptively torn from the roll, in a little willow basket. Amused, I wondered whether Orthodox Jews were allowed to flush the toilet on Shabbat.

Eight

That night I lay awake. The whole evening passed before my eyes. Every single thing.

The photos of Monsieur. Elzira had shown three: one of just him, one of him and her, and one of the dachshund and its new mistresses. Their grandmother: she was still alive, her hip and her zest for life were whole again. Sara: enjoying life on her own in Antwerp, apparently. The wedding of Abigail and Simon, the photos and all the explanations that went with them. Simon had met Abigail in Amsterdam at a wine tasting. He himself had taken the initiative to approach her, and at first Mr and Mrs Schneider hadn't been too pleased. They'd had other plans for their eldest son, but Simon was not to be deterred.

Jakov: his infectious enthusiasm as he'd talked about his international studies. My feeling of slight jealousy at the ease with which, time and again, he and his people settled into new places. I envied them their extensive ties with the world beyond the country of their birth; the social, religious and professional networks on which they, Orthodox Jews, could count anywhere in the world. They only had to go three times a day to the same *shul* to be recognized, received, acknowledged, understood, assisted. All of this thanks in large part to their lingua franca, modern Hebrew. I tried to picture myself in a similar situation. That film was short and not very pretty. Yet Abigail, who'd only just moved to Bnei Brak, already had a job and was involved in voluntary work. Had

Nima's sister found herself in such a world full of contacts back then, things would have gone very differently. The social control, which hung like a shadow over everything, was something that I passed over. But I mistrusted the ease with which they entered into international marriages. They formed alliances across every geographical border. How could that be: didn't it matter from which country or culture you came, as long as you shared a religion? Was religion the glue that kept all relationships intact, no matter what? Like in our Catholic Flanders? I remembered the first teacher to get divorced at my school in Meulenberg. I was about eight at the time. She was instantly dismissed. No one protested, but there was a lot of gossip.

I just couldn't get to sleep. I tried lying the other way round, with my head at the foot end of the bed, but that didn't help. I switched on the light, then quickly switched it off again—it was Shabbat.

I was kept awake by the bad marriage between Jews and Palestinians. By the many daily humiliations that hundreds of thousands of Palestinians—young and old, sick, healthy and pregnant—had to endure, close to the bed in which I lay. By the colonization strategy with which the Jewish state, despite the protests of the United Nations, took more and more land from Palestinians. By the image of Simon as a young soldier, the image of innumerable Simons and Simonas who temporarily defended Israel tooth and nail, then went back to their countries of origin, but who were given the authority to make decisions about the lives of Arab inhabitants. How deeply could you wound the Palestinian soul? How many souls would hate and fear kill, on both sides? Why couldn't there be joint peace and shared sovereignty? Why had we avoided this subject so consciously during the meal? Didn't silence mean complicity? Had the children become more radical? Did they no longer believe in a two-state solution, as we—especially Jakov and I, at his desk—had often discussed?

Under the light sheet I dwelt on all the memories that welled up. My time at the Schneiders' home. Elzira, who now had to laugh at herself and at how difficult she'd sometimes been. Abigail, who often, to her own annoyance, said Elvira instead of Elzira, because the name Elzira inadvertently reminded her of a German relative who'd died in Sobibor: "But let's not talk about that." Elzira, who got so good at chess that she beat Jakov. Jakov, who said that he let his little sister win.

The three had told me what they'd thought of me all those years and how, when I started, they thought that I'd soon give up, just like the other students. They joked about my skull-print trousers and my short, spiky hair. Other things amused them too. How little I knew about their laws. How, in the early days, I'd ring them on Saturdays to say I'd be coming a bit later the next day—something I'd forgotten or repressed. How even after six years I didn't know when their main holidays were, and how they couldn't understand it: surely it wasn't so hard to remember that Rosh Hashanah was celebrated on the first day of the month Tishrei, that Sukkot fell on the fifteenth day of that month, and that Yom Kippur, the Day of Atonement, was celebrated ten days after Rosh Hashanah, i.e. five days before Sukkot, the Feast of Tabernacles, which lasted seven days?

How I'd thought that Jakov was pulling my leg when he had told me about Shavuot, a holiday in early June, with its tradition of studying all night until sunrise. The Jewish people had overslept, it was said, the morning that they received the Torah. By studying all night, they were still atoning for such laziness all these centuries later.

My high heels: it hadn't been the height that had bothered them, rather the noise that they'd made. Did I really think their crêpe soles were an expression of militant feminism? Hadn't I grasped that women's heels weren't supposed to make a noise? Because women shouldn't attract attention?

Sometimes Jakov, Elzira, Simon and Abigail had talked to each other in Ivrit. There could only be one reason for that, I was sure, lying in bed: that they didn't want me to know what they were talking about.

The deep affection with which they spoke about their parents kept coming back to me. Affection and a respect that seemed almost too great to be true. Their gratitude to their father, who had worked hard to pay for their studies abroad: "Daddy says the Jews know better than any other people that no one can take away their intellects. Our brains, our knowledge—we can take them with us wherever we go."

The air conditioning in the guest room hummed. So did my head. Even though there were no mosquitoes the night seemed endless.

Jakov: "Do you remember how Daddy always drove a second-hand car, so he could pay for our studies? He bought a Volvo that was at least six years old, and drove it for a good six years or so."

Me: "But you guys are filthy rich."

Simon: "Our parents possess nothing besides their children, their house and their intellects. No savings. *Nothing*."

Me: "You're filthy rich. You have domestic staff who are there all day, from early to late. You all have your own bathrooms. If it rained, you went to school by taxi. Your parents paid me. I could go on."

Of course that once again prompted the question of why *I* didn't have any children. And as in all such discussions, it led to the invariable assurance that I'd be a good mother, yes, really, I shouldn't have any doubts on that score.

They spoke of the great faith their parents had had in *them*. Which meant I'd been allowed to work in their bedrooms, with the door shut. That this seclusion had been a test whose results Mummy and Daddy had known in advance. It was in this context that I had to see Bnei Brak and the strict seminary. The Schneiders

had precious little in common with Haredi Jews. They could just
as well have sent Simon and Jakov to the rabbinical school Yeshiva
Etz Chayim, which was close to Antwerp. Yes, they believed that
the Messiah would arise from their ranks, someone who would
rid the world of all poverty and injustice. But they didn't believe
that the whole of Western humanity was one big tragic mistake.
In the spiritually confined surroundings of Bnei Brak they'd get to
know their Jewish soul better than in Tel Aviv, was the thinking.

"Mightn't your parents have also hoped that if you were beset by
carnal urges while still single, you'd be safe here, Jakov?" I teased.

"How come?" asked Jakov.

"Remember Amsterdam," I said.

I couldn't see if he blushed, it was too dark for that.

Elzira didn't understand, and asked what I meant. Turned out
she knew nothing of the whole condom affair.

I also reviewed my own life as I lay in bed. Nima, our friends from
the Middle East, Turkey and Morocco. The friends who split up
when we did: oil and water. Limburg. My work for the Schneiders.
Meulenberg, where I'd gone to school with children from ethnic
minorities and myself belonged to a minority: of my classmates,
only the Flemish children had gone to university. First-generation
immigrant children weren't expected to continue their education
after school. The idea didn't even occur to anyone, least of all their
parents: "She should train for a job in childcare. So that when we
go back to Turkey or Morocco she'll at least have a diploma." The
institute that advised pupils on study and career choices automatically steered immigrant children into vocational education. A
university education, it was felt, was only an option for youngsters
whose native language was Dutch. Or who were Catholic: Spanish
and Greek boys and girls were given a little encouragement. But
later in my professional life I never even encountered them. Some

had returned to their countries of origin. Others worked in the Houthalen tobacco factories. The lowest social class remained low, was kept low.

My past, I realized, featured more *couleur locale et sociale* than the present in which I found myself. For someone intending to make journalism her vocation, that realization alone was enough to keep me awake.

Nine

In Jerusalem Elzira told me she wanted to get married.

"Oh, you've fallen in love with someone here!" I exclaimed, enchanted and curious. "And you're telling me *now*? Don't your brothers know yet?"

"I've asked Mummy and Daddy to set the matchmaker to work," she answered.

We were strolling around the busy Mahane Yehuda market, where the vendors of fruit and vegetables, spices, nuts, cake and other delicacies were loudly praising their wares; their collective calls sounded like one big choir.

I don't know why I responded as I did. I acted as if I hadn't heard what she'd said. I said I was delighted she'd fallen in love, then I drew her attention to the Hebrew and Arabic being spoken around us; it was the first time during my visit to Israel that I'd heard these two languages dancing together.

"Many of these Arab vendors speak Hebrew," Elzira said, and instead of asking what had got into me, took my arm and guided me to a biscuit baker whose stall dripped with honey and sugar.

"If these Arab merchants know a fair bit of Hebrew, then the same must be true in reverse," I said.

"Sure. Especially the people who work for Shin Bet."

"Shin Bet?"

"The internal security service. We have our men and women everywhere."

She too said "we" and "our". With her sweet face, dear little studs in her ears and her hair, strictly parted in the middle and plaited into a ponytail, she didn't look like someone who thought about internal security services.

In the middle of the baker's long table, every millimetre of which was covered with Bundt cake, plaited bread and baklava, stood a layered tower of dishes full of orange, glazed angel-hair pastry so sticky that just *seeing* it made me run my tongue anxiously over my teeth.

I thought: she's too young and beautiful to get married, she's so happy right now, she's at such an important stage of her life.

She bought a syrupy wedge of angel hair. It smelt of rosewater and was studded with chopped pistachio nuts, under which a layer of cream cheese peeped out invitingly.

"You have to try this *knafeh*," she said, "you'll be hooked."

Within the space of five minutes we'd bought a second wedge that we shared with relish, sitting on the doorstep of a house in one of the sloping side streets. Elzira, her legs slightly spread, caught every crumb in her skirt. She collected the little pile on a spit-dampened index finger, then licked it clean.

"You will come to my party?" she asked. "My wedding party."

I gazed at her intently. She seemed to glow, desirable as the ripe pomegranates on the stall across the road. That she was deadly serious I didn't doubt. Yet I hoped she'd suddenly burst out laughing.

"I've already been introduced to a young man. I really like him. He's from a good family. He lives in Switzerland. We met once, briefly, in the company of others, in Jerusalem, when he was here on business. Daddy and Mummy came over. He works in a bank He knows about my dyspraxia. He *has* to know. It's on the list of particulars that the matchmaker has about me. It's important, *très important*, that my future husband knows as much as possible about me, especially *tous les trucs* that our children might inherit from me. And we know all about him. Our *shadchan* made sure of that. As did we. My brothers looked up everything they could about him, so did my parents. I think I like him."

I nodded. So her brothers knew. How should I respond to this news?

"Do you want to move to Switzerland?" I asked.

"I'd rather not."

"So will he move to Belgium, then? Will you live in Antwerp?"

"*Non.*"

"In Israel?"

"*Non. En Suisse.*"

"But you just said you'd rather *not* live in Switzerland. So why are you seriously considering him as a suitor?"

"He suits me. And maybe I would suit him."

"Why do you think that?"

"Because I find him nice and *mignon.*"

"What do you find nice and sweet about him?"

"Everything."

"What do you mean by 'everything'? Does he look cute?"

"I don't know when a man looks cute."

"Yes you do. Do you remember Alex? That boy who lived quite near you. Sometimes we'd bump into him when we were walking Monsieur. You thought he was nice. Cute. Exciting. Sweet. Mischievous. And you said he came from a good family. If you compared Alex to your suitor, who would you choose?"

"I don't know Alex."

"I'm talking about intuition. Which of the two interests you more? To whom are you intuitively most attracted?"

"Intuition isn't something we do."

"For heaven's sake, Elzira! This whole conversation is *meshugga*— and I just can't understand how you could opt for a matchmaker!"

The Yiddish word made her laugh, and in the end I laughed too. There was no point resisting Elzira and her tradition. Not like this, anyway. Our cultures saw love differently. Her choice of an introduced marriage—"Never say arranged, because it isn't, I can choose from the candidates who are introduced to me, and nobody is forcing me to do anything"—wasn't a whim, but the result of pure will, in accordance with her tradition. The mind ranked higher than the heart. First intellect, then feeling; the latter would follow automatically.

"I can't wait to get married," she said. "I want to be a mother. And have a big family."

"What about your studies?"

"That's not something I think about so much."

As we talked it dawned on us both that Daddy and Mummy Schneider were behind my visit to Israel. It wasn't Elzira who'd pressed for me to come to Israel. It was her parents, who felt their daughter should have a talk with me. When she'd ordered them to find a husband for her, they'd urged her to take her time. Daddy Schneider: "You still have plenty of time, Elzira, you don't yet have any obligations. Why don't you study a few more years? These days young women can even wait until they're twenty-five before they get married, if they're studying." But if Elzira wanted, she didn't even have to keep on studying. She could just come back and live with them. The family would have to face up to possible gossip and backbiting, of course. "Anyway, nothing to worry about. A young woman's market value is determined more by her dowry than her age!" That was how Daddy Schneider, pragmatic as ever, jokingly summed it up.

The Schneiders considered it high time that Elzira had a woman-to-woman talk with someone "completely different". They knew their daughter would tell me her marriage plans. They knew I'd respond. And they knew I had some influence over their daughter.

*

Under the striped awning of a fragrant coffee house terrace on Mahane Yehuda I spoke to Elzira as a young, adult woman about to take the most important step in her life. And she responded to me in kind. Like someone who knew what she wanted, like a young person with newly acquired pride.

By now, I'd already spent three days in Jerusalem. Each day I'd tried to work out the layout of the historic city centre. Each day I'd got lost, even in the neighbourhood where I was staying.

Even with a city map in my hand, even with the main religious sites marked in orange, I couldn't conquer the four chambers of the city's circular heart—the Catholic, Jewish, Islamic and Armenian quarters—without having to retrace my steps. Whenever I felt sure of my route it turned out I was going in the wrong direction. Whenever I thought I was headed towards one religion, I'd end up in the middle of the other.

This lack of spatial awareness came back to me during my conversation with Elzira. She never seemed to stray, or even to doubt the route she wanted to take. I don't mean she wasn't afraid of what she might encounter—because she was. But she seemed to possess all the orientation points she needed so as not to go around endlessly in circles.

And her choice wasn't just purely personal. That too, she tried to make clear to me, explaining—without the least pretentiousness—that she wanted to play a part in a greater story. She was now realizing, she said, that Judaism required her to live as good a life as possible, that her religion and her history demanded the highest possible moral standards of her, that she wanted to shoulder her responsibility within the greater whole. She tried to explain to me that, out of respect for Him, she wanted to live according to the principles of her ancestors; she wanted to follow paths that all those before her had followed, for generations, often at their peril.

"You're not going to take religion too far?" I asked nervously.

"I'll have to find my own form of Judaism," she said, sounding much too grown-up to my mind.

She didn't look at me as she said it. Presumably because she felt I couldn't understand the divine task that she was assigning herself. Which was true.

"He's called Daniel," she whispered in my ear.

Ten

I don't have them any more. I never made copies, or kept drafts. But Mr and Mrs Schneider possess most of the letters I wrote to Elzira during her time in Israel.

When I found out that those letters, personally addressed to Elzira, were at her parents' house in Antwerp, I was shocked. It turned out they'd read most of our correspondence, a possibility that had never entered my head when I put thoughts to paper. Had I known, I'm not sure I'd have written to her any more, certainly not spoken to her so freely.

Why her parents had read along with us—albeit a couple of years later—I don't know. Was it curiosity? An urge to control? Because Elzira wanted to prove something with those letters? Or did the Schneiders, within their family and community, simply have a different take on privacy than what I was used to?

Of all those letters, one is particularly dear to them. It's an epistle whose contents surprise me. If Elzira or her parents hadn't had me reread my words, I'd never have believed I'd written them. In my own life I showed remarkably little talent when it came to relationships. Yet in writing I displayed such wisdom on the subject that, looking back, I can't help but wonder if I missed my vocation as a matchmaker!

The letter was a reply to one from Elzira, appealing for advice on potential bridegrooms. Two men were interested in her, and she in them, and she didn't know which to choose. One was a British

Jew of Syrian-Egyptian origin, the other a man of Dutch ancestry who'd been born in New York and lived and worked there. Daniel, the man from Switzerland, was no longer in the picture. No idea why: "these things happen". The two new candidates had been thoroughly screened by Mr and Mrs Schneider. Elzira had met the man with Middle Eastern roots through her brothers. The other had been proposed by the matchmaker. The fact she wasn't trying to find suitable candidates through the rabbi of her Antwerp synagogue was because of the "provisions" her future spouse had to meet. One of those provisions—conditions, really—was her preference for someone who wasn't from Antwerp.

"Why shouldn't he be from Antwerp?" I'd asked.

"Can you still remember how I learnt to ride a bike? How I could only cycle over the cobblestones for short stretches at first, and often fell, because I was scared? Until one day I wasn't scared any more, and cycled home in one go? I want to be Jewish like I cycled. At top speed. *Sans peur*. Fearlessly. I can't do that in Belgium. But in the US or in England maybe I could. They, other Jews, say that everything there is easier. Especially in America, where everyone eats bagels and cheesecake, so Jewish cuisine is daily fare. We're on the menu. We help to shape that country's character and flavour."

My letter was a response to her announcement that she'd now twice met the man from New York, first in the lobby of a hotel near Bryant Park, then at a restaurant in Riverdale, the kosher part of the Bronx. She wrote that it was *très rare* that a girl went to a boy, that by tradition it should be the other way round. "But I was with Mummy and Daddy and a bunch of cousins in the Borscht Belt, just north of New York City, so we all thought it would be convenient to meet there."

Isaac had landed her with a huge problem: he met all her wishes, and she his. Their personality tests had confirmed the hunch that they were made for each other. Which frightened her.

"How can I be sure of him?" She wrote. "How can I know he's the man I should marry?"

"You can never be sure of anyone," I wrote to her. "You can't even be sure of yourself."

Then I grew very serious.

I wrote that I knew her to be someone with a strong mind. I sketched how I'd seen her grow from a withdrawn girl to a confident woman, who wouldn't let anyone divert her from her path. I stressed her unique character, her honesty, her persistence, her determination to be her own person. I expanded on the strength of her intuition, illustrating it with concrete facts and memories. Her talent for empathy, much greater than that of her siblings.

I told her I'd never be able to understand the traditional Orthodox Jewish approach to affairs of the heart; that, in my view, an element of chance and romance was vital to love. But that if she felt she absolutely *had* to find her partner the Jewish way, she should play that game as well as possible.

Then I went into agony aunt mode: I advised her to draw up lists and to discuss them in a businesslike way with her intended. Isaac should do the same. If they were to assess their potential compatibility they needed to scrutinize every little thing.

I drew up a list of questions. What do I like? What don't I like? What makes me happy? What doesn't make me happy? Who are my friends? Why are they my friends? What do I expect from family? From in-laws? Do I want a job? How much time should that job take up? What values are important to me? What values are alien to me? How would I want our children to be brought up? How many children do I want? How important is a son? What if we only have girls and no boy—how many daughters am I prepared to have? What makes me laugh? In what language will we bring up our children?

To this day Mr and Mrs Schneider maintain that, when considering their future together, Elzira and Isaac took that letter as their compass, and that it was pivotal to their elder daughter's happiness. Personally, I'd rather not consider the scary possibility that I played any role at all in her choice of partner. When I wrote that letter I was probably just winging it. Very likely with a pile of women's magazines at my elbow: *Feeling, Elle, Marie-Claire*, heaven knows what. I think there's a very real possibility I was drunk when I dispensed good advice so liberally.

Eleven

Their next meeting was to take place in Antwerp, the city of Elzira's birth.

She called me: "What's the nicest public place in the city?"

"What do you mean by public place? Most beautiful monument?"

"No, a restaurant or a cafe that's very beautiful."

"In Antwerp? Outside the Jewish neighbourhood?"

"Yes. For me and Isaac."

"But surely you can't eat out if you're not in the Jewish neighbourhood? The places I know aren't kosher."

"Can you recommend a place that tourists go to where I can invite Isaac for a soda? It's important that I make a good impression."

"You could go to De Pelgrom. It's a historic cellar in a street near the cathedral. Lots of tourists go there, but the locals like it too. It's the sort of place you show people who are visiting Antwerp for the first time."

"A cellar, did you say?"

"Yes, of a mediaeval building. They've got a big selection of Belgian beers. Americans like that. And you can eat there. Typical Belgian fare."

"I can't meet a man in a cellar. It must be a transparent place."

"Transparent?"

"The outside world must be able to see us. A man and a woman who are not married may not sit opposite each other in a space that is not open."

"There'll be other people in the cellar."

"A cellar doesn't sound good. Can't you think of another place? With lots of windows? Where the outside world can look in?"

I listed a few other possibilities. None fitted the bill. "Let me have a think. I'll call you back."

The next day I recommended Zuiderterras. Perfect for her needs and close to the sights. The restaurant stood at the end of a floating esplanade on the river Scheldt, level with Suikerrui, so it was really central. The two of them could—let's play all the aces at once—stroll across Groenplaats via the statue of Rubens to the impressive cathedral, then from there to the Brabo fountain and the magnificent town hall to the black-and-white minimalism of Zuiderterras.

"So if I go to that terrace on the Scheldt, he'll get a good impression of Antwerp?"

"He'll fall in love with Antwerp," I assured her. "The cathedral is the largest Gothic church in the Low Countries, tell him that. And there are paintings by Rubens inside, some real gems."

"We're not going to go into a church."

"Not to pray, Elzira. To look at the artworks."

"We don't do that either. Only if we have to. For work or something."

"Well in that case go to the town hall. It's a palace—the staircase alone is worth it."

Isaac had never been in Antwerp or Belgium. He knew Amsterdam a little, though. Elzira: "And his family knows Abigail's mother's family—it's an amazingly small world, isn't it?"

"Have you got a photo of Isaac?" I asked.

"Yes," she said.

"Send it to me! I'm curious. Fax it. Or email it to me: I'll give you my address."

The fax machine was on its way out. The Internet had been born. To get online, you had to call a modem. Often the connection was broken halfway through and you had to start all over again. The hooking-up process always began with a shrill, scratchy ringtone.

"I can't send it just now. Perhaps later."

I'd expected Elzira to look me up during Isaac's visit to Antwerp. To briefly introduce him to me. She didn't. But to my surprise I *did* receive a postcard with a view of the cathedral. "Thank you, a thousand times," it said in her scrawly writing, "I didn't know the old city was so beautiful. *Dommage* that I hadn't been before. And the Zuiderterras: *sublime!! Bisous* from Elzira. And Isaac greets you too."

Twelve

And then in the middle of the night I got a phone call. It was Elzira. In a terrible panic. In floods of tears. In New York.

"Calm down, Elzira, calm down."

"It's *terrible*." She sobbed uncontrollably.

"Take a few deep breaths, poppet. I'm not going anywhere. We can talk all night. There's no rush." She was so far away: the term of endearment was an attempt to pull her closer.

I had no idea why she was so distraught. But I did know that she didn't get upset easily. Also that if she was distressed, she was more likely to rely on her own courage and determination than share disappointments or dramas with others. And now she was ringing me up in tears because something *terrible* had happened in New York? I feared the worst.

"Are you on your own?" I asked, when I heard her breathing slow down somewhat.

"Yes. I'm staying with friends of Mummy's and Daddy's. I'm in Brooklyn. It's *terrible*. I don't know what to do."

I was overcome with dread. She hadn't been assaulted, had she? Whose idea had it been, anyway, to send her to New York? In Antwerp she wasn't even allowed to go to the city centre by herself or anywhere else outside the Jewish neighbourhood. But now, after a brief sojourn in Israel, that overprotected child could suddenly take on the world? Just because Jews lived all over the globe? How old was she? Twenty-two? Twenty-three? I'd never been to New

York. I knew the iconic buildings, bridges and yellow taxis only from movies. A crime-ridden city, to judge by what I'd seen.

"Where are your parents?"

"I went too far," she sobbed. "I was on the water and he was there too."

"What are you talking about, Elzira?" I asked. She wasn't making any sense. Had she taken some kind of drug? Why was she ringing me of all people? And in the middle of the night? The only other people who'd ever done that were Nima's parents.

"It was a present from him," she said.

"What? From whom?"

"From Isaac."

"Oh, so you're with Isaac?" I said. I immediately felt less worried.

"Did I wake you up?"

"It's five in the morning here."

"I just got back. I couldn't ring anyone else. I did something my parents and brothers would never approve of. I couldn't think of anyone else I could tell this to." She blew her nose loudly, next to the receiver.

She's been to bed with him, I realized. She's lost her virtue and needs to share that with me.

It took a while before Elzira could knit disjointed facts into a reasonably consistent story. In short it amounted to this: Isaac was the man of her dreams and she was the woman of his dreams—this neither of them doubted for a moment, they intended to get engaged. He had passed all the tests of his future parents-in-law, including cross-questioning about the Torah. She had likewise satisfied his parents' requirements. The two looked forward to forming a happy family together—in fact they couldn't wait!

By tradition, their engagement would take place behind closed doors. But before that happened, Isaac wanted to give her a very special introduction to New York, the city where the young couple would live.

His first plan had been to treat Elzira to a helicopter tour above the Big Apple. That way, his future wife could admire all the famous skyscrapers—the Flatiron, Empire State and Chrysler Buildings, the Trump and Twin Towers—from above, and she'd see with her own eyes that Central Park, where they would stroll with their children, was as big as Belgium. However, he'd gathered from the last conversation he'd had with Elzira that she wasn't so crazy about air travel: on long flights she took a pill her mother gave her. "Mummy suffers from a very acute fear of flying. If it was up to her, she'd be given a general anaesthetic just after fastening her safety belt."

So Isaac didn't charter a helicopter but a luxury yacht. "A kosher private yacht, with captain, cook and waiter. We sailed through New York harbour and past the Statue of Liberty."

Me: "So while you were afloat Isaac got down on his knees and proposed to you?"

She: "We, *les juifs*, don't kneel. Not when we pray. Nor when the man asks the woman to marry him."

Unfortunately it was raining when they set off. And as they'd left the shelter of the harbour the weather had got worse; a grey curtain of rain and mist had hung between them and the Manhattan skyline the whole time. The boat had rolled. She'd found the heat of the cabin oppressive, but it was too wet to go on deck for a breath of fresh air.

She'd tried her hardest to enjoy the cruise, had strained every sinew to keep smiling and not betray the fact she'd rather have been dropped into the subway blindfold than toss about on the Hudson in this vile weather. She knew how important this trip was to them both. She appreciated the effort Isaac had made, didn't want to hurt her future spouse, didn't want to mess up the engagement. Not even when she saw the soup in her plate sloshing back and forth.

She'd grown dizzy and nauseous. She'd wanted to massage her temples to relieve the pressure in her head, but she was scared to show how ill she felt: he might think her affected. So she'd placed her hands on either side of her plate. The wind whipped up, attacking the boat. Ever bigger waves thudded against the side and washed over the deck. In a panicky reflex she'd grabbed hold of Isaac's arm, held on to it, squeezed it. "That's against Jewish laws, *c'est terrible, on n'est pas marié, zelfs niet fiancé*—not married or even engaged—and I touched him."

We talked for over two hours. By the end of the conversation I'd managed to get her to laugh. But she refused to see the harmlessness of this "slip".

I learnt that the young couple, in consultation with their families, had already pencilled in some possible wedding dates. All they had to do was pick the best one, and *bien sûr*, of course the wedding would take place in Antwerp; she and Mummy still had to find out whether the hotels, preferably the ones in the Jewish neighbourhood, would have enough rooms on those dates and not charge top rates.

"We're getting married in the Romi Goldmuntz cultural centre."

"Oh, so not in your synagogue?" I asked, after all these years still ignorant of the most basic customs and rituals.

"You can, but you don't have to," she said. "The rabbi conducts the ceremony, but he can do that anywhere, so we'd prefer it to be at Romi Goldmuntz in Nerviërsstraat, which has big function rooms. Lots of weddings and parties are held there, really lots. Jewish weddings don't take long. Don't *have* to take long, I should say. Sometimes it's almost like in Las Vegas. If you don't watch out, you're married before you know it. It is *suffisant* that, in the presence of two kosher witnesses, a man says 'Harei at mekudeshet li b'tabaat zu k'dat Moshe v'Yisrael' to a woman and hands her a ring, and *les deux sont mariés!*"

"Can I be a kosher witness?" The stupid question popped out before I knew it.

"You hear stories about jokers acting out such a ceremony as if it were a play. And girls falling for it. They joined in the play—as they thought—creating *leur propre drame*—their very own drama. Only an official divorce could free them again."

I didn't tell her, but after a few years of brief romantic escapades, love had once again entered my life. I was lying naked, unmarried and unengaged, telephone in hand, in the arms of Martinus.

"You'll really like Isaac," Elzira was sure. "He's smart and so funny."

Thirteen

If I occasionally had the temerity, even briefly, to think I could penetrate the millefeuille of Jewish culture, I was soon disabused of this idea.

By now I'd chosen to live by my pen, and was writing articles for newspapers and magazines. Reporting out-of-the-ordinary stories in our seemingly ordinary world: that was my forte. I wanted to write a story on the *shadchan*.

I called the Schneiders. I still knew their telephone number by heart. Still know it even now. In an age of phones without memory buttons, I must have dialled it hundreds of times.

Mrs Schneider was surprised and pleased to hear from me. I told her a little about my work, and my wish to write an article about the Jewish tradition of matchmakers.

"Jakov's essays helped you well," she laughed. *"Votre journalisme est né chez nous*. Your journalism was born at our house."

I didn't tell her I'd started on my first novel.

She said that in her community, marriage mediation was regarded as an *affaire religieuse*, a sacred matter, and that I would have to treat the issue with delicacy.

"Could you give me an introduction to a *shadchan*?" I asked.

Mrs Schneider didn't see any objection. She gave me the telephone numbers of two Antwerp-based matchmakers, adding that I should pass on her respectful greetings, and in the case of Mrs Rosenbaum her most cordial greetings, because Mrs Rosenbaum had matched Elzira and Isaac, and the two would marry shortly!

I rang Mrs Rosenbaum.

"You are *qui*?"

"A journalist and a friend of the Schneiders."

"Aaron *et* Moriel Schneider?"

"Yes. Mrs Schneider asked me to pass on her most cordial greetings."

"But you are not Jewish?"

"That's correct, Mrs Rosenbaum. I'd like to write an article about your profession: how you tackle the matter of mediating between people, and why your knowledge and expertise are so important within your tradition."

"We have nothing to gain by allowing others to pry into our affairs. I refuse to talk to you."

"But Mrs Schneider—"

"I will ring Mrs Schneider."

The conversation with the other matchmaker followed an almost identical pattern. *Unglaublich*, this *shadchan* muttered several times at the other end of the line. And: "The less people know about our way of life the better."

"I'm sorry, I—"

She hung up without saying goodbye.

That same day Mrs Schneider was rung by two furious match-makers. Their reactions had stunned her, and she rang, apologet-ically, to tell me so. The fact that her community closed ranks to keep outsiders at bay wasn't new to her: when I appeared on their horizon she herself had been a fervent supporter of this approach. But Mrs Schneider had got used to my presence. And that was the nice thing about the whole affair: she'd forgotten that I too was an outsider. Over the years, the Schneiders had come, in some tiny way, to regard me as one of them.

I experienced something similar with Elzira.

In the run-up to getting married, she moved back in with her parents for a while. She made good use of these months to plan the wedding. And to get her driving licence.

She asked me to help her with the theoretical part of the driving test. Not that she needed my help; she could have managed perfectly well on her own. But any excuse to relive old times just once more was good enough for her and me.

"So your father's teaching you to drive," I said.

"No. I'm taking lessons."

"How's that possible?"

"I don't understand you," Elzira said.

"How is it okay for you, as an unmarried Jewish woman, to be taught by a man? A car is an enclosed space, right? Or do you always have a chaperone?"

She grinned. "You know more about us than some liberal Jews."

She admitted that driving lessons for women were a borderline case. Her parents didn't have a problem with it. Nor did she. And Isaac hadn't objected. As long as it didn't have tinted windows, she and her circle regarded a car as a transparent space. In the daytime, at least. As soon as it got dark, there was no way she should sit in a car with a man who wasn't a relative, not even if he was an instructor.

She was being taught by a non-Jewish driving instructor who specialized in Jewish pupils.

"He can even a little Yiddish!"

"Can even?"

"Can even speak."

"So he can speak Yiddish?"

"That's what I said!"

"Well, I've never seen a Hasidic woman driving," I joked, "neither here nor in Bnei Brak."

"Some of them drive, you know, don't underestimate them!"

"Where do they learn?"

"Oh, if you saw them drive, you wouldn't ask." She chuckled. "They look like they've never had a lesson in their lives. But their menfolk are worse! Hasidic men haven't any idea how to drive in a city. Have you never encountered them? In your own car? Have they never nearly knocked you off your bike or run you down on the pavement?"

She sounded cheerful, as if she felt good about life. That made me happy.

"How *do* those women learn to drive?" I wanted to know the answer.

"They go to a driving school. But no one's allowed to know. That's the difference with me. I have the instructor pick me up at home, and from here *l'école* starts. Hasidic women have themselves picked up at a place where no one knows them. They take the bus to a suburb where they're sure they can practise without being seen. Or they get their husbands to take them there. A bit like when I learnt to ride a bike," she laughed. "It has to be done in secret."

"A female friend could go along."

"Sometimes that happens. *Mais on ne veut pas stimuler les* women to get driving licences. It's not encouraged. Not by Hasidim. Or by our community. Mummy's been driving since she was eighteen. She just hates parking in cities, especially when there are other cars behind her." Another peal of laughter. Israel had given her a more relaxed, mature perspective on her religion.

When the time came for her test, she asked if I wouldn't mind sitting in the back of the car. "Then perhaps I'll be less nervous."

She did the test drive perfectly. Though she was briefly flummoxed when, before we all got in the car, the examiner shook her hand. Afterwards she told me: "I'd been told by other girls that he'd do that. I shook his hand, it wasn't a problem for me. Some girls refuse, and some examiners react by being stricter on them, even failing them, some say, but I don't believe that."

"It's kind of weird that I'm only asking you this now, but why *don't* you shake hands? Everyone knows that in our society, shaking hands is socially desirable. You put yourself at a disadvantage by not doing it. And the same will apply in your new home, the United States."

"If a man touches the skin of a woman who is not his spouse, he can get *envie* in her, become desirous of her. It's out of respect for his spouse and respect for the other woman that he maintains a distance. And of course he never knows if a woman is having *ses règles*. Losing blood. Even a single drop is unclean."

"But the examiner who shakes your hand isn't Jewish. And you're not married. So what's stopping you?"

"I told you, didn't I, that I didn't make an issue of it. But if I can choose, I'd rather not be touched by strange men."

"Couldn't I write a nice story about that, about Jewish girls, their driving instructor and their driving test? And about all the quirks and complexities when it comes to touching others?"

"Shall I ask my teacher if you can accompany him and some of his pupils during their lessons? So that you can ask them questions," she said, "and see how it is in practice?"

Of course, it didn't get that far. When Mr Schneider heard of our plan, he made it plain, in very few words and without an accompanying joke, that we should put that idea out of our heads right away. Elzira's protests died away almost instantly: her mind was on Isaac.

Fourteen

Martinus and I went to Amsterdam: he to visit family and friends, me to be introduced to them.

On the train to Amsterdam the subject of "the Schneiders" came up.

As we slid out of Central Station on the raised railway track we passed the main Antwerp synagogue, belonging to Shomre Hadas, the modern Orthodox Jewish community of which the Schneiders were part.

I told Martinus what I knew about this synagogue, which was looted and destroyed during the Second World War by Nazis and Flemish pro-Nazi groups, and later renamed the Romi Goldmuntz synagogue, after the man who had invested in the restoration of this place of worship. The same Romi Goldmuntz—a diamond merchant who had survived the Holocaust—as the one in whose cultural centre Elzira was to marry Isaac—by now we had received the invitation, soberly printed in white and silver, in four languages. A wedding list had been enclosed. I loathed wedding lists and was disappointed that this invention, which put efficiency and covetousness above spontaneity and generosity, had even been adopted by Jewish people. Wedding lists should be banned, I felt. They were an insult to the giver and his heart.

"Well it's high time another Romi came along," Martinus replied, "the paint's peeling right off it." He tried to read his paper.

"The synagogue was designed by a Russian *and* by a fellow countryman of yours," I said.

"*Ach ja*, we Dutch are just like Jews: all over the place," he joked.

"The architect's a Dutch Jew, actually. Called De Langhe, if I remember rightly."

"What a fate: to be born Dutch *and* Jewish," he twinkled. He looked up again from his newspaper.

"De Langhe designed lots of buildings in Antwerp, it turns out. Like the coffee-roasting factory by Zuiderdokken, you know, near our place. And his Russian associate, Isgour, was also a Jew— he'd fled to Brussels with his family when he was a child, because anti-Semitism was on the rise in Russia."

"Okay, we'll talk till Roosendaal. Then I get to read till Utrecht. Then you can talk again."

"Do you know where this Isgour guy designed a lot of buildings just after the Second World War?"

"Is this a quiz?"

"In the Limburg mining region. Zwartberg, Meulenberg. Where I went to school. He designed the Houthalen casino, where I often went as a kid. By then it had been turned into a cultural centre. I watched loads of plays there, and when our school put on a play— about a bear called Brammetje Brom—I appeared on stage there lots of times. I was in the choir. Brammetje was played by a Moroccan boy. He was only ten, but he was *really* good. Those performances were the only ones where the audience was mixed. Mixed in the sense of immigrants and locals. But I'm losing the thread. Isgour had a lot to do with the design of the *cité*, a kind of model village for the mining community. He built the engineers' houses on Koolmijnlaan—we used to pass them on our way to school. And he designed the school I went to, with all those immigrant children. The ones that also had Koran teachers."

I looked at Martinus expectantly.

"Tell me about Brammetje Brom. And about your schooldays."

"Not now. Some other time. Don't you think it's strange that a school where children were taught the Koran turns out to be built by a Jewish architect?"

"*Now* it's strange. Right after the war it probably wasn't that strange. I don't know."

"I think it's *really* strange. Just as I find it pretty amazing that the same Jewish architect who helped design Antwerp's chief synagogue also shaped the landscape of my youth! That the man who built the place where the Schneiders worship also designed my nursery and primary school classrooms. I only found this out recently. This Isgour guy even designed the Sint-Lambertuskerk where I took communion," I said. "Was forced to take it."

"Tell me about when you were little."

"I only know six Jewish people, you know. Orthodox Jews, I mean. And they're all from the same family. And a grandmother, I mustn't forget her. So seven religious Jews. If I hadn't done any tutoring, I'd never have met them. Their world is so closed. We don't know anything about them. We don't even know about their contributions to our society," I said. "Why don't I know about the history of Jewish architects in the Limburg mining region?"

"Gosh. Doesn't the same apply to non-Jewish contributions? Don't we rarely know what people do exactly? I wouldn't split people up so much, actually. Since when have you been so into architecture?" He tucked his paper away.

"Nima's parents were architects. We sent them photos and newspaper articles about interesting buildings. They asked us to. They wanted to see Europe."

"And it's through them you heard about this Sigour?"

"Isgour. No, I found that out by chance. Heard something, then went and looked him up."

"I think that Dutch Jews are less closed than Flemish Jews. That's the impression I get, but I could be wrong. In Flanders, each community seems to be more like a separate, mini-society. Lots of little islands alongside each other. In the Netherlands, a lot of Jews work in television. They're politicians, lawyers, businesspeople, writers. They're more anchored in our daily life. Because they're more liberal. I think. But I could be wrong."

"Why is that?"

"I don't know, love. They've lived in Amsterdam for many centuries. That must play a role. Along with the Dutch tendency to be open-minded. Flemings are more inward-looking, you know that as well as I do. Dutch people are always ready to be charmed: everything and everyone is '*leuk*' (nice) or '*enig*' (delightful). The Flemish say the Dutch are more superficial. That's certainly true. But it would be wrong to think that, just because they tend to make an issue out of everything, people have more depth. Though I admit that too much superficiality can be very tiring."

I was reminded of Abigail, Simon's wife. After just one day, she'd treated me much more spontaneously than Elzira, even after six years. And the American woman I'd shared the *sherut* with in Bnei Brak: more communicative than the average Fleming. What was there in our tap water that made us roll down the shutters of our existence as soon as anyone showed the slightest bit of curiosity or spontaneous joy? And hadn't some of our Flemish friends and acquaintances, after meeting Martinus, reacted just as they had when they met Nima, using the word "real" like Milena, when she talked about Jewesses? "Oh, but you're not a 'real' Dutchman, you're like one of us." By which they meant that Martinus wasn't insufferably loud and didn't urinate against the cathedral.

"Do you think it's nice, the synagogue?" asked Martinus, dragging me back from my thoughts.

"The De Langhe and Isgour one? It's kind of austere. And you're right, the paint *is* peeling off."

"Inside, I mean!"

"I don't know."

"But it's the Schneider family's synagogue?"

"Yes."

"And you've never been inside?"

"Never."

It had never occurred to me. In all the years I'd lived in Antwerp, I'd never been inside a synagogue. I'd never even peeked in the Dutch Synagogue, right across the street from where I'd studied. Nima and I had photographed and filmed its oriental facade: it was the most beautiful *shul* in Antwerp, perhaps in the Low Countries. Not until this conversation in the train did I realize I'd only seen the building's grand exterior. Yet on study trips to Barcelona I *had* visited the Old Synagogue on Carrer Marlet, even had it explained to me by a rabbi and a tourist guide. Not till Barcelona did it dawn on me that, unlike churches, you seldom saw a hearse outside a synagogue. I learnt there that a Jewish body is seen as ritually unclean; the dead and their rituals have no place inside a sacred Jewish place, unless the dead person was named Cohen, the Hebrew word for priest. How was it that in Antwerp, where there were over fifty synagogues and where I'd lived for nearly fifteen years, I'd never been aware of this custom?

"In a place they don't know, people are perhaps a bit more daring," Martinus reassured me, "and that certainly applies to Flemings."

"Going into a synagogue has nothing to do with daring," I said.

"It *does* have to do with leaving your comfort zone," he replied. "How many people never use public transport in their own town? But once they're somewhere else they suddenly don't have a problem travelling by metro, bus, tram and taxi. Until they return home. Then they get back in their cars again. Even to go to the baker's on the corner."

I looked out of the window. We were passing through Heide-Kalmthout. Once, many Jews had lived here, close to the Dutch border. The history of Mrs Schneider's family, which had been nearly entirely wiped out, had happened in this place. That much I'd grasped from the odd remark she and her children had made. More than that, and the fact that almost none of the Jews who lived here had survived the war, I didn't know.

A deep sigh escaped me. I just couldn't shake off the Schneiders. Martinus slid next to me.

"If you let me read the paper now, I'll treat you to a taste of Jewish Amsterdam very soon." He stuck his arm through mine. "We'll go to Sal Meijer's and have a salt beef sandwich."

Fifteen

I'd never had a salt beef sandwich before. At Sal Meijer in Amsterdam's Scheldestraat I ate two in a row.

"I don't know any place like this in Antwerp," I said. "We don't even have this type of pastrami."

Martinus: "I used to work in a cafe near here; in the small hours we'd drop in at Sal's."

We were in a cheerful mood: the family visit had gone well. It had been a very Dutch affair. People found me *leuk* and *enig*, but also a bit odd, because I didn't say very much. We had sat in a circle around a few bowls of crisps and drunk coffee and soft drinks. More than once people commented that when I did open my mouth I spoke such lovely Flemish, and once I was asked to repeat an idiom, because it struck them as so expressive—much more expressive than the Dutch equivalent. In this company, I suddenly felt myself back in the role of outsider, entering an unfamiliar *tableau vivant*, but I didn't mind.

Sal Meijer's looked like it dated from the 1960s or 1970s. White tiled walls, men with aprons, old-fashioned crockery, plain rolls amply filled with high-quality meat and fish, nothing fancy. No frills, unless you counted the Amsterdam accent, which filled the small space.

The customers were young and old, Jewish and non-Jewish, Orthodox and liberal. Nearly all the tables and chairs had been taken, outside too. The atmosphere was relaxed. A rabbinical certificate hung on the wall. If someone ordered a ham roll, they'd get a roll with beef sausage or salt beef shoved under their nose without comment. No one asked where the pork was. Milk and butter didn't exist in this establishment.

"Ah, you're from Belgium." An older man addressed us. He was drinking tea at the table next to ours.

"Well spotted," I said.

"Guess you're on the lookout for Dutch celebrities?"

"What do you mean?" I asked.

"Sonja Barend. Bram Moszkowicz. Ralph Inbar, that guy who hosts *Banana Split*. Hanneke Groenteman, they all come here."

"We're just here for the sandwiches," Martinus said. "I really wanted her to see this place."

"Oh, so *you're* Dutch. How nice. You're quite right to bring her here. Jews and Amsterdam: they go together like peas and carrots," the man went on.

"Are you Jewish?" I asked.

"What do you think?" he said.

"Jews and Amsterdam go together like peas and carrots? Only one fifth of the Jews came back after the war," I blurted out. "In Belgium, there was more resistance to the Nazi genocide."

I had a tendency to do that, I'd noticed. To stick up for Belgium when I was in the Netherlands, or talking to Dutch people. As if I felt called upon to defend my country, my place of origin.

The man fell silent. He finished his cup of tea. I could feel him sizing me up.

Before he left, he asked if we wanted to hear a funny story, typical of Amsterdam Jewish humour. I nodded without much enthusiasm. Martinus sounded keener.

The man, Jacky, told a story about a student who used to help out at Sal Meijer at peak times.

One day, Jacky, a regular at Sal's, said to the student: "Give that young lady some cutlery for her beef sausage sandwich." (Some customers ate their sandwiches without cutlery, he told us, whereas others absolutely insisted on a knife and fork.) Jacky had pointed discreetly to a woman sitting at a table by the window.

The student had held out a knife and fork to the woman: "*Alstublieft*, here you go."

Then he blushed bright red. The customer turned out to be a thalidomide victim. Born to a woman who'd been prescribed the drug during pregnancy, before it was known to cause birth defects. One of her arms ended in a stump.

"Now *that's* Jewish humour," Jacky said, and he burst out laughing. The men in aprons roared too. Martinus joined in somewhat hesitantly. I shrugged in mock stoicism. I was confused and didn't know what I preferred: Mr Schneider's jests or Jacky's mockery, drenched in pain and self-loathing—only blacks can make jokes about blacks.

Sixteen

It was the first time I'd seen Elzira's intended; Isaac was white as a sheet and looked as if he might faint at any moment. Two men led him to the *chuppah*: his father and Mr Schneider. Tall, thin and gangly, his wide-brimmed hat looked more substantial than he did. He wore a white robe over his suit. He didn't have a beard and I caught myself being relieved to note that.

Isaac stood under the silk canopy. The rabbi spoke and chanted. The women's gallery, where I was sitting, was abuzz with chatter; sometimes voices were raised loudly, like in a market. All the women, except me, had a lot to discuss. They stood up, sat down again, strolled around the gallery. They were dressed to the nines. They laughed, made phone calls. In addition to Dutch, French and Hebrew, I mainly heard American English around me. Only the odd snatch of Yiddish. Children ate sweets and chased each other around. No one was concentrating. I had to bite my tongue so as not to tell them off: "Hey, pipe down a bit, this *is* Elzira's and Isaac's wedding, you know!"

As far as I could tell, I was the only non-Jewish woman there. But I might have been mistaken. After all, I myself could have passed for modern Orthodox. I was wearing a black, floor-length dress. My hair was shoulder-length and dark brown. No wedding ring gleamed on my finger, so I didn't have to wear a wig. The dress code surprised me: I'd expected dark colours to dominate. There was plenty of dark blue, but lots of the ladies were wearing pastel or bright shades. A few could have gone straight onto the cover of a glossy magazine.

I looked for Abigail, Simon's wife, and Sara, but couldn't spot them. I couldn't see anyone I knew or recognized. Close relatives were probably somewhere else, nearer the bride and groom. Two hundred to two hundred and fifty guests, I estimated. Where was Granny Schneider? I really wanted to say hello to her; how long had it been since we'd seen or spoken to each other? I didn't know how many granddaughters she had. But I knew she was fond of Elzira.

I was sitting right at the front, at the balustrade, and could see the men on the floor below. Martinus was nowhere in sight. He would surely have hooked up with other guests by now, had probably already been invited to coffee by somebody. In addition to his social skills he had another trump card: Isaac's family had Dutch roots, so the guests must include Amsterdammers. Perhaps he'd seen someone he knew. At the entrance, a man had handed Martinus a blue velvet *yarmulke*. My boyfriend could be taken for a Jew, especially in the dark suit he was wearing.

In defiance of the wedding list, we'd bought the young couple a lovely and (for our budget) extremely expensive duvet cover. King-size. White satin with silver stripes. The same colours and motifs as on their wedding invitation. As I sat there waiting for what was to happen, I suddenly realized we should also have bought an identical duvet cover for a single bed. I'd completely forgotten that Jewish women slept in a separate bed when they were menstruating. How could I have been so stupid?! We should have followed the wedding list.

I'd already caught a glimpse of Elzira as we came in. The bride-to-be was sitting on a decorated throne. She looked lovely. Corkscrew curls, flowers in her hair, pink blusher on her otherwise pale, translucent cheeks. An intense look in her eyes. Her hands resting in her lap. A crowd of people surrounded her; I'd kept at a distance. My eyes welled up. I was nervous for her. For Moses, the sea split in two; for this young couple, men and women split into separate camps.

Elzira. In a small way *my* Elzira. The bride. The *kallah*. Her mother and Isaac's mother led her to the canopy. In a plain, white wedding dress and train she advanced slowly and calmly towards Isaac, her face covered by a veil. She'd chosen a beautiful sleeveless dress from the Natan fashion house, carefully modified by tailors to meet Orthodox Jewish norms. With the two mothers, candle in hand, she circled Isaac seven times. It was one of the few rituals I was familiar with. The world had been created in seven days. She was creating seven bulwarks around her marriage; enough, hopefully, to protect it from external harm. A lot happened. I can't remember any more in what order. My mouth felt dry. The rabbi began to speak; he gave his blessing, in many words and long sentences. Wine was drunk from one goblet, and from another. Mrs Schneider took away the veil that hid Elzira's face. Isaac looked at her. She smiled. I saw all the tension flow out of him. He had a disarming smile. The rabbi talked again. The women around me looked at the *chuppah* where Isaac was sliding the ring over Elzira's right index finger. The rabbi continued to talk and read aloud. I waited for the moment when Elzira would place a ring on Isaac's finger. There was a time I'd have been worried she might drop the ring. Now I had no such worry. But Isaac didn't get a ring on his finger. Elzira fiddled with hers, put it on one of the fingers of her other hand. The young couple signed a form whose contents the rabbi had, I supposed, just read out. After the signing Elzira handed the document to her father. Mr Schneider had to fumble for his handkerchief.

Then Isaac stamped on a glass, breaking it. The shards—another thing Elzira had told me—symbolized the ruins of Jerusalem, the fragile peace in Israel and, by extension, the imperfection of the world.

"Mazel tov!" everyone shouted.

My eyes scoured the floor below. I so wanted to be with Martinus!

PART III

2001–the present

One

Funnily enough, years after my sojourn in Bnei Brak, it wasn't Elzira but Jakov who I saw first.

Returning from a stay in San Francisco, Martinus and I had, on a whim, added three days in the Big Apple to our trip. Both Jakov and Elzira lived in New York.

"Why don't you give Elzira a call?" Martinus asked.

"It's Friday."

"Still early afternoon, though, not yet Shabbat."

"You can't do that!" I said. "Just suddenly ring someone up after you haven't seen them for years and say: 'Hello, it's me—surprise surprise, I'm in town, and I'll be on your doorstep in a minute!' Elzira has a family, she's got her own life now."

But there was more to it than that. I couldn't just knock on the door of an Orthodox Jewish family without mental preparation. I couldn't hop from one moment to the next to a life full of religious laws—certainly not after a stay in Frisco. One day, I'd certainly visit Elzira. But she and I would prepare for that thoroughly, and well in advance.

Over time, our relationship had changed, of course. We didn't see each other any more. The contact I still maintained with the Schneiders' married children was unstructured. Sometimes I wouldn't hear anything from them for a year, nor they from me. When their children were born, I usually got a card or an email. Since nobody was being born at my end, I occasionally looked for other reasons to get in touch. Like the time I ran into Opris, asked after Monsieur, and was sorry to hear that the little dog had died.

"Why don't you ring Jakov, then?" Martinus persisted.

"He's got even more on his plate than Elzira. His wife and children. His job. Living in New York is super expensive."

"What's *that* got to do with it?"

"I don't want to bother them, Martinus."

"I'd like to see Jakov. And so would you, right? You miss the Schneiders, so why not look them up while we're here?"

"You don't even *know* Jakov."

"Yes I do. I talked to him for ages at Elzira's wedding party."

"Ages? A quarter of an hour at most! And that was years ago! We can't just suddenly rock up without warning."

"I'm sure Jakov would be pleased to see us."

"I don't want to be pushy."

"That's such a Flemish mindset. Why shouldn't Jakov be happy to hear from us? What the Dutch call nice and considerate, the Flemings called pushy." He pulled a face to show he didn't get it at all. A face that also signalled I was wrong.

"Why don't *you* call him, then?"

"What's his number?"

Within hours, Jakov was striding through the automatic doors of the hotel lobby. In my mind's eye, I see him wearing a lightweight K-Way rain jacket. A red one. Though I'm not sure this is actually true. It's quite possible I invented this red jacket later, attributing a colour to the relaxed impression he made. I do know, though, that he was wearing dark-blue Levi's, "because of Levi Strauss, of course, the Jew who taught the world to wear jeans".

"How cool to see you so unexpectedly!" Jakov thumped Martinus's shoulders till they were sore, and gave him a crushing handshake. I received a cordial, happy nod. "Welcome to New York, best place in the world. What brings you to my city?"

I thought: How big he's grown. Big in the sense of grown-up. Serious too. I panicked a little: what if we didn't know what to talk about, if we just exchanged platitudes. I was scared we might end the day with a gulf between us.

Jakov took charge. He wanted to show us a local food truck. "They sell the *best* Brussels waffles in the world." Gesturing expansively, as if he were an enthusiastic tour guide, he told us that the importer of the kosher waffle dough was a Jew from Antwerp: imagine, a Jew makes New Yorkers passionate about Belgian waffles, while you'd scour Belgium in vain for kosher waffles baked on the spot.

He took the lead. It had always been the other way round. The constellation had changed.

"Speaking of Belgium, don't you miss it?" I asked, for something to say.

"Yes and no," he answered. "Sometimes I'm homesick for my family, for Beni's Falafel, for friends. But I'll never go back for good. New York's a great place to be a Jew."

He walked between us. Like so many Orthodox Jewish men in Antwerp he walked quickly. I could scarcely keep up with him. I felt like sticking my arm through his, so as to keep pace with him better. I also felt like a nice glass of wine.

"Only now that I'm one of the one and a half million Jews of New York—twelve per cent of the city's population!—do I know what it means to be a modern Orthodox Jew as a matter of course," he went on. And European Jews were different to American Jews, he said. "We, Europeans, have a different type of humour. We dress and act differently. We love soccer. We look each other up, even in New York. By the way, more and more Antwerp Jews are moving here. Including friends of mine, of Simon's and my sisters'. I think I've started a trend," he joked.

"Elzira beat you to it."

"Yes, Elzira's intuition was always spot on," he said.

"What language do you, European Jews, speak amongst your-selves?" I asked. I was playing our old language game.

"I've still got a school friend who speaks broad Antwerp dialect," he laughed. "In fact he knows you," he said, "we even talked about you not so long ago."

"He knows me? Apart from you, I don't know any Orthodox Jews."

"Sure you do. You wrote his essays!"

Everything he said about his wife Thirza, there at the waffle truck, radiated admiration. She'd been born in New York. She'd got a PhD in physics, but preferred—and found it made more financial sense—to join her parents in their jewellery business. There, she didn't have to work nine to five. And she didn't have to explain about Shabbat.

He talked about his parents-in-law. Thirza's father had been born in Antwerp. After the war, in which he lost practically his entire family, Europe felt like a tainted place. He'd boarded a ship to America. Aged sixteen, he lied to the US immigration authorities that he was an adult. Eventually Thirza came along. His daughter had been introduced to Jakov through a *shadchan*. They had two children. "I'd like five, at least, so you can see why it's handy for Thirza to keep on working in the family business."

He seemed to have put away his us-and-you grin. His spectacles had been traded in for lenses; I got the impression he saw the whole world differently, with more colour.

Jakov told us about the business he'd started up, developing dig-ital cameras. He already had ten people working for him. "I'm still making a loss at the moment, but we're going to grow, to boom." To set up the business, he'd borrowed money from a wealthy Jewish real estate broker. At first, the man had refused to invest in Jakov; he didn't think his plan would work. But Jakov hadn't given up. For weeks, he'd gone to the same *shul* as the property magnate. When that didn't lead to a breakthrough, he spent three successive nights in a sleeping bag outside the real estate broker's front door. On the third morning the man said "Come in."

Jakov paid for the waffles, which were indeed excellent. We talked about this and that. About his parents: their health, how Mrs Schneider's fear of flying ruled out visits to the US, though she would take the train to Amsterdam, where Simon and Abigail lived with their two children. About Sara, who, to everyone's amazement, never volunteered for the Israeli army. The youngest of the four children had stayed in Antwerp, marrying a Jewish man of Turkish origin. We talked about Elzira. He saw his older sister only occasionally. They might live in the same city, but New York was so big, and Elzira lived in Brooklyn Heights and he up in Fresh Meadows, to the north of JFK. At least an hour's drive, assuming there wasn't a hold-up. But there was always a hold-up. And they both led separate lives, went to their own synagogues, lived within their own Jewish communities. "No, my Thirza doesn't wear a wig. She's a young Madeleine Albright, if you know what I mean. We don't even live in a neighbourhood with an *eruv*, can you imagine! Elzira and Isaac do. There are lots of *eruvin* in New York, about ten or so just in the south of the city, I believe."

Then Martinus told his story about Elzira's wedding.

During the reception, some of the guests had held a hat, a tin platter or a money box under his nose, muttering something in Hebrew or Yiddish. Each time, Martinus had got out his wallet. First he had given them notes. When he didn't have any notes left, he switched to coins. He assumed this ritual was part of the wedding; all the contributions would go towards a present for the young couple, or perhaps to cover the accommodation costs of foreign guests. But the hats and platters kept coming. He asked the man next to him what present they would buy for Elzira and Isaac with the money they collected. The man had started to laugh heartily.

It turned out that the collectors represented all kinds of Jewish voluntary organizations. They liked to drop in on weddings, because there they found lots of good-humoured, generous people all in one spot. What's more, the peer pressure was considerable: one person could see how deep into his pockets another was prepared to reach in the interests of *tzedakah*, a God-bidden act of charity.

Without knowing it, Martinus had sponsored all kinds of—possibly ultra-Orthodox—schools, youth movements, *shuls*, associations for the elderly, kosher meal providers and ambulance services.

"Fantastic," chuckled Jakov, after hearing the story.

"Well I felt pretty stupid," Martinus said.

The two got so immersed in conversation that I felt left out. They talked about migration. About the travel bug that infects the Dutch, making Jakov think of his people: the history of Jewry had traditionally been one of migration. They talked about IT, getting all geeky and technical. Sometimes Dutch tripped off Jakov's tongue, sometimes American English. The language he spoke depended on the subject and on his memories, the time events took place. The two men swapped email addresses.

As we sat next to Jakov on a little stone wall near Penn Station, waiting for his train, I saw he was wearing black socks with the days of the week embroidered along the top. It was a Friday, but they said something else. What's more, Jakov was wearing a different day on each foot. Discovering that felt like coming home.

Two

I was just sorting out my mailbox when the message arrived.
At first I thought it was from Elzira. She and Isaac had a shared
email address featuring both their names. But it was from Isaac. It
boiled down to this: he hoped all was well with me and Martinus.
He didn't want to bother me, he said. He told me that their elder
daughter had recently had to undergo major heart surgery. The
operation had been a success, thank God (that was what he wrote).
But Elzira couldn't shake off her worries. Because the 9/11 attacks
had happened just as their daughter was being operated on. He
wondered whether I might like to come and stay for a few days. He
wrote that they had plenty of room for guests. That it would do his
wife good to talk to me. That for the time being he'd prefer to keep
my visit a surprise. So it would be better not to email him back.

He gave me three telephone numbers. In a postscript he added
that he would like to pay for my flight.

Three

I stayed for five pleasant days.

Elzira and Isaac had three daughters and a son. When I went to bed, I would find sweets and little notes under my pillow. Every day, I found sweet Post-it messages and drawings on the bathroom mirror.

The house was full of song. The youngest daughter made off with my high heels and transformed the sitting room into a cat-walk. The oldest, who'd had the heart operation and afterwards been passed fit as a fiddle, couldn't believe I'd ever tutored her mummy. She must have asked me at least fifty times. The middle one wanted everything I said to be repeated to her. When we played with his toy cars or I helped him make a sandcastle in the sandpit, the little boy could gaze at me fixedly for minutes at a time. He was a dear little chap, not quite three. In accordance with the Torah, his hair wouldn't be cut until his third birthday, so his corkscrew curls tumbled down his cheeks. Elzira was more strictly observant than her parents. Her children spoke English and Hebrew, and a smidgen of Dutch. They loved waffles and *frites*. And cheesecake from Kleinblatt's in Antwerp's Provinciestraat—I'd brought some with me, which made my popularity soar.

The Latin American home help lived on the attic floor. When she romped with the children, her laugh made the whole house vibrate, as if an engine had been switched on. The young woman was mainly responsible for the laundry and other domestic chores.

Elzira did the cooking herself. And it was she who helped her children with their homework. Despite her deep concerns about her family, she radiated the good-humoured, self-assured contentment peculiar to mothers who have consciously chosen to devote their lives to their families, and who lack for nothing financially.

After her first pregnancy, Elzira, whose name I only now discovered meant "devoted to God", had given up her clerical job at a Jewish school. Since then she'd focused on voluntary work. She'd metamorphosed into the selfless linchpin around which local—Jewish—community life in Brooklyn Heights revolved. If, when leaving home, she didn't immediately get into her khaki-coloured four-wheel drive, she was very likely to be buttonholed by a local resident. "I get on well with everyone, though I do find some of the JAPs trying," she said. "JAPs?" I asked. "Jewish American princesses. Rich Jewish women who are out of touch with the real world. The Paris Hiltons of our community. I try to be super friendly, and I'm very patient with them. But inside I sometimes think: grow up!"

She knew the local families and what was going on in their lives. Her insight, her efforts and her refusal to judge had a wide social reach. If she hadn't been a woman, she'd have made a good Orthodox rabbi.

"You could still become a *shadchan*," I grinned.

"Yes! Dating agency Elzira, more reliable than Al Jazeera," she laughed.

But we didn't discuss 9/11. Not in essence, anyway. The debris, the dust, the commotion in the hospital on the day her daughter was lying on the operating table: *that* was talked about at length. She'd seen some of the severely injured brought in as she sat in the waiting room, praying for good news from the heart surgeon. She'd gone on praying for days.

*

My stay with Elzira's family included one Shabbat.

I asked her if she'd be okay with me taking the children for a walk this Friday afternoon, instead of helping her in the kitchen.

"Of course," she said.

I was too unfamiliar with the dietary laws to feel confident about what I was doing, and wanted to avoid that stress. I still didn't know which ingredients were allowed to lie side by side, which plates I could rinse in which sink, which pans I was allowed to use. Whether I could touch the knobs of the gas cooker—because wasn't turning up the flame the same as lighting a flame? The fridge, with its light that went on and off: was it okay to open and shut its door? Somewhere I'd heard that even the transport of kosher foodstuffs was strictly regulated: if a truck's last load had consisted of non-kosher products, the back had to be thoroughly cleansed before it could be reloaded. "Who *comes up* with these things?" had been my response. And: "No wonder kosher food's so expensive."

Despite this, I still slipped up that evening as we sat at the table. I was taking notes after the candles had been lit, the blessings pronounced, completely forgetting that writing fell under the list of prohibited activities. I just hadn't internalized Jewish laws.

Elzira and Isaac's youngest daughter put me straight in no uncertain terms: "That's not allowed," she piped up. "You must put away your pen. And switch off your phone. I know, Mummy and Daddy say you can do what you want, because you're not Jewish. But I'd prefer it if you didn't confuse us."

Four

A few years later I sent Elzira an email unlike all the ones I'd sent before. Without elaborating on the threads of life I'd briefly lost hold of, I told her I felt a need to see her and her family.

"Come whenever you like," she answered.

Despite my belief in the adage "Guests, like fish, start to smell after three days," this time I spent seven nights at their—new—brownstone in Brooklyn Heights, where I stayed in a spacious guestroom with en suite, and slept in the same bed as Mr and Mrs Schneider when they came to stay.

I was given the key to their home and the code for the alarm system. "There are ashtrays in the garden house," Isaac said, after I came back from a stroll through the neighbourhood—he must have smelt that I'd had a furtive smoke. He gave me the key to the garden house, which was like a country retreat, and featured a bar stocked with spirits of the finest brand, some with kosher certificates, including a bottle of Jack Daniel's Old No. 7. Besides soft drinks, the fridge contained Duvel and Maredsous (beers without additives were kosher) for friends from Belgium who regularly came to stay. Their American friends were partial to them too. Isaac told me of Hasidic men who loved to drink Duvel. Picturing this made me smile.

The volumes in the garden house bookcase included my debut novel. I leafed through it. Here and there Elzira had marked passages and made notes; I recognized her handwriting.

I went for a lot of walks. On my own or with the children. Sometimes with Elzira, sometimes with Elzira and Isaac. She and her husband almost never touched each other familiarly when I was there. But from the playful interplay of their words, silences and covert glances I could tell they'd created their own language and their own world, and felt at home in it.

On my outings, I saw every branch of Judaism. Within each branch I encountered every conceivable gradation. Within each gradation I came across every conceivable individual difference.

For the first time in my life I was aware that a homogeneous Jewish community just didn't exist.

Short-skirted Jewish girls walked alongside Hasidic women in ankle-length dark skirts, fake-hair wigs and beige tights featuring a thick, vertical seam so the nylon couldn't possibly be mistaken for the potentially erotically charged skin of the lower leg.

In New York, women in antique garb seemed less anachronistic than in Antwerp. That realization surprised me, because on the Old Continent, past and present were more interlinked than in this New World metropolis.

I talked to people of all kinds. In these conversations I noticed that Jews addressed me with an openness I'd never encountered in Antwerp. In the course of a week I spoke to more Orthodox Jews than I had in the quarter of a century I'd lived in Antwerp. Perhaps because, as a visitor to the city, I opened up more to the world around me. Martinus had once put forward a theory along those lines, and there was a lot of truth in it. But the reality was more nuanced than that: the people, young and old, who I started conversations with on the street, or in the subway or lift, weren't bent on concealing their lives. They weren't bolting and chaining the door to their world. On the contrary. They wanted to share it with me.

These exchanges made me recall the teacher who'd gone with Jakov's class to the Anne Frank House and had initiated a debate in the train about Jewish self-confidence. Apparently, the DNA of Jewish New Yorkers contained less fear, and more pride and *joie de vivre*. How had Jakov put it again? That the naturalness with which he could be a Jew here boosted his self-confidence? As I saw it, the collective self-confidence also benefited from the advantages of New York. As if the people here didn't bear the weight of the grim history of European Jews on their shoulders, didn't perpetually fear a repetition of these horrors, weren't constantly surrounded by traces of their extermination. As if there were more light here, and more future.

During those seven days, Elzira never asked me what was wrong. She watched over me in silence.

Five

On the occasion of Mrs Schneider's sixty-fifth birthday, Elzira secretly rounded up her sister and brothers. On their mother's birthday, the four gathered in Antwerp, where they stood singing at her front door.

It just so happened that the week before, I'd sent another how-are-you-doing-it's-been-ages email to Elzira. She'd immediately responded with an invitation. Couldn't Martinus and I drop in too, at her mother's birthday party? "That'd be great, it'd be just like the old days, Mummy and Daddy won't believe their eyes, I'm not even going to tell Daddy: he's in on the whole surprise plan for Mummy, but we won't say anything about you coming."

There are people who never shed the past versions of themselves. Mrs Schneider was such a person; she accommodated all her ages in her and was as inscrutable as always.

But that afternoon of her birthday she seemed completely at sea. She had the look and the gestures of someone who's lost something important but doesn't know what. Like when you leave the house in the morning feeling you've forgotten something. You sense— you *know*—that something's not right, but you just can't work out what's missing. You pat your pockets. It's not your wallet. Not your bag. Not your coat, your scarf, your jewellery. But what *is* it then?

I've no idea what Mrs Schneider was missing during her party. Time, perhaps. Three of their children had gone abroad when they were eighteen or so. Since then they'd only been home occasionally, for brief periods. Never, since secondary school, had all four stayed in the parental home at the same time. Certainly not by themselves, without spouse or children. Sometimes Mrs Schneider had to reach for her handkerchief. Like when she picked up a photo of Granny Pappenheim from the sideboard.

"*Grandmère* died peacefully. During her afternoon nap, while visiting her sister in the Netherlands."

I didn't tell them I'd driven to the Jewish cemeteries in Putte a few times. Not to visit grandmother Pappenheim, because I'd only recently learnt of her death. But because I'd heard they were the last resting place of some Flemish and Dutch Jews who had gone down with the *Titanic*. I'd smelt a story. I never managed to get into the cemeteries though: the gates were locked, and I couldn't read the instructions next to the code lock, which were written in Hebrew.

Although I'd felt greatly honoured by the invitation, it felt strange and confrontational to be with all the Schneiders again in their home after all those years. Inevitably, like all reunions, this one was a disappointment. And like all reunions, this one fed off everything that was past. We'd all taken our own separate paths in life. We'd all changed: grown fatter or thinner, more open or closed, more energetic or rheumaticky, more religious or atheistic, older in years, but sometimes younger in ways of thinking and acting.

Sara had grown chubby, but hadn't lost any of her old energy. Simon looked good, and still had that air of seniority. I thought: if he lived in my neighbourhood, I'd make him my doctor straight away. Elzira was enjoying it all. Jakov seemed slightly ill at ease. For once, he was quiet, more an observer than a participant. Father Schneider was in seventh heaven. The way he looked at his wife, surrounding her with small gestures—like a shy young man of almost seventy, convinced he'd found the woman of his dreams. Their behaviour towards each other belied my views on the institution of marriage.

Martinus and I stayed for a good hour. In that short space of time, during which I never relaxed entirely, I noticed that every-one was doing their best not to bring up any memories of Nima. I appreciated their discretion, but at the same time it felt oppressive. I knew they didn't want to hurt Martinus. But in this house I'd always faced the same dilemma, and it was no different now: where did respect and caution end, and taboo start? Must I be silent about Martinus's failed marriage and the children tangled up in it, because the Schneiders, devout as they were, couldn't handle the truth? Or because I knew that one of the conditions imposed on all their children's potential spouses had been: "May not be the child of divorced parents." I didn't want to be silent. I didn't want to restrain myself. No way. But the Schneiders saw a divorce in their family tree as the beginning of the end. And a child of divorced parents could never grow into a stable, mature, modern Orthodox partner. "Those who lie down with dogs get up with fleas," was Mr Schneider's comment on the subject. So I myself was flea-ridden and shared table and bed with a man even more infested with vermin.

My toes curled. I tried to connect with Elzira. For once, she didn't see how ill at ease I was. She busied herself carrying plates from the kitchen to the living room. Opris dropped by to say hello. Unlike everyone else, she looked miraculously unchanged. But Opris couldn't distract me from my concerns. I searched for the right words to tell Mr and Mrs Schneider about Martinus. I was proud of my life and my choices, I was proud of our fleas. My muscles tensed, ready to take on any hint of superiority and to meet any judgement, whether spoken or silent.

"How are your children—Elzira tells me you have two?" asked Mrs Schneider, turning to my boyfriend. Followed by at least ten other questions. About whether they were healthy, how they were doing at school, about their aptitudes and characters. "It can't be entirely easy for you," she said, addressing me. "How do you handle the situation?"

Yet my visit felt like a finale: the very fact we'd grown so close over the years made the distance between us now all the greater. Back then, *force majeure* and children had overturned the laws. Now, *mitzvoth*, appointment diaries and adulthood had regained the upper hand. Our relationship was at its end. It was, I feared, just a question of postponement. That afternoon, Mr Schneider said at least three times that he and his wife regarded me as their eldest daughter—though each time he said it, he fixed his gaze on Martinus. Like a father trying to get the measure of his son-in-law.

Six

"Daddy, can you teach me how to shave?" The boy jumped off the sofa where I'd been sitting with him, leafing through a photo album full of rabbis. I'd once heard Elzira's little son ask the very same thing.

A year had gone by since Mrs Schneider's birthday party. Jakov and Thirza had invited Martinus and me to spend a few days with them in Fresh Meadows.

"Why do you want to shave, Benjamin?" asked Jakov.

"Because I don't want a beard," the little boy replied.

"You don't want a beard?!" asked Thirza, who was sitting at the computer. How she and Jakov managed to combine their private, professional and religious lives with such serene good humour was a mystery to me. By now they had four children. Alexander, the oldest, was eight. They lived in cramped, basic accommodation. They worked incredibly hard, partly because the children's schools—all private—were eye-wateringly expensive: up to twenty thousand dollars per child per year.

"I don't want a *long* beard like the men in that book," Benjamin said.

Thirza's eyes twinkled.

"I'll teach you how to shave," Jakov promised.

"Now?"

"Not now. Later this week."

Reassured, the little chap rejoined me on the sofa. I told him that when Daddy was a boy, he'd had posters of men with beards next to his bed. Thirza, amused, raised an eyebrow at Jakov.

"Do you know Daddy's daddy and mummy?" asked Benjamin, clambering onto Martinus's lap.

"I've often visited them at their home."

"Do you think they're nice?"

"Your Granny and Grandpa Schneider are *very* nice."

"Daddy's Daddy was a little boy in the war."

I nodded.

"I want to hear stories about the war," the boy said. "My grandpa, Mummy's daddy, lived on a farm. He sat on the back of an ox. He told me. And he told me he made butter from the milk of a real cow. I don't know anything about Daddy's daddy. Can you tell me about him?"

I shook my head, but couldn't suppress a smile: so *someone* would certainly try and winkle out their stories. "Perhaps you should ask Granny and Grandpa Schneider when you see them."

"Granny is scared of planes. She almost never comes. And Grandpa doesn't like to travel by himself."

"When are you going to Antwerp again? When will you stay with them next?"

"I think in summer."

"Well, write down all the questions you want to ask them."

"I can't write properly yet! Only my name and a few sentences. But I can read. English and Ivrit. Do you know how old I am? Five. I'm already five."

"You could ask Mummy or Daddy to help you. Or Alexander. Or I could help you. Wait a minute."

"Is that why you always have those notebooks with you: because you're scared you might forget all the important things?"

★

It happened that our stay with Jakov's family coincided with Sukkot, the Feast of Tabernacles. Of course I was familiar with this most domestic of festivals. But it was only here that I grasped its significance, or had it explained to me: that this eight-day holiday celebrates the Jewish Exodus out of the desert, commemorating the improvised shelters used by the Jewish people during their wanderings in the wilderness.

The fact we'd picked this special week was entirely accidental: Jewish festivals aren't on my radar, and in Belgium, despite the large Jewish community, there's little to remind me of them. It just so happened that cheap flights were on offer that autumn.

On this visit, the presence of Jews in New York life struck me even more than on previous occasions. From improvised street stalls in and around Manhattan, Jews were selling the four religious symbols associated with this festival: branches of palm, myrtle and willow made up into bouquets, along with *etrogim*: ochre-yellow, wrinkled, citrus fruits with a very characteristic aroma that are kept like diamonds in ornate silver boxes. Customers scrutinized the fruit with magnifying glasses. The largest, finest, most symmetrical and pristine specimens were extraordinarily expensive: over a hundred dollars, if I recall correctly. The stallholders' calls echoed through the streets.

Notices were stuck up at the tills of shops and supermarkets: "Keep calm and have a happy Sukkot". All the papers ran articles about the festival. Public and private *sukkot*, or tabernacles, were displayed all over the city, like you might see nativity scenes in December. Martinus said: "I think this is going a bit far. Religion should be a private affair." I agreed, while at the same time gazing at it all in fascination.

We helped build and furnish Jakov's family's *sukkah*. With the aid of a wooden frame, the flat roof of their annexe was decorated with leafy boughs of palm and willow, and transformed into an outdoor hut.

Jakov and Martinus put two sun loungers and a long table in the *sukkah*. Thirza and I sat at the table with the children, making drawings with finger paint. The neighbours' children came to help, and joined in the art sessions. We made posters saying "Welcome to our *sukkah*" and stuck them to the walls with drawing pins. We balanced on a stepladder, attaching strings of little lights—it seemed quite Christmassy—to the walls and home-made ceiling. We blew up dozens of balloons, tied strings to them, and hung them everywhere we could. Thirza and her daughters placed the *menorah* on a pedestal.

The children, all ten of them, had a nap on the sun loungers, which had been covered with sleeping bags. They were given biscuits and tea. They fantasized aloud about the stars they'd be able to see peeping through the leaves at night, while we, the adults, cleared everything away and went inside to drink tea in the kitchen.

A quarter of an hour later, Renate suddenly ran into the room, in floods of tears.

"Laura," she sobbed. "Something really bad happened to Laura."

Thirza flew off, closely followed by Jakov. Martinus had gone pale. My heart was in my throat.

It turned out that the children had tied Laura to one of the sun loungers with the nylon string we'd used for the balloons. Alexander and Benjamin had helped. As had all the other children. Even the littlest, Renate—who'd afterwards turned out to be the bravest, by coming to tell us. Together they'd lashed Laura to the bed in true cowboy and Indian style, by her hands and feet. Laura had protested, but in her way, with silent tears.

Jakov and Thirza sent the other children home and took Alexander, Laura, Renate and Benjamin aside. Aside, meaning in their kitchen; Martinus and I felt unsure as to whether we were in the way.

Thirza talked to the children about their bodies. She told them that everyone was the boss of their own body. She explained why it was important, especially for young girls, to know that their bodies belonged to them and to no one else. She spoke about boys' superior physical strength; flexed her arm muscles to illustrate her words, asked Jakov to flex his too. In her explanation, supplemented by Jakov, Thirza explained to the children that neither boys nor girls should ever tolerate anyone touching them against their will. That if anyone did something to them they didn't want, they should do something about it. That their bodies and their sexuality were their own.

I was deeply impressed by this lesson. Thirza was a woman after my own heart. An impression that was only strengthened after the end of her assertiveness course, when I caught her secretly pinching Jakov's bottom.

Seven

O ne day, as I was cycling past the Schneiders', I saw a removal
van. A crane was busy lifting furniture and boxes to the first
and second floors. I stopped. Was someone moving, was the dumb
question I asked one of the men unloading the van. He asked me
if he should call the new occupants, because they happened to be
inside.

No, there was no need for that.

Once home, I emailed Elzira. I attached a photo I'd taken with my
phone: their beautiful white facade with the crane leaning against it.

The answer came quickly. Their parents had sold the house and
now lived alternately in a flat in Antwerp and one in New York.
They wanted to spend half the year in the city where most of their
grandchildren lived: Elzira and Jakov had nine between them.

Mrs Schneider had gone on a course to cure her fear of flying.
"And if the turbulence gets really bad there's always Xanax."

Elzira added a few attachments to her email: photos of Mr and
Mrs Schneider, dressed in pyjamas, dressing gowns and slippers,
waving off Elzira's children as they got onto the school bus in the
morning. There were also a few snaps of the children themselves.
Surrounded by their friends, they were looking a little askance at
their grandparents: no teenager thinks it's cool to be waved off at
the doorstep by people in dressing gowns.

The photos of the children made me laugh; the ones of Mr and
Mrs Schneider didn't. That was because Mr Schneider reminded me

too much of Dustin Hoffman in his role as Arthur Miller's travelling salesman. Though that might just have been me; never before had I seen Mr Schneider dressed in anything other than a dark suit and white shirt. Suddenly there he was in pink fluff.

Eight

I emailed Mr and Mrs Schneider to pass on our best wishes for their new, split life. To my great surprise, Mr Schneider rang me as soon as the email arrived.

"We're in New York. We live near Elzira."

"Congratulations. You must love being so close to the children and grandchildren. How is Mrs Schneider?"

"I don't like to hear American around me. Americans talk as if they've always got chewing gum in their mouths. I'm glad my grandchildren are growing up in the United States, but I think it's a shame they won't absorb all the languages they would in a European setting."

"I'm just as sorry about that as you are. Though there is one comfort at least: everyone speaks English. With that language they can explore the world."

"Thank you for your email. My spouse and I were very happy to receive it."

"You're welcome."

"I'm worried about our Jewish youth, you know. Asia is investing heavily in education. If we Jews want to continue to play a leading role economically, intellectually, artistically and academically, our grandchildren will have to make a greater effort. I'd feel happier, more reassured, if they spoke more than one language."

"They can speak modern Hebrew too, surely?"

"They can speak Ivrit, but they can't all read it well. They know the basics, that's all. That's America for you. Not much depth. Loss of tradition."

"You sound so pessimistic. That's not like you."

"I'm thinking about the future."

"You're worried."

"China's a rising power. What if it soon calls the shots? America's economy would suffer, and that would have a social impact. Maybe our children would no longer be welcome there. Since time imme- morial, Jews have settled in places where the economy and com- merce flourish. But would China be open to them, to us?"

"Can you see your grandchildren going to China?"

"I'd like them to study Chinese, certainly. But I wonder whether Jews can put down roots in Asian soil. And the Chinese are a closed people. What's your opinion?"

"The Jews are also a closed people."

"Do you think so?"

"Don't you think so?"

"Have we been closed towards you?"

"Had it not been for your children, we'd never have had any contact. Children lower thresholds. Adults build walls."

"Do you think that applies to me and my spouse?"

"I think it applies in general."

"I'm not sure."

"I think it certainly applies to the Orthodox Jewish community. Why are you too frightened to open the doors a little wider, so everyone can peep inside?"

"Are you talking about Antwerp? Or the US?"

"Antwerp."

"But you are a writer. You are a journalist. You always want to know what's going on behind the scenes!"

"I'm saying this as a family friend. Not as a writer or journalist."

"You think in terms of stories. You always have."

"Is that bad?"

"No. As long as you don't write about us."

"What if I do?"

"Are you planning to?"

"You're giving me ideas."

"Well if so, I hope you never use our names. That you won't reveal who we are."

"Who is this 'our' and 'we'?"

"All the Schneiders and Pappenheims."

"Jakov and Elzira wouldn't mind my writing about them. I think Jakov might even brag about it."

"You are very dear to us, my spouse and me. Our children, especially Elzira and Jakov, are very loyal towards you. Please don't abuse their and our loyalty."

I didn't want to oppose him. I didn't want to say that their children were grown-ups now. I knew he was right. Jakov and Elzira would make their own decisions, very likely different to those of their father and mother. I didn't want to drive a wedge between them. They were dear to me too. All of them.

"We, the Jewish community of Antwerp, cannot be open. Not as you would like," he went on. "You know a little bit about our history. So you should understand that. That it's better for us to lead our own lives in silence."

I was sorry about the direction this conversation had taken.

He didn't stop. "I cheer for Kim Clijsters," he said, "and I walk through Central Park wearing my Anderlecht baseball cap. That's how proud I am of my country. Yet you reproach us for a lack of openness. For failing as Belgian citizens."

"That's not at all what I meant. I'm trying to say that diversity, like love, is a work in progress, Mr Schneider. Diversity takes blood, sweat and tears from all parties."

"You could get a job writing for politicians. You talk in slogans."

"Do you think so?"

"Our friendship is unique. The bond you have with Elzira isn't something that can be replaced. Let us not jeopardize that."

"No, of course not!" I was shocked.

"I hope you will continue to see our children. My spouse hopes that too."

"We regularly email each other, Elzira and I," I said, in an attempt at reassurance.

"You can't keep up a friendship by email. When we are in Antwerp, you can stay in our little flat in New York."

"That's incredibly kind of you, but—"

"Is this not the diversity to which you refer?" he asked. Then, immediately afterwards: "Have you heard the one about the Jew, the Frenchman and the Englishman who all get washed up on a desert island?"

Although I tried to bite my tongue, I couldn't stop myself. "You, Mr Schneider, who pride yourself on being Flemish *and* Belgian," I objected, mock-humorously, "why do you talk about 'a Jew', alongside 'a Frenchman' and 'an Englishman'? As if the Jew couldn't also be a Frenchman, an Englishman or a Belgian."

There was a long silence.

"You are right. Thank you for your observation. Have you heard the one about the Flemish Jew, the Frenchman and the Englishman who all get washed up on a desert island?"

AVAILABLE AND COMING SOON
FROM PUSHKIN PRESS

Pushkin Press was founded in 1997, and publishes novels, essays, memoirs, children's books—everything from timeless classics to the urgent and contemporary.

Our books represent exciting, high-quality writing from around the world: we publish some of the twentieth century's most widely acclaimed, brilliant authors such as Stefan Zweig, Yasushi Inoue, Teffi, Antal Szerb, Gerard Reve and Elsa Morante, as well as compelling and award-winning contemporary writers, including Dorthe Nors, Edith Pearlman, Perumal Murugan, Ayelet Gundar-Goshen and Chigozie Obioma.

Pushkin Press publishes the world's best stories, to be read and read again. To discover more, visit www.pushkinpress.com.

A WOMAN IN THE POLAR NIGHT
CHRISTIANE RITTER

MEMORIES OF LOW TIDE
CHANTAL THOMAS

MAZEL TOV
J.S. MARGOT

DAYS IN THE CAUCASUS
BANINE

THOSE WHO FORGET
GÉRALDINE SCHWARZ

YOUNG REMBRANDT
ONNO BLOM

THE WORLD OF YESTERDAY
STEFAN ZWEIG

NO PLACE TO LAY ONE'S HEAD
FRANÇOISE FRENKEL

DREAMERS
VOLKER WEIDERMANN

A CHILL IN THE AIR
IRIS ORIGO

RED LOVE
MAXIM LEO

A WORLD GONE MAD
ASTRID LINDGREN

ON THE END OF THE WORLD
JOSEPH ROTH

THE ALLURE OF CHANEL
PAUL MORAND

CLOSE TO THE MACHINE
ELLEN ULLMAN

SORROW OF THE EARTH
ERIC VUILLARD

A SORROW BEYOND DREAMS
PETER HANDKE

MEMORIES: FROM MOSCOW TO THE BLACK SEA
TEFFI

IN SEARCH OF LOST BOOKS
GIORGIO VAN STRATEN